Praise for **The Walk-On**

"This book truly resonates with anyone that is chasing their dream. Following Tommy's pursuit in basketball as he grows up in the powerhouse basketball state of North Carolina is truly inspiring. If you're a fan of a true underdog tale, this is a story for you. Personally, this book gave me instant nostalgia, bringing back memories from my time at UNCG. I think everyone can relate to Tommy's story and for sure bring back your own nostalgia from your youth."

- Kyle Hines, UNCG Hall of Famer & Retired Jersey 4-Time EuroLeague Champion

"It's a Wonderful Life meets Hoosiers in this heartwarming story about love, life, and basketball set in small town North Carolina."

- Alan Gratz, NY Times bestselling author of Refugee and Allies

"I have to admit I'm not an avid reader, but when I was asked to read **The Walk-On**, I was definitely intrigued. And as soon I started to read it, it was hard for me to put down. Having been a player at UNCG during the time period the book was set, it really hit home for me. But the more and more I read, the more I realized that a connection to UNCG or Greensboro wasn't necessary to enjoy the book. Whether you like a sweet love story or one of perseverance by an athlete or any young person, or you're a teenager in the midst of life's ups and downs, or you're an adult struggling to be happy for your kids no matter what path they choose, **The Walk-On** has something for you!"

- Scott Hartzell, UNCG Hall of Famer & Retired Jersey Point Guard for the 1995-96 Championship Team

"Heartwarming. Tommy's passion for the game of basketball and his pursuit of true love will keep you glued to this story set in a state where hoops are a religion. For anyone who enjoys a heated rivalry and likes to pull for the underdog, this is an authentic tale that brings back memories of your youth. For those of us who were there when UNCG joined the Division I ranks and first experienced the sweet success of March Madness, it's a must-read."

- Ty Buckner, Former UNCG Associate Director of Athletics

"***The Walk-On*** is not only about the Spartans, it's *for* the Spartans. More than that, it's a relatable coming-of-age story that will leave you laughing, crying, and remembering the awkwardness of youth. You'll cheer Tommy on from page one."

- Lynn Chandler Willis,
Award-winning author of the Ava Logan series

"Tommy was able to overcome so much adversity and it was refreshing to see his perseverance pay off. I felt that same vibe Tommy described about UNCG. That place is special and will always be somewhere I hold near and dear to my heart. Reading Greensboro street names and references to campus buildings brought back so many memories. For the aspiring players please note that it takes more than just pure talent to be a basketball player."

- Courtney Eldridge, UNCG Hall of Famer & Retired Jersey
Point Guard for the 2000-01 Championship Team

Also by Ross Cavins

Follow The Money
(A collection of interconnected short stories)

Follow a briefcase of $3 million dollars as it changes hands from idiot to idiot. A botched kidnapping, a money scam, a not-so-average convenience store holdup … each story flows (with the money) through a series of interesting and bizarre plots.

Barry vs The Apocalypse

Meet Barry Glick, a middle-aged superhero with Super-Strength, Super-Speed, and a mullet. He thought he'd retired twenty years ago. Now in his mid-forties, after years of apathy, selfishness, and using his X-Ray-Vision on lottery scratch-offs to get by, Barry is once again goaded into action when a Homeland Security agent disappears.

THE WALK-ON

A NOVEL ABOUT LIFE AND BASKETBALL

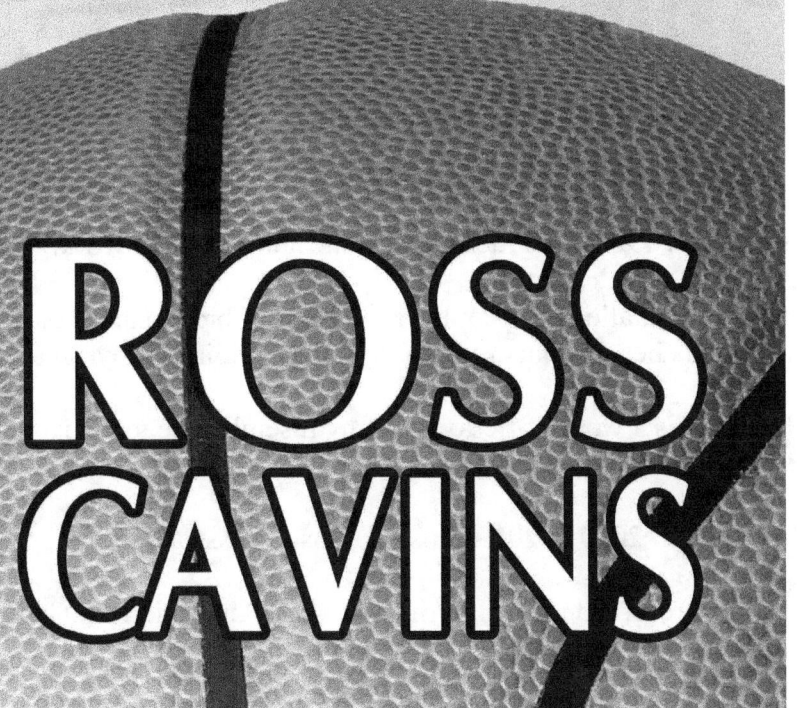

ROSS CAVINS

RCG PUBLISHING

Ross Cavins has asserted his right under the Copyright, Designs and Patents Act 1988 to be identified as the author of this work.

Any representations of people or products or brand names or trademarks here within are property of the original copyright holders.

This book is a work of fiction and any resemblance to actual persons, living or dead, is purely chance.

Copyright © 2010 & 2019, Ross Cavins – RossCavins.com

All rights reserved under International and Pan-American Copyright Conventions.

Published by RCG Publishing – RCGPublishing.com

Trade Paperback ISBN-10: 0-9827720-8-4
Trade Paperback ISBN-13: 978-0-9827720-8-9
Ebook ISBN-10: 0-9827720-9-2
Ebook ISBN-13: 978-0-9827720-9-6

For all mid-major basketball fans.

You know who you are.

Like The Beach Boys said once,

"Be true to your school."

Special Thanks to ...

Jennifer Pearce ... for being my first-level editor and alpha reader way back in 2010 when I first wrote the story with a different focus. Thank you for your corrections and direction.

All my beta readers: Lynn Chandler-Willis, Micki Bare, Karen Fritz, Norma Caviness (mom!), Amy Schwartz (wife!), Jordy Kuiper, Scott Hartzell, Ty Buckner, Kyle Hines, Courtney Eldridge, Francis Alonso, Alan Gratz, and everyone at the SEMWA Outer Banks Retreat I asked for advice ... Thank you for your frank input, whether or not I wanted to hear it. That's what a beta reader is for.

And everyone else I've not mentioned that had a hand in helping me down this long journey.

Chapter 1

Tommy Chandler drifted through the back door and tossed his book bag onto the kitchen counter. Helen Chandler picked it up and handed it back to him. "In your room."

Tommy took the bag and stalked off. She yelled after him, "How'd you do?"

He didn't answer.

In his room, Tommy plopped onto his bed. Today had been the last day of high school basketball tryouts. Tomorrow the list would be up outside the coach's office. But tonight, Tommy could only worry.

For some guys, there was no question. Patrick Hart, for instance, always got everything he wanted. He drove a new car, dated Laura Novak, and he would surely start for the basketball team. His parents were boosters. They'd donated the money for the uniforms, and rumor had it they'd chipped in for half of the new computer lab.

Patrick was set for life.

Then there was Nick, Tommy's best friend. He'd make the team, maybe even start beside Patrick at the other guard position. Nick was the best shooter Tommy had ever seen. He could make a hundred free throws in a row, and then switch to his left hand.

Tommy's little brother, Brant, appeared in his doorway.

"How'd you do?"

"Leave me alone."

"Think you got cut?"

"Go away."

Brant stood there until Tommy raised his head, saying, "What do you want?"

"Mom said for me to tell you to wash up good. She doesn't want supper to smell like a locker room."

"Bite me."

Brant didn't move.

Tommy sat up and threw a fuzzy basketball at Brant. It hit the door jamb.

"What do you want, dorkhead?" Tommy asked.

"Mom told me to make sure you washed up."

Brant was twelve, four years younger than Tommy, and took a lot of things literally. Tommy shook his head, then got up and lumbered past Brant and into the bathroom. He took a quick shower and threw on a pair of shorts and a t-shirt before sitting down to dinner. The aroma of fried pork chops had assaulted him as soon as he came through the back door but it hadn't truly registered until now. His stomach grumbled.

"You going to answer me now?" his mom asked.

Tommy shrugged and dragged a pork chop to his plate. "I did okay."

"Just okay?"

"I don't know." Tommy loaded his plate with mashed potatoes and gravy.

His dad cleared his throat and spoke to the food in his plate, "I could have used some help at the store today."

"Gene." Helen Chandler said only one word, but it was the clipped way she said it that added meaning.

"All I'm saying is the delivery truck came in."

"You could have had it delivered tomorrow when you knew Tommy would be free." Helen was now glaring at Tommy's dad.

"We were out of whole wheat bread."

"People eat regular bread too."

Gene Chandler turned his attention back to his food as Helen looked at Brant.

"How'd your day go, honey?"

"I got an A on my math test."

"Very good, Brant." She smiled.

Brant said, "I could help out at the store."

"You're too young, honey," Helen said before Gene could answer. "We've agreed you won't help at the store until you're fifteen."

"But I want to help."

Helen smiled at her youngest son and passed him a bowl of green beans. Brant took them with a frown and spooned some onto his plate.

They ate in silence for a few minutes until Gene Chandler said, "So you don't even know if you made the team?"

"Gene."

Gene glanced at Helen, eyebrows raised in surprise. "It's a valid question."

"It's the way you asked it."

"How did I ask it?"

Helen stared at him as she took a bite.

Gene paused a second before turning to Tommy. "Well?"

"I'll find out tomorrow."

"You don't have any clue how you played compared to the other boys?"

Tommy shrugged.

Gene's voice raised a notch. "You've had tryouts for a week and a half, and you don't know how you did?"

Tommy pushed his green beans around his plate and took a bite of his biscuit.

Helen said, "Okay, Gene. Let's just have a nice dinner."

"What?" Gene snapped his head toward his wife. "I told him he was too undersized to make the team. And even if he did, he'd never start and probably wouldn't get any playing time. What good is being on the team if you never get in the game?"

"Do you always have to be like this?"

"Like what? There's no point in playing if you know you're going to lose before you suit up."

Helen put her fork down. "Sometimes you have to finish second before you can finish first."

Gene humphed and shook his head. "If you don't finish first, you might as well come in last. Second place gets the same damn thing last place gets. Nothing." His fork had halted inches from his face, a huge sliver of pork chop stuck to it, dripping gravy onto the edge of his plate.

"Language." Helen sat up in her chair, skin taut against her chin as she thrust it toward her husband.

Gene held her gaze for a moment before returning to his food.

"Maybe if I had new shoes," Tommy offered.

"New shoes!" Gene exploded. "You think those grow on trees?"

"But my shoes aren't real basketball shoes."

"Boy, shoes are shoes. In my day, we wore Chucks. They didn't have no special arches or zippers or whatever. They worked just fine."

But to Tommy, Sears shoes were not real shoes. They weren't made for basketball like Patrick Hart's Air Jordans. Tommy slipped his hands beneath the table and brought up one of his shoes.

He waved it over his plate. "These aren't made for basketball. They give my feet blisters if I try to do too many moves."

"Get that off the table," his mom said.

"They're not even real leather," Tommy added. "They're *pleather*." He held the shoe away from the table. "And they creak when I walk."

"You're not getting new shoes just for basketball unless you buy them yourself," Gene Chandler said.

"With what?" Tommy replied. "You barely pay me anything for all the hours I put in at the store."

Gene held his eyes steady. "You can't put a price on experience."

"Experience won't buy me new shoes."

Gene stared at his son, impassive. "Keep it up, boy."

"Gene," Helen scolded.

Gene kept his gaze on Tommy, eyes firm, unforgiving. The look conveyed the speech Tommy had heard a million times.

Grandpa Chandler started the store and handed it down to his oldest son, Tommy's dad. It went without saying that the same was expected of Tommy, Gene's oldest son, to learn the business and take it over when the time came. Gene made it no secret that the store was the family's only source of income. And it was more than just a business, it was a family heirloom, like the big Bible that sat on Maw Maw Chandler's coffee table; it was a keepsake to be passed down from generation to generation, with reverence and thanks. The store was not an optional way of life, it was *the* way of life.

* * *

Helen stared at her husband, wishing he was easier on the boys sometimes. He didn't have to be perfect, just a little more understanding and lenient.

"Can I be excused?" Brant said, breaking the moment. He'd cleaned his plate and finished his tea.

A second passed and Helen turned to him, smiling. "Yes, honey."

As he slid his chair back, she asked if he'd finished his homework. He said he just had some reading in his history book.

"Go do it now."

"But, mom, I can do it right before I go to bed."

"You can do it now before you watch TV."

"Mom," Brant whined, elongating the word into more syllables than needed.

"No arguments."

Brant dropped his dishes into the sink and slunk from the kitchen.

Helen nodded toward Tommy, "Don't play with your food."

Tommy had formed a word with the green beans. When his dad raised up to see what it read, Tommy messed it up with his fork.

"May I be excused, too?" he asked.

"Who's Laura?" his dad said.

Tommy jerked his head up. "No one."

"Who's Laura?" Gene looked at Helen now.

"The Novak's daughter," she said. "Bill and Janie?"

"Janie Matthews?"

Helen licked her lips and squinted her eyes. "Yes, that one."

Gene held a hand up, a grin forming over his thin mouth. "I didn't say anything."

"You didn't have to."

Tommy's dad tilted his head. "What? You gonna hold a memory against me now?"

Helen's eyes narrowed.

Gene tapped the table to get Tommy's attention. "She good-looking, this Laura?"

Tommy's mouth opened, but he said nothing.

"Gene."

"What?" He turned back to his wife. "I'm just trying to see how far the apple fell from the tree." He grinned and looked back at Tommy. "You going steady?"

"Gene, " Helen said, shaking her head. "They don't go steady now."

Gene frowned. "What do they do?"

"They *go together*. Isn't that right?" She turned to Tommy.

"Mom."

Brant stuck his head into the kitchen. "Tommy's got a girlfriend. Tommy's got a girlfriend."

"No I don't!" Tommy slid his chair out. "We're not going together!"

"Tommy's got a girlfriend." Brant launched into a sing-song version of the chant. "*Tommy's got a girlfriend, Tommy's got a girlfriend.* "

"Boys." Their mother's voice was drowned out by Brant's singing. "Brant, go to your room."

"But—"

"Go." She pointed. "Homework, now."

Brant smirked as he twisted on a heel and strolled down the hall humming. Helen turned to her older son, eyes relaxing. His seventeenth birthday was approaching soon. He was growing fast now. She had noticed it this past summer when she had to buy school clothes. None of his jeans had fit. Tommy called them high-waters. Some terms never went out of style.

Tommy's boyish features had begun sharpening in this last year, his body developing. His voice changed octaves, it seemed, almost overnight. And she'd noticed the fur forming on his upper lip.

She knew this would happen one day, but it had arrived too soon. Wasn't Tommy just in diapers? He'd just cut his first tooth. Taken his first step. Had his first haircut.

And all of a sudden, he had his first girlfriend. It was too soon.

"Stop it, Mom," Tommy said.

Helen blinked. "Stop what?"

"Stop looking at me like that. I know what you're doing."

He really was growing up, she thought. Able to read her like a drive-thru menu.

"Do you want to talk about it?" she asked.

"I'm not going with anyone." Tommy leaned forward and made impressions in his mashed potatoes with his fork, little railroad tracks from one side to the other.

Helen studied her son with a gaze only a mother could offer. She set her silverware down. "We can talk about anything."

Gene Chandler continued to shovel food into his mouth.

"Mom," Tommy said. "There's nothing to talk about, really."

She sighed. "And I suppose nothing happened at school today, either?"

"Only basketball tryouts." Tommy fidgeted in his seat. "Can I go now?"

Helen picked up her fork. "Go ahead. Do your homework before you get near the TV. I mean it."

Tommy cleared his plate and left the room.

Helen watched him leave and turned to her husband. He paused mid-bite, saying, "Don't look at me like that."

Her eyes moistened. "He's growing up so fast."

"I'm just glad he's into girls."

"Gene."

"What? I am. There are worse things, you know. He could be one of those kids who don't know what he likes. I heard the Granger's son is a fairy."

"Stop it."

He shrugged and filled his mouth with buttered biscuit.

Helen sighed again. "Once it starts, you know, there's no going back. Girls will preoccupy him from now on." She paused, the sides of her mouth turning down. "And he'll get his sweet, little heart broken."

"Jesus, Helen. He's sixteen." Biscuit crumbs shot from his mouth. "He's not a kid anymore. It'll be good to get his heart broken. Make him a man."

"That's an awful thing to say."

"And if you're gonna have a girl break your heart, it might as well be Janie Matthews' daughter."

"What's that mean?" Helen jerked around in her seat so she was facing him.

More biscuit crumbs tumbled from Gene's mouth. "All I'm saying is that if you're going to get your heart broken, shoot for the stars. You know? What's the point in—where are you going?"

Helen had pushed away from the table and stood with her plate. "I'm suddenly not very hungry." She dropped her plate in the sink as Gene watched. She passed by him, saying, "And I think I feel a week-long headache coming on."

She narrowed her eyes at him and disappeared down the hallway toward their room.

Chapter 2

Thanksgiving came and went, and Christmas was fast approaching. While cold winters had already settled in for much of the country, North Carolina was enjoying a relatively mild December.

Nick picked Tommy up in his Jeep. He ground the gears as they jerked out of the driveway.

"Don't you ever wash this thing?" Tommy said.

Nick shrugged. "Gives it personality."

"No, the stuff people write on it gives it personality."

Nick glanced at Tommy.

Tommy laughed. "You've got something written on the passenger door, and it doesn't say WASH ME."

"Crap." Nick shook his head. "We'll go through the car wash before we pick up the girls."

"And who's this girl you got me stuck with?"

"Stuck with? You're a lucky man. Britney's a babe. She goes to Grimsley. I told you about her before. She's Destiny's cousin."

"Uh-huh."

Nick laughed. "I'm serious, man. She's hot. Imagine Destiny with bigger boobs and shorter hair. You'll worship me after tonight."

"I'm still a little fuzzy on how you got this set up."

Nick shook his head. "All Destiny had to say was you were on the basketball team. Britney digs athletes."

"That's comforting."

"Hey, you just have to get your foot in the door. It don't matter if it's because you play basketball or have money or drive a nice car. You can't get laid if you don't get a date first. I'm telling you, man, you're gonna worship me after tonight."

They drove another half mile before Nick said, "There's just one thing."

Tommy closed his eyes and turned toward his best friend as he opened them. "I knew there was a catch. What is it? She missing teeth? Have a lazy eye? She bigger than me?"

Nick waved his hand as he turned into the automatic carwash. "No, no, nothing like that. She's a freshman."

Tommy hesitated. "In college?"

"No."

Tommy said, "Wait, a freshman in high school?"

Nick shrugged. "She's old for her age."

Tommy shook his head. "What does that mean?"

"Well, you're a junior, but you're sixteen, right? She's a freshman, and she's fifteen. You guys are only like a year apart."

"She's a freshman, Nick."

"Yeah, but like I said, she *looks* older." Nick cupped both hands in front of his chest and jiggled them up and down.

Tommy snorted. "Does she have a permission slip from her mother?"

"Destiny said she started growing her boobs when she was eleven." Nick paused. "And ain't stopped yet."

Tommy squinted his eyes. "So if nothing's wrong with her, why's Destiny pimping her out?"

Nick dropped quarters in the machine and pulled himself back in, rolling up the window. "That's my doing. I asked Destiny to find someone for a double-date." He eased the Jeep into the Wash-N-Dri building until the green light on the far wall switched to red. He nodded at Tommy, "If you don't ever use that thing, I hear it'll fall off."

Tommy grinned. "It gets used."

"I'm not talking about autopilot. You gotta let somebody else drive it every once in a while or the battery will go dead. You know, get the oil changed, drain the fluids before they build up."

"Hey. Speaking of ... your brother get the new month yet?"

"Oh yeah, Christmas edition."

"And?"

"It's got twins. Redheaded twins. Santa was definitely good to all the naughty little boys."

They both laughed as the car wash drummed the Jeep with hot water and suds, the rollers with brightly-colored flap scrubbers following closely.

Thwump, thwump, thwump.

Nick nudged Tommy as they pulled out of the car wash. The radio was set on 98.7 KISS FM, blaring REO Speedwagon through the Jeep's ratty speakers. He turned the music down.

"You got one in your wallet?"

"You're kidding, right?"

"Do you?"

Tommy twisted in his seat. "You don't honestly think that's going to happen on a double-date in this little Jeep, do you?"

"Gotta always be prepared."

"Plus, you said Britney's fifteen."

"A mature fifteen," Nick said, nodding.

Tommy laughed hard. "So are you planning on traveling back in time to find us a drive-in to go to?"

Nick sniffed. "As a matter of fact, I'd planned on us all going to Ham's, then if everything went well, we could drive out to the Rock."

"It's going to be chilly tonight, Nick."

"I brought blankets."

"You're crazy."

"I figured we could take turns in the Jeep. One couple could take a long walk, then switch with the other couple."

"You've actually thought this out."

Nick smiled and nodded.

Tommy rolled his eyes, but Nick didn't see him. They pulled up to Destiny's house two minutes later and Nick motioned to Tommy. Tommy exhaled loudly, then scrambled between the seats to the back. Destiny opened the passenger door and hopped in, pausing to exchange spit with Nick.

Tommy coughed from the back which earned him two middle fingers, one of which was slender and feminine. Destiny said, "Hey, Tommy."

"Hey, Destiny."

"Where's Britney?" Nick asked.

"At her place."

"She's not here? You mean we gotta go pick her up?"

"We're going to town anyway aren't we?"

Nick shook his head and backed out of the driveway. He stripped the gears twice before he finally got the Jeep in first.

"You excited?" Destiny asked, turning in her seat.

"I'm not a charity case," Tommy replied. "It's not like I can't get a date."

"We just figured we'd give you a little push."

"Was I supposed to bring a bib or is she bringing her own?"

"Funny," Destiny said. "Britney is very mature for her age."

"That's what I've heard. If she's got her learner's permit, maybe we could let her drive some."

Destiny grinned. "You're in a rare mood tonight."

"I wasn't aware I was ever in a *common* mood." Tommy raised an eyebrow as Destiny turned in her seat.

"Oh yeah, she's gonna love you."

"What's that mean?"

"You'll see."

Tommy thought on that as they drove along, listening to Tiffany's remake of "I Think We're Alone Now."

Destiny directed Nick to Britney's house, a huge two-story brick home with a double-garage and pristinely landscaped lawn. Before Nick could come to a complete stop, Britney popped out the front door and bounded down the walk.

Destiny smacked Nick on the arm. "Quit staring."

Nick shook his head and pretended to check the gas gauge. Destiny stepped out of the Jeep and hugged Britney. Then she tilted the seat forward.

Britney smiled and introduced herself as she squeezed in beside Tommy. Destiny hopped into the front and closed the door.

Nick smiled back at Britney and jerked his head forward as Destiny pinched his leg through his jeans. Tommy smiled at her too, his name spilling out of his mouth like stringy drool. "Hi, I'm Tommy."

Britney wore a heavy coat, unzipped in the front, and she settled into the coziness of the small back seat with the ease of a longtime friend. "I'm Britney."

Nick flipped the heater to high to replenish what had escaped when

Britney got in.

"Chilly tonight," Britney said with a wide grin. She shivered and ran her hands down her bare legs. She wore a mini-skirt.

"Yeah, chilly," Tommy said.

Britney tapped Tommy on the shoulder. "I'm up here."

Tommy looked up, immediately flush. "S-s-sorry."

Britney laughed with gusto. "I'm used to it. No big deal." Looking up front to Nick and Destiny, she asked, "Where we heading?"

"How about Ham's?" Nick offered.

Everybody nodded.

Nick pulled out of the drive and Britney swiveled toward Tommy. "Destiny said you were on the basketball team."

Tommy nodded. "But I'm not a starter."

Britney snorted. "Only five guys can start, but it takes a team to win."

"Yeah, but I've only played in one game so far, and that's because we were getting blown out by twenty."

"And how did you play when you were in?"

Tommy shrugged, but Nick yelled from the front, "He scored a three-point play. Drove to the basket, faked the guy out, then shot over him and got fouled."

Britney slapped Tommy's knee. "That's something."

"Yeah," Tommy said. "But they had in their scrubs too."

Britney was shaking her head. "What matters is what you did with your chance when it was yours to take."

Nick had stopped at a red light and turned around. "How *old* are you?"

Britney let loose an infectious laugh. "Sorry, my dad's a coach. I guess it's in the blood. I've heard him so many times it's ingrained in me." She turned to Tommy. "The point I'm making is you can't twinkle until a light is shined on you, and it's those times that you should focus on. Not the other times."

Tommy nodded, taking in for the first time the fullness of Britney's cheeks, the smile lines around her eyes, the faint aroma of honeysuckle and roses emanating from her presence.

She continued, "When the light's not on you, that's when you work hard to pull the light back. You do whatever it takes to attract the light, whether it's shooting more free throws after practice, running an extra mile, or staying in the gym till it closes." She paused. "Geez, I do sound like my dad, don't I?" She shook her head, smiling. "I'll shut up now."

Nick stepped on the gas, saying, "Hey Tommy, I'll bet that's the first pep talk you ever received on a date."

"I feel like I should hit the showers now," Tommy said. Everybody laughed and Tommy said to Britney, "Anything else before I go in, coach?"

Britney smiled and hit the seat in front of her, "I like this one, Destiny. You did good."

"I told you," Destiny said.

"He's even cuter when he blushes," Britney said, eyeing Tommy.

Tommy didn't know what to do. He'd never met a girl so bold. He felt like a different person around her. More mature. He wondered if all city girls were like this. They surely didn't grow them like this in the country.

"It's warm in here," Britney remarked. Nick went to turn the heat down, and Britney said, "No, don't. I'll just take my coat off."

She leaned forward and struggled, then asked Tommy to help her. She got her left arm behind her, trying to grip the sleeve with her right hand, but the space was too tight.

"Pull my sleeve down," she said.

Tommy reached over and tugged on the sleeve. Britney turned right, then left, then up. Before Tommy knew it, Britney's breasts were shoved in his face.

Tommy jerked up and hit his head on the roll bar. Britney chirped out a laugh and asked if he was alright.

Tommy rubbed his head and said yeah.

"You two need a room already?" Nick yelled over the noise of the engine and radio.

Britney caught Tommy's attention. "You're gonna have to reach around behind me and grab my sleeves, then pull down."

Tommy paused. "Do I really?"

Britney squinted, then said in his ear, "No, not really. But it's a lot more fun than me doing it myself. Don't you think?"

Tommy reached around her and found the sleeves. Their cheeks touched, and he felt Britney's warmth. Her chest grazed his, and he felt the heat rush through his body.

He finally freed her arms, and she kissed him on the cheek. "Ever such the gentleman," she whispered, pulling away. "Thank you."

All Tommy could do was smile sheepishly.

"If you two are done back there," Destiny asked, "We're here."

Nick pulled the Jeep into Ham's parking lot. It was Saturday night, and the place was packed. They sat in a booth, couples beside each other, and ordered a bowl of homemade chips with ranch dressing as an appetizer. The chips came straight from the fryer, thick and curled from the heat with a light dusting of salt.

Pitchers of beer passed by them like cars on a highway, full ones headed toward tables with college kids, empty ones headed back to the bar. TVs in each of the corners were turned to various sports games.

UNC was playing Syracuse, Duke at Temple. A toy train chugged around the restaurant along tracks suspended two feet below the ceiling.

Nodding at the Carolina game, Britney asked, "What positions do you all play?"

"Shooting guard," Nick answered.

"Point guard," Tommy said.

"Point guard?" Britney said, her voice rising. "Really? Well, we've got more in common than you know. I was a point guard when I played."

"You played?" Tommy said.

"Sure did."

"But you don't anymore?"

Britney shook her head.

Tommy scrunched his face. "Why'd you stop?"

Britney smiled and shook her shoulders, "Because it's hard to dribble three basketballs down the court at one time." Nick and Destiny laughed as Tommy turned pink.

Britney leaned over and hugged Tommy's arm, then said to Destiny, "I love the shy ones. They're so innocent."

Destiny added, "You just love to corrupt them."

Britney laughed. "There's that, too."

They ordered burgers with chips and watched the games.

"You know," Britney said. "You can't be shy on the court when you're a point guard."

Nick said, "He's an animal with a basketball in his hands."

"I am not." Tommy rolled his eyes.

"Yeah, he is," Nick said. "You should see him. Slicing and dicing through defenders like a Ron Popeil invention."

"You're stupid."

THE WALK-ON

Britney tilted her head. "Why don't you start then?"

Tommy looked at Nick, but it was Destiny who answered, "Because Patrick Hart's parents give money to the school."

Tommy shook his head, "Patrick's really good. I've heard the coaches talking. They say he's going to play in college. He's already got the attention of some schools. They say he'll probably get a few offers this year."

Britney placed her hand on Tommy's. "That must be hard to play behind someone like that."

"Naw, it's easy. You just sit there. Anyone can do it."

Britney's eyes softened, then she said, "Well, there's something special about any point guard. They run the team; they're an extension of the coach. When the team's on the court, everybody looks to the point guard for instructions. It's his team, for better or worse. Even if you're a second-string point guard, you're still a point guard."

Tommy was quiet for a moment. "I just want a few minutes each game. That's all. Just a few minutes to prove myself."

They ate their burgers, watching the games and commenting on calls and plays. The sounds of the restaurant ebbed and flowed with an invisible tide, influenced by the action in the games and laughter and random outbursts. Tommy lost himself in the moment, three high school juniors and a mature freshman, out for a Saturday night on the town. He soaked himself in the freedom of youth, reveling in the absence of responsibility, without consciously knowing it was a magical time in all their lives.

It was one of those nights he'd look back to in thirty years and remember the smallest things. Like how some of the chips were soft and others were crispy. Like the way Britney's skin felt when her arm brushed his. Like the way all four of them yelled, "Walk!" at the same time when Duke's point guard started his move before he put the ball down.

The girls left for the bathroom and as the boys slid back into the booth, Tommy froze. Nick followed his gaze. A couple had just entered the restaurant holding hands: Patrick Hart and Laura Novak.

As they stood waiting for the hostess, Nick said, "Hey, don't worry about them."

After Angel's thirteenth birthday party, Patrick and Laura had begun going together. They walked around school holding hands, sneaking kisses in the hall when there were no teachers around. They'd been seeing each other off and on for the last four years.

Tommy scratched his forehead. "I'm not worried about them."

"You know, you should just get over her."

Tommy looked at Nick. "I was never into her."

Nick smirked. "Whatever you say."

"That's what I say."

Nick exhaled and shook his head. "You forget how long I've known you. I know you liked Laura before liking girls was cool. You've drooled over her since the first day she moved to school."

Tommy stared at Nick, then said, "You suck."

Nick laughed. "I know, but I'm telling you, man, she's just a girl. There are plenty more in the world. Look at Britney. She's awesome, huh?"

Tommy smiled. "Yeah, she's nice."

"Nice? She's hot, smart, funny."

"Don't forget fifteen."

"Ha. Yeah, fifteen."—cupping his hands in front of him—"with huge"—

Destiny smacked the back of his head, and Tommy laughed. Nick turned around, flustered, finishing his sentence, "tracts of land."

Tommy tried to get up to let Britney in, but she shooed him over, then sat beside him. She said to no one in particular, "I love Monty Python."

Now it was Nick's turn to redden. He said, "I ... I'm sorry." He slid over for Destiny.

Britney flipped her hand at Nick. "I've had these things for years. I've heard it all. Yes, they have different zip codes. My last three boyfriends are still lost somewhere down in there"—pointing to the modest cleavage that peeked out from the neck of her t-shirt—"And my personal favorite, I have to order my bras from a parachute company. Although that isn't as funny, it's not far from the truth."

When they left the restaurant, Tommy diverted his eyes from the booth where Patrick and Laura sat, both on the same side, his arm around her. It was enough to survive her cheering Patrick on at the games; he didn't need her popping up at other times too, reminding him he wasn't good enough for her.

Tommy was the dreaded "funny friend." It was a prison very few boys ever escaped from once they were relegated to its dark recesses. He was close enough to invite to a birthday party. He was nice enough to sit with at lunch. He was funny enough to laugh with over a teacher's miscues.

But he was not boyfriend material. That was reserved for guys like Patrick Hart, guys with perfect hair, perfect teeth, and large allowances.

Nick was right about two things that night, Tommy thought to himself. Tommy needed to get over Laura, forget her ever being more than a casual friend he saw at school and the mall. And second, Tommy had indeed fallen head over heels for Laura the very first moment he met her.

Chapter 3

It was the first day of second grade, and little Tommy Chandler was excited. He had on his favorite shirt and a new pair of shoes. They squeaked when he walked, and he thought that was cool.

His mom took him to school, and they checked in at the front office. He waved to Nick in the hallway. They'd just had a sleepover on Saturday night, and they hoped they were in each others' classes.

On the way to his new classroom, he saw other kids he knew with their parents. Angel Keller, Melody Bruner, Barry Foreman, Yvonne Winston, Michelle Garrick, Terrell Baker, Greg Farmer. They were all there.

Mrs. Mims greeted Tommy's mom with a stiff handshake. She was old, and Tommy thought her face resembled a horse's. It was thin and long and sagged a little. She looked tough. Second grade might not be as fun as he and Nick thought.

Tommy took his new seat directly behind Nick, and they immediately began jabbering away about the things this year would hold. There were rumors they'd get homework for the first time and during recess, they'd get to play dodge ball every Friday. This was going to be a great year.

Eventually, the parents left, and Mrs. Mims strolled to the blackboard. She grabbed a piece of chalk between her bony fingers and

The Walk-On

wrote her name in big block letters, saying, "My name is Mrs. Mims."

She stepped to the side and pointed at the board with a long, knobby finger: her middle one.

It was enough for Tommy and Nick to break into giggles. Mrs. Mims cut her eyes at them. "Is something funny?" she asked stiffly. "Perhaps you'd like to share with the class."

Tommy and Nick knew darn well everybody had seen what she'd done, but none of them had laughed. And neither Tommy nor Nick was about to say anything about Mrs. Mims' middle finger for fear of getting sent to the principal's office. That wouldn't be a good thing to happen on the first day of class.

Mrs. Mims pursed her lips and narrowed her eyes a few seconds, glanced at the seating chart on her podium, then said, "Thomas Chandler? Let's have you change seats with"—peeking at her clipboard again—"Susanne Hinshaw over here." She pointed in front of her with her middle finger, and it was all the boys could do to keep from bursting into laughter. Did no one else see she pointed with her middle finger? Her middle finger!

Tommy gathered his new notebook and freshly sharpened pencils and changed places with Suzy Hinshaw while Mrs. Mims erased and scribbled on her clipboard.

Tommy was now in the front row center of the classroom. Directly in front of Mrs. Mims. The teacher smiled at him with grayed teeth as he settled into his new rectangular desk.

It wasn't level and rocked toward the front-left. The chair rocked the other way, to the front-right. Tommy hunched over, a dark cloud gathering over his new seat assignment. Second grade was shaping up to be no fun at all.

It was a whole hour before Mrs. Mims told them to break into pairs to practice their cursive writing. She had stood at the front the whole time, going over math and spelling, writing endlessly on the blackboard, pointing at her work with her middle finger, daring anyone in the room to react. Tommy got up to go find Nick, and Mrs. Mims told everyone to take their seats. "Everyone on the front row, turn around and partner with the student behind you. Then the third row do the same with the fourth. Fifth row with the sixth."

Tommy twisted his chair around and looked into the biggest honey-colored eyes he'd ever seen. The girl had long brown hair, silky and shiny, that fell over her shoulders. The right side was tucked behind her ear revealing a tiny golden heart earring.

She was a new girl.

"I'm Laura," she said.

"Tommy."

Laura smiled and Tommy stopped breathing. It didn't make sense. She was just a girl, why did his chest hurt? Why did his face get warm and his ears beat like conga drums?

They practiced their cursive writing, Tommy watching Laura as her pencil glided across her paper. Her hands were slender, her fingers delicate. They reminded Tommy of silk curtains. Graceful as they slid her pencil across the page in an effortless exercise.

Laura murmured the words as she wrote. Tommy watched her lips, and he found himself saying the words with her. She was like a doll, her skin smooth and perfect.

He wanted to touch her hand, to see how soft it was. He wanted to hold it, to draw on its warmth. He wanted to brush her cheek and breathe in her scent.

And for the first time in his life, Tommy Chandler wanted to kiss a girl.

He'd seen it done in movies and never understood exactly why it was done with someone who wasn't family. With aunts and uncles, you kissed them on holidays. With moms and dads, you kissed them at bedtime or when they went out and left you with a babysitter.

But Tommy didn't know anything about Laura, only her first name. And yet, he felt an urge to place his hand on hers, to touch his lips to her lips. Gently. Carefully. Tenderly.

"You're not writing," Laura said.

Tommy blinked and looked down at his paper. Had she caught him staring? His face warmed, and his mouth dried up. "I was watching how you did your *L*s."

Laura grinned, saying, "I can show you." Before Tommy could respond, Laura hopped up and came around beside him. She set her paper down beside his and leaned over it. Her shoulder touched his, and she said, "It's easy. You start over here at the top, curve it around, then down and around and back up at the end."

She turned to him, their faces inches apart. "I like to put a little curly thing on it at the beginning." She smelled like the wind blowing through his Paw Paw's apple orchard.

Tommy swallowed, the touch of her shoulder keeping him off-kilter. He had to think of something to say while he could still form words. "I can't do the curly thing," he said.

"Sure you can." Laura smiled at him. She showed him how to do the curly part again, but Tommy found himself watching how her fingers held the pencil instead. How they skimmed over the paper as naturally as if she had been born with the ability to write a perfect cursive *L*.

Suddenly Mrs. Mims towered over them. When she spoke, the world sped back into reality. "What are you doing out of your seat, young woman?"

Laura looked up, startled. "I was showing Tommy my *L*."

Tommy heard nothing else after that. She'd remembered his name, said it aloud. It was as if a rainbow had spoken after a rainstorm, announcing that everything would be alright, the bright happy sun was here now. Nothing else mattered when the rays of her angelic voice caressed his skin. She had spoken his name, and the world approved.

There was certain strength in the weakness that washed over him.

"Return to your seat," Mrs. Mims clipped. She looked at Tommy's paper. "There's nothing wrong with your *L*s."

Tommy spent the rest of the writing time making *L*s until he could add the curly part at the beginning. Then he filled in the rest of the name after each *L*. *Laura, Laura, Laura.*

Recess was announced thirty minutes later, and Tommy was slow rising from his desk. They filed outside, Tommy watching Laura step in line with Angel Keller, the two girls chattering about Angel's new dress. He listened while Nick told him how Bobby Black drew pictures of Mrs. Mims in a witch's costume on the back of his writing paper. Bobby didn't know he was going to have to hand it in when they were done so he balled it up and threw it away on his way out of the room.

"We have to hand it in?" Tommy said, jerking his body toward Nick.

"Yeah. You didn't hear her say that?"

Tommy hadn't, and he'd filled the paper with the new girl's name. He turned to run back into the classroom, but Mrs. Mims was already coming out with all the writing paper in her hands.

Tommy felt all the air leave him.

"What's wrong?" Nick asked.

"Nothing." Tommy shook his head in slow motion. "Nothing at all."

Tommy and Nick hit the seesaws first, Tommy with his back to the old storage building. Every time Tommy rose in the air, he scanned the playground. Laura and Angel went from the monkey bars to the merry-go-round to the swings. It was as if Angel was giving Laura a tour.

Most of the kids were running around playing tag or chasing each other for no real reason.

When they'd had enough of the seesaw, the boys walked around. The place looked the same as last year. Nothing had changed; nothing new had been added, and nothing was taken away. They took turns teetering across the balance beam, then scrambling through the tire tunnel, then swinging across the ladder bars.

"Tommy and Nick smell like farts!"

The boys turned to see Angel Keller and Laura making faces at them. She had her nose crinkled and tongue stuck out. There was only one thing they could do at that point: They gave chase, what all boys did at that age when taunted by a girl.

Screeching, Angel and Laura turned and fled. Around the swings, narrowly missing Deanne Henderson as she descended in a broad arc, around the merry-go-round, past the big tires—through the last one—skirting the dodge ball slab, through another group of kids playing keep-away with Darrell Bowder's glasses—he was having a real hard time seeing who had them.

As the girls sprinted toward the big trees, Tommy and Nick stopped, picked up some rocks, and threw them, missing far to the right.

"Angel Keller eats turds for breakfast!" Nick yelled, his hands cupped around his mouth.

"Laura too," Tommy added. The response was a chorus of giggles as Angel and Laura peeked out from behind the safety of huge oak trees.

And thus, the ritual had completed as quickly as it had begun. As the players age, the ceremonies get more diluted, more complicated. Extra steps are added, dressed up, reshaped. Promises are made and sometimes kept. Expectations grow. Hearts are courted and broken. Lives are built, altered, fulfilled.

But at its most basic level, the ritual is always the same. It never changes.

Girl yells at boy, boy chases girl, boy throws rock, boy gives up, girl delights in newfound attention. Boy is clueless.

Chapter 4

It was a gym class of jocks: basketball, baseball, and football players. Taking gym wasn't mandatory as juniors and seniors, but if you played any sport for the school, it was an unspoken rule.

Coach Barrows had decided on basketball as the activity that day for three reasons: it was Friday, it was basketball season, and he was the basketball team coach.

All twelve members of the Varsity basketball team were in this particular gym class, a feat that did not happen by accident.

Coach blew the whistle, and everyone gathered at mid-court. Even though they knew the routine, he still made a show out of explaining what was going to happen.

"Okay," he began, "I want Patrick, Jalen, Nick, Austin, Dave, and Miles over here. Tommy and the rest of you over there."

Patrick Hart's team consisted of the five starters and the first guy off the bench. Tommy's team was made up of the rest of the second and third-string. They were to go head-to-head on the first court under the coach's careful supervision. On the other court, the rest of the class would play a game wrought with excessive fouls and arguing. They were mostly football players.

From the beginning, Patrick's team dominated. Patrick was an inch taller than Tommy, and a step quicker. He could beat Tommy off the dribble every time and when on defense, never let Tommy by him. Tommy would usually have to settle for quick jump shots. And they were always contested.

Patrick brought the ball down, strutting, and calling out a play.

"Come on, Tommy," he said loud enough for everyone to hear. "Can't you stop me just once? You know what play we're getting ready to do, and yet I still run all over you."

Some of his team laughed. Tommy said nothing, only concentrated on Patrick's dribbling.

Patrick said, "I'm going to fake left, then go right. You ready?"

Tommy steeled himself with his hands out in ready position as Patrick dribbled toward him.

Then Patrick made his move. He faked left, and went hard right. Tommy couldn't recover from the fake, and Patrick went around him with ease, driving to the basket for an easy lay-up.

The laughter rang in Tommy's ears. He heard someone say, "Broke his damn ankles."

Patrick patted Tommy on the head before he jogged back down the court. Tommy went to deflect him, but Patrick was already jogging off, laughing as he high-fived Miles Flaherty.

It was even worse in practice. The taunting, the ridiculing, the jeering. And the coach did nothing. He saw it though he never showed it. That kind of inaction was as good as condoning the behavior as far as Tommy was concerned.

After gym class, Tommy knocked on the coach's door.

"Yeah." Coach looked up, then said, "Come on in." When Tommy stepped into his office he asked, "What's up?"

At first, Tommy didn't know how to say what he came to say. Then he just blurted it out. "Can't you just tell Patrick to stop?"

Coach narrowed his eyes. "You mean his picking on you?"

Tommy nodded, glancing at his feet. "Yeah."

Coach turned back to the bookcase he was sifting through, saying, "Not really."

Tommy hadn't expected that answer. Maybe "I'll look into it" or "I'll say something to him," but not a no. He stared at the coach's profile.

Coach Barrows looked up from the bookcase and said with a shrug, "Get better." Then after a second, he squared himself to Tommy and added, "Do you really think me telling Patrick to cut it out is going to work? He'd just pick on you in the halls and after school." He shook his head. "No, the only thing that'll stop somebody like him is for you to beat him at his own game. Get better and shut him up on the court."

Coach grabbed a basketball sitting in the chair beside the bookcase and tossed it to Tommy. "Beat him with that. Practice. Get faster." He paused and frowned. "Just get better."

"But Coach," Tommy said, his hair still dripping from his shower. "He's bigger than me."

"I know," Coach responded, nodding. "But here's the thing, all you boys are still growing. As a matter of fact"—pointing at Tommy—"you've only now started to grow. You're going to catch Patrick Hart and I wouldn't be at all surprised if you passed him in that respect." He removed the whistle from around his neck and plopped into his chair at his desk. He swiveled toward Tommy, rubbing his knees. "I ever tell you about my best friend growing up?"

Tommy shook his head, and the coach motioned toward the chair in front of the desk. Tommy slid into it as the coach continued.

"My best friend and I, growing up, were as close as two guys could be. We did everything together. Listened to the same music, tried for the same girls, played all the same sports." He laughed. "We were so competitive that if you didn't know any better, you'd think we didn't like each other once we were on the court. When we stepped onto that hardwood, we took no prisoners. Especially when we were on opposing teams."

Coach leaned back in his chair and propped his foot on his trashcan.

"By sixth grade, Joey had hit his growth spurt. You look at pictures of us back then, and he's a whole head taller than me. Then, by our junior or senior year, I don't remember which, I was suddenly a head taller than him. I was a late bloomer, Tommy, just like you.

"The height will come. Trust me. But you have to try harder, practice more, be more determined. Height won't give you experience and talent."

Coach leaned forward. "You watch college basketball on TV? What do you watch?"

Tommy frowned. "What do you mean?"

"I mean exactly what I said. What do you watch? The coaches? The refs? The cheerleaders?"

Tommy smiled. "I watch the ball," he replied, straightening.

"Wrong." Coach waited for Tommy's face to cloud before continuing. "What position do you play?"

"Point guard."

"Then what should you be watching?"

Tommy hesitated, then grinned. "The point guards."

"Right. On both teams. Watch how they defend, how they penetrate, how they see the court. They sometimes don't know what they're gonna do until the split second before it happens. But what makes great point guards different than the good ones is that they know all the possibilities right before they happen. They're prepared, expecting those openings to present themselves. And when those opportunities arise, they grab them."

He paused and wiped the sweat from his forehead. "Let me ask you something. If you got better at passing and dribbling, what gets easier?"

Tommy thought for a minute. "Shooting?"

Coach smiled. "Exactly. They have to back off you because they don't know what you're going to do. The biggest humiliation a point guard can have is to get beaten off the dribble. Am I right?"

Tommy remembered all the times Patrick blew by him.

Coach continued. "So if your defender has to lay back to prevent you from humiliating him, a little fake here or there will open you up enough space for an uncontested jump shot."

Tommy nodded, taking in the wisdom like a broken-in sponge.

"Why do you think you made the team?" Coach Barrows asked, leaning back and propping a foot atop his trashcan again.

Tommy shrugged.

Coach pursed his lips, then said, "You weren't one of the best guards. In fact, if I had chosen players based on that fact alone, you would've been out."

Tommy swallowed, but his throat was dry.

"Any guess?"

Tommy looked down at his hands and noticed he needed to cut his nails. He raised his head. "My sense of humor and good looks?"

Coach Barrows laughed the hardest Tommy had ever seen. "That's part of it. Your attitude. The other part is your potential. You're at the beginning of your development, and you've got talent. But it's raw." He dropped his foot back to the floor and straightened his chair. "What you've got to do is work harder than anyone else if you want to get better. If you practice the same amount as everyone else, you'll get better at the same rate. And you'll still be behind them. Some below you will practice harder, and you'll actually drop back a few spots. You understand?"

Tommy nodded.

"You know what a gym rat is?"

Tommy shook his head.

"Gym rats show up to practice early. They run extra laps. They practice free throws every chance they get. They *live* in the gym." He paused. "You understand?"

Tommy thought about it. "Yeah."

"If you truly want to get better, be a gym rat. That's something that can't be taught or coached. It has to come from inside you. You have to really want it, or you're just going through the motions."

Tommy nodded again. "I get it."

"Do you?"

"Yeah, I do."

"Good. Now get out there before the bell rings." Coach nodded at the door.

Tommy thanked the coach and walked back out into the gym where everyone was waiting for class to officially end. The aroma of soap and deodorant mixed with sweat and testosterone. It was the smell of every high school gym in America.

As he walked toward Nick, Tommy passed by Patrick Hart. Patrick was leaning against the painted cinderblock wall, performing for a rapt audience.

"Yeah, Laura made us go see some stupid movie about a princess bride. Best thing in it was Andre the Giant," he was saying, "Anyway, after that I took her to The Rock. We parked way out at the edge of the field, over where it drops down. You know where I'm talking about?"

Miles Flaherty and Austin Brenner nodded, their bodies tilted

THE WALK-ON

forward, eager for the gritty details. Patrick sneered out of the right side of his mouth.

"She put out?" Miles asked, his eyebrows rising.

Patrick scoffed, then pushed off the wall and raked his hips forward. "She couldn't get enough of the Hart Train." They shared raucous laughs as Patrick kept rocking, his arms bent, chugging at his side. "Even after I was finished with her, she wanted more."

Tommy's fists clenched as Miles asked Patrick what he did then.

Patrick stopped chugging, and his face looked like he'd drank sour milk. "I told her to get off me. I'd give her more when I was ready."

"Hell, yeah," Miles said as he high-fived Patrick.

Tommy had to force his legs to keep moving forward. By the time he reached Nick, he was breathing hard, teeth clenched.

"What's wrong with you?" Nick asked.

"Nothing," Tommy answered.

"Was it something the coach said?"

"No." Tommy turned and glared in Patrick's direction.

Nick followed his best friend's eyes. "Oh, him. Don't let Patrick get to you, man."

"That's what everybody says."

"It's good advice."

"But guys like him ..." Tommy was shaking his head.

Nick brought his hand up in front of him. "He'll get his in the end. Some way, somehow. Somebody will give it to his preppy ass."

Tommy still shook his head, eyes transfixed on Patrick. Patrick made obscene gestures with his mouth and hands, the boys around him laughing and copying him. Tommy didn't need to hear what they were saying, it was obvious to everyone within sight.

The bell rang and everyone filed toward the gym's double doors.

Patrick yelled out from behind, "Hey, Tommy! Where'd you get the high-waters, your little brother?"

As laughter broke out, Nick put himself behind Tommy and railroaded him into the hall, repeating, "Just keep going. Keep going."

Chapter 5

Tommy dribbled left, stopped, went right, faked left, then lifted high in the air for a ten-foot jumper that swished through the rim. "Five-three," he chirped.

"Lucky shot," his dad said, tossing the ball to Tommy as he gathered himself at the top of the key.

It was not unheard of to have a sixty-degree day during December in North Carolina. This Saturday was no exception, and Tommy found himself challenged by his dad to a game of one-on-one.

Tommy took the ball, fighting back a smile. "You ready?"

Gene Chandler nodded, adjusting his shorts and breathing heavy. He wiggled his fingers. "Come on."

Tommy allowed himself a slight smirk as be began dribbling. He went right first, then left, continuing the dribble with his left hand—something he'd been practicing. He pushed left, starting and stopping twice, before whipping a crossover dribble just out of his dad's reach. The move accomplished his goal.

Gene lunged for the steal, but Tommy was already gone, dribbling around his dad's left side. Tommy elevated for an easy lay-up. He imagined himself in a movie he'd seen a few years ago, *Hoosiers*. Ever since the talk with the coach, he couldn't get it out of his head. He felt like one of the country bumpkins on the team, waiting for his chance to shine.

"Six-three," Tommy said as he jumped back to the top of the key.

"You carried the ball," his dad said.

"No, I didn't."

"Yeah, you did, but I tell you what, I'll let it go this time." Gene sucked in some hard breaths and rested his hands on his knees.

Tommy eyed his dad, then bounced the ball to him. "Check."

Gene bounced it back, harder.

Tommy started his dribble and realized his dad was giving him more room now. Afraid of being humiliated.

Tommy switched to his left hand, and his dad still stayed back. Tommy faked left, then shot a jumper from where he stood.

The fifteen-footer clanked off the back of the rim, and Gene grabbed the rebound. He dribbled out past the three-point line and turned.

"You've made your last shot, boy."

Tommy grinned and wiggled his finger at his dad. "Come on."

Gene did. Hard. He dribbled straight toward the basket like his son wasn't standing in the way. He barreled right over Tommy, but Tommy was able to strip the ball away.

"Foul," Gene said.

Tommy picked himself up from the concrete driveway and walked out to the top of the key with the ball still in his hand.

"What are you doing?" Gene chopped. "You fouled me." He thrust his hands out for the ball.

Tommy pulled the ball back. "You ran right over me!"

"You were moving."

"No I wasn't."

"Your feet were moving. That's a blocking foul. Gimme the ball."

Tommy still held the ball back. "My feet were moving because you knocked me off them."

By this time, Brant had come outside and sat on a chunk of fat log turned on its flat side. "What's the score?" he asked.

Tommy looked up. "Six-three, me."

Gene took the distraction as a chance to swipe the ball out of Tommy's hands. "My ball," he said.

Tommy grimaced but held himself back. He checked the ball, and Gene took an immediate jump shot. It banked in.

Tommy whistled and looked at his bare wrist. "I didn't know the bank was open after five unless you called first."

"Get the ball, smart ass," his dad replied as he slumped, his hands grasping his knees while he wheezed.

Brant hid a smile as Tommy retrieved the ball and checked it.

"Six-five."

Tommy straightened. "Six-four."

"I just made a shot. Six-five."

Tommy turned to Brant. "What was the score?"

"Six-three."

"So you add one to that?"

"Six-four."

Gene Chandler cleared his throat. "Whatever. Six-four. You wanna cheat, go ahead. I'll teach you a lesson about what happens to cheaters."

Gene began dribbling to his right. He jerked left, then knocked down another jump shot.

He laughed. "You can't stop me out here."

Tommy tossed him the ball. "You got no choice but to shoot out there." Smirking, he added, "You can't get by me."

Gene sneered. "Six-five." Then looked at his youngest son. "Unless the scorekeeper has it different?"

Brant threw up his hands.

Gene started dribbling, faking left, then right. Tommy held his ground, knowing his dad couldn't keep shooting from the outside. He was right. Gene faked hard left, then went right. He faked a shot and rose into the air, letting loose another jump shot, only this time, he was closer to the basket, and Tommy was able to get a piece of the ball. It clanged off the front of the rim, and Tommy snatched it up before his dad could recover.

He dribbled out top and turned to find his dad almost on top of him. Gene swiped for the ball, hit Tommy's arm, and sent the ball out of bounds off Tommy's foot.

"Out. My ball," Gene said.

Tommy exploded. "That was a foul!"

"Bullshit."

"You didn't even touch the ball. You got my arm."

"It was a love touch. What are you, a girl? I barely breathed on you."

Tommy scooped the ball up, shaking his head. "It was a foul."

Gene turned to Brant. "You see how he cheats? First the score, then this."

"I'm not cheating."

"Hey." Gene raised his arms. "If you can sleep at night."

Tommy threw him the ball. "Six-five." Gene threw it back, harder.

Something had changed. This was no longer a friendly contest. No longer a nice Saturday afternoon diversion. No longer a casual game of hoops between father and son. What had begun as an innocuous way to pass a sunny December day had turned into war. A full-fledged, all-out war.

Tommy tucked his head down and concentrated. He dribbled left, then right, went behind his back left, behind his back right, faked left and went right hard. Gene recovered in time to fall for the fake shot. Tommy leapt past him and laid the ball in with an old-school finger roll.

"Seven-five."

The next possession, Gene backed off, and Tommy popped a twelve-footer that garnered him a pumped fist from his little brother.

"He don't need no damn cheerleader, boy."

Brant smiled as Tommy said, "Eight-five."

Gene checked the ball, and Tommy dribbled left-right-left-right, continuously switching dribbling hands. He'd been working on going left because he'd seen a lot of college guards were going to their weak side with enough frequency they no longer had a weak side. So this time, Tommy went left. He faked left, faked right, then went left hard.

Gene had not expected Tommy to go left; he went for the fake right, shifting the entire weight of his body. By the time he recovered Tommy had shot past him and elevated for another lay-up.

Gene jumped to block the shot, but at the last second, Tommy switched hands and finished with his left. Gene crashed into him hard, but the ball was already in the air. It bounced off the backboard and danced around the rim before dropping through.

Tommy picked himself up off the ground, brushed the dirt from his body, and said, "Nine-five." He shared a secret smile with Brant as he returned to the top of the key.

Gene, breathing hard, grunted as he kicked the ball to Tommy.

Tommy picked it up and dribbled. His dad was playing off him so the jumper was open, but Tommy didn't want to win that way. He wanted the satisfaction of putting the ball up right by his dad's face, just out of his reach.

He wanted to hold the ball out and when his dad went for it, pull it back and say, "Too slow."

He no longer wanted to just win. Tommy wanted to humiliate his old man, to repay all the times his dad had humiliated him on the court. And off.

Tommy dribbled left, between his legs back to the right, crossed over to the left. He changed directions a few more times, keeping his dad off balance, slowly inching his way toward the basket.

Then, by the way his dad had set his feet, Tommy saw his chance. He faked left, rocked the old man back on his heels, and drove right. Tommy soared into the air for a little baby-hook he'd seen Magic Johnson do hundreds of times, but his dad had recovered quicker than Tommy thought he would.

Gene crashed into him before he could release the ball. Tommy went flying off to the side, skinning his knee as he landed on the concrete.

"Foul," Tommy said as he rose.

"Foul? What, are you wearing a skirt now? That wasn't a foul."

"You knocked me five feet." Tommy was close to yelling.

"It's a contact sport."

"Yeah. That much contact gets you thrown out of a game."

Gene shook his head and caught his breath. "You got so much to learn, boy. Stop crying and play. Life ain't always going to be fair. You gotta learn how to shrug off the things that don't go your way and play on."

Tommy shook his head. "But that was a clear foul."

Gene rolled his eyes. "If I wanted to hear this much whining, I'd go to a tampon convention." He turned and limped toward the house.

"Game's not over."

"I'm done." Gene slammed the back door, and Tommy turned to Brant.

"That went well," he said.

The Walk-On

Brant laughed. "When did you learn to do all the dribbling stuff?"

"What do you mean?"

"You know, behind the back, between the legs. That stuff."

"Oh." Tommy shrugged. "Watching other guys on TV. I've been practicing."

They walked inside, Tommy promising to show Brant how to do the moves after he got some Mountain Dew. They popped into the kitchen and paused, taking a moment to sniff in the smell of fresh-baked goodness.

"You boys want some cookies?" their mom asked. She had just pulled a pan of cookies out of the oven and the kitchen was warm with hazelnut and cocoa.

They eagerly hot-potatoed three cookies onto napkins and began nibbling, blowing on the cookies before each bite.

Helen nodded toward the kitchen window which opened out to the back yard. "It was getting pretty rough out there."

"I was winning," Tommy said, looking for the Mountain Dew.

"Your dad doesn't like to lose."

Tommy laughed. "You don't have to tell me."

"Well, if I were you, I'd steer clear of him the rest of the day."

"That goes without saying." Tommy looked up. "Who's working the store today?"

His mom thought for a minute. "I think it's Steve."

Tommy nodded. "We're gonna get a drink, you need anything else while we're there?"

She ticked on her fingers. "Flour, bananas, pecans, eggs."

Tommy raised his eyebrows. "No side of beef?"

Helen smiled and began scooping cookies into a holiday tin. "You want banana nut cake for dessert tomorrow or not?" She opened a cupboard and said, "Might as well add some powdered sugar to that list while you're at it."

As they were heading out she stopped them. "And take Steve some cookies." She handed Tommy a baggie with some warm cookies, then paused. "I'll call and let Steve know you're coming. Maybe he can have most of it ready by the time you get there." She added, "And I'll let him know to expect four cookies." She held up four fingers and mouthed, "Four."

Tommy shook his head, grinning as the storm door closed behind them.

* * *

Helen found Gene in the tub soaking, an open box of Epsom salts steadied on the edge. "You all right?" she asked.

"Leave me alone."

"I brought cookies." She held out a plate.

Gene lifted his head and winced, groaning as he closed his eyes and relaxed again.

"He beat up on you pretty bad, did he?"

Gene's eyes flashed open, and he cut her a sideways glance. "He didn't beat me."

"I know," she said, moving the Epsom salts so she could sit on the side of tub. "I was watching out the window." She paused. "You quit."

Gene said nothing.

"He reminds me of you at that age," she continued. "He doesn't give up easily."

"I didn't need all that fancy dribbling when I was his age," Gene spit out.

"If I remember correctly, you didn't have to worry about defense too much either."

Gene raised his head. "What's that supposed to mean?"

Helen held a cookie out while Gene took a bite. She said, "And I don't remember your dad being so rough with you on the court."

Gene huffed. "Not when you were around."

"Do you have to be so rough on my son?"

Gene stared at her a second. "He'll never get better if it's easy for him."

"He'll never get better if he's always picking himself up off the ground either."

Gene looked away. "He needs to be toughened up. He's undersized."

Helen smiled. "I remember you were small back then. Skinny as a rail."

Gene swiveled back toward her. "It was different back then."

"I know. You didn't need any fancy dribbling."

Gene squinted his eyes at her. "He'll never be a starter unless he's willing to take some punishment. He's too little. They don't start little guys."

Helen fed him another bite of cookie. "You started."

"And my dad was hard on me. Taught me the importance of inner strength."

"All I'm saying is, you could let him win every once in a while."

Gene's mouth gaped open. "Let him win? Are you crazy, woman? The world won't just let him win whenever he needs to feel good about himself. The world will beat him down and keep on beating him till he's senseless."

"But you're his father." Helen stood. "Your job is to prepare him for the real world, not kill him before he gets there."

Gene raised his voice and sat up. "My job is to make sure he doesn't fail."

"Like your father did you?"

"What the hell are you saying?"

"You know exactly what I'm saying. He held you back from the one dream you had. Don't you dare do the same thing to our son."

"He's the oldest; there's no choice. Just like—"

Helen narrowed her eyes at him. "I'll never forgive you, Gene."

Gene pursed his lips and Helen stepped toward the door. "Leave the cookies," he said.

Helen turned and glared down at him. She smiled and turned the plate over the tub. Gene threw his hands up and gasped as cookies splashed in his lap.

"Enjoy your bath," she said and slid out the door.

Chapter 6

Tommy picked Britney up at precisely six o'clock in his mom's old Buick. They had plans to go to dinner and then see *Dirty Dancing* at the movies. Britney really wanted to see it, and although Tommy had his heart set on seeing *The Princess Bride*, he gave in.

Mrs. Denton let him inside and asked him how he was doing.

"Cold," he answered, blowing his hands.

She smiled and said Britney would be down in a minute. He followed her to the kitchen where she asked if he'd like anything to drink.

"No thanks, ma'am."

"Oh please, don't call me ma'am. It makes me feel old." She motioned for him to sit at the kitchen table. Coupons were strewn everywhere; she looked to be organizing them.

Mrs. Denton held one up, "Fifty cents off Glad trash bags." She looked at Tommy. "We don't even use them, but I always save the coupon."

Tommy grinned. "We always get an off-brand."

"We do too. Whether we go to Winn Dixie or Food Lion, we always get the store brand. Which grocery store do you go to usually?"

"My dad owns a little store out near Forest Oaks. We get all our stuff from the store."

Mrs. Denton was nodding. "Of course you do. Britney told me about that. I'd forgotten." She shuffled a few coupons around. "So I understand you work there after school some days?"

"Yes, ma'am." Tommy winced after he used the word, but Mrs. Denton waved him off. "And every other Saturday."

"Do you like it?"

Tommy shrugged. "It's alright."

"There's a lot to be said for running your own business. Being your own boss."

Tommy shrugged again. "Yes, ma'am." He winced again.

Mrs. Denton laughed. "Just go ahead and call me ma'am. It's nice to meet a young man with good manners these days. It seems like your generation isn't being taught such things as we were."

"Yes, ma'am."

A few seconds of silence.

Mrs. Denton asked, "Do you know what you want to do for a living?"

Tommy shrugged. "Not really."

"You'll possibly take over the store? I understand it's been in your family a while."

Tommy looked down at the coupons. "My grandfather started it way back. Then my dad took over." He looked up. "But I don't think I want to do it."

Mrs. Denton studied him. "So you want to strike out on your own? Blaze your own trail, as they say?"

Tommy nodded. "I figure I'll find a direction in college."

"Well, that's a good thing." She smiled. "College is about more than learning out of books. You'll learn a lot about life, too."

Britney popped into the kitchen. "I don't know who's a better recruiter, Mom, you or Dad."

"I am," Mrs. Denton said, straightening. "Who do you think recruited *your dad*?"

Britney rolled her eyes and turned to Tommy. "We better hurry before she starts asking you about your SAT scores."

Tommy stood and nodded as Mrs. Denton stood. "Nice meeting you again, ma'am," he said.

"Nice meeting you ... which one is this again, Britney?"

Tommy's face warmed as Britney said, "Mom, stop it."

Mrs. Denton smiled. "Tommy knows I'm kidding." She walked them to the door, saying, "You just keep doing what you're doing, Tommy. The rest will come to you when it's supposed to."

They bounded down the steps, leaving Mrs. Denton at the door. Before she disappeared inside, she yelled, "Ten o'clock tonight, Britney. It's a school night."

Britney waved behind her as she followed Tommy. When they pulled out of the driveway, her mom was still standing at the glass storm door, waving.

Britney smiled and waved in return, then turned to Tommy, the smile gone. "God."

"She means well," Tommy said.

"She's so nosy."

"Wouldn't you be?"

"You think she was just being nice in there, but really, she was mining you for information. I see she got all the way to the college question."

Tommy slowed for a stop sign. "Actually, I think I'm the one that brought that up."

Britney stretched her legs out. "So you got a college in mind? Anywhere you want to go?"

Tommy bit his lip. "I don't know."

"You don't know? Well, what do you want to do?"

He hesitated. "I don't know."

Britney turned to him. "What are you good at? What do you love to do most?"

Tommy shrugged. "I'm okay at a lot of things, just nothing stands out. I don't have a dream job."

"You go to college for a career, not a job."

They listened to the radio as Tommy drove to Swensen's in Friendly Center. Britney ordered a grilled chicken sandwich with fries and Tommy got a cheeseburger with fries.

"Carolina's having a good year," Britney finally offered.

Tommy perked up. "I think they're good enough to win it all."

"Duke'll give them a hard time in the ACC."

"Wake's doing good too."

Britney nodded and sipped her Coke. Other couples were in the restaurant, sharing banana splits or root beer floats, laughing and making googly eyes.

"We play Grimsley next week," Tommy said. "At Grimsley."

"I know. I'm planning on being there."

"Which side you gonna sit on?"

"Probably the Grimsley side. All my friends will be over there." She smiled. "But if you get in the game, I'll scream my lungs out for you."

Tommy shook his head. "Hope for a blowout then."

"You really don't think you'll get any playing time?"

"It doesn't matter how good I do in practice, Coach has his starting five. Plus, I've heard him say he wants to keep Patrick happy."

"Why's that?"

Tommy shrugged. "Probably got something to do with all the money

THE WALK-ON

his parents give to the athletic program."

"That's not fair."

"I hear they even donated the computers in the computer lab."

Britney wiped her mouth. "Patrick's such an ass."

"You know him?"

"You can tell a lot about a person by the way they play on the court. Especially a point guard, because they run the team. And Patrick is a grade A ass."

Tommy laughed. "You don't know the half of it."

"What do you mean?"

Tommy waved his hand. "Don't worry about it. It's just a bunch of little stuff."

Britney dipped a fry in ketchup and popped it in her mouth. She chewed for a second before saying, "Did he do something to you in particular?"

Tommy shrugged. "He's just one of those guys, you know?"

"No, I don't. Tell me."

"I don't know. He's always talking and saying stuff under his breath. Know what I mean?"

Britney scrunched her face up. "Are you saying he's a bully?"

"No, he's not a bully. He's just ... I don't know ... he's just one of those guys. I don't know, forget about it. Why are we even talking about this?"

Britney raised her eyebrows and looked down at her plate. She ate a few more fries and said, "What time's the movie start?"

"Seven forty-five."

Chapter 7

Southeast was up fourteen over Grimsley with a minute to go. Coach put the second string in the next dead ball. Forty-five seconds.

The entire game, Tommy had glanced up at Britney on the far side of the court, talking and laughing with her friends. She waved to him twice. He smiled back.

In the forty-five seconds he actually played, Tommy racked up an assist, a steal, and two points off a lay-up.

Afterward, Britney rushed to him. "You played great."

Tommy shrugged. "I did okay."

"Are you crazy? That crossover you did? You left their guard sucking his thumb."

Tommy then noticed Laura Novak make her way to Patrick Hart. They hugged and kissed.

"He was another scrub," Tommy finally replied, looking back at his girlfriend.

"He may be, but Tommy"—she grabbed his sweaty face in her hands—"You are not."

Tommy was about to say something when Coach Barrows yelled his name. Tommy turned as the coach caught up to him.

"You've got to get to the hospital," he said, out of breath.

"What happened?" Tommy asked, alert as his face hardened.

"It's your dad. He's had a heart attack. He's at Wesley Long."

Tommy suddenly had a thousand questions. The coach answered the most important with his next statement. "He's okay, but your mom's frantic for you to be there."

Tommy was stunned. He couldn't move. They'd just played ball together the other night, and his dad had seemed fine.

Tommy couldn't be there to help unload the truck today because he had a game. His mom told him not to worry about it, but his dad glared at him all breakfast long. And now ...

"I'll drive you," Britney's friend said. "It's just down the street."

They didn't speak during the five-minute drive. The friend dropped them off, and Tommy got his dad's room number at the front desk. They navigated the maze of sterile halls, following sparse signs to the cardiac wing. The antiseptic aroma emanating from the rooms they passed added to Tommy's anxiety. According to the old lady at the front, his dad was in a room of his own.

When they arrived, Britney stayed outside as Tommy cracked the door. He saw his mom first. She broke into a sad smile and held her arms out. Tommy rushed to her.

The hug was strong and unyielding. It spoke of sadness and relief. Of the mortality and frailty of life. It was a hug that conveyed more than the unconditional love of a mother.

It also communicated that one minute you could be unloading a truck or shooting a jumper; and the next, you could have plastic tubes shoved down your throat, wires protruding from sticky patches on your chest, and beeping machines reminding everyone around you that no one lived forever. No one.

Dad was steady, Helen told Tommy. Not out of the woods yet, whatever that meant, but the doctors were no longer worried. She had been crying. Her face was splotchy, her eyes red.

Brant sat in a chair beside his dad, watching the breathing machine as its insides bellowed up and down. He smiled thinly at Tommy.

"Did I see Britney out there?" his mom asked.

Tommy nodded and Helen went out to talk to her. Tommy slid over beside Brant. Brant never took his eyes off the machine, as if doing so would suddenly cause it to cease functioning.

"Steve called 9-1-1," his brother said. "Then he called mom."

Tommy glanced at his dad. He was pale and looked small for some reason. "Was he unloading the truck when it happened?"

"Just finished."

Tommy's guilt pressed in on him like a vise. If he wasn't playing basketball, he'd have been there. He'd have helped unload the truck. He'd have carried the heavy items. His dad would be fine right now, maybe propped up in his recliner sucking down a beer, bitching about his distributor raising the prices on toilet paper. Not laying here in an adjustable bed, his skin gray and clammy, face slack and lifeless. He'd have a remote in his other hand, switching between games, yelling at the TV like he was in the stands and could affect the outcome.

Suddenly the machines beeped faster, and Gene Chandler came to life. He made choking noises and clawed at the tube protruding from his mouth. Tommy ran to grab his mom, but nurses were already filing in. They had everyone wait outside.

The family was let back in ten long minutes later. Gene Chandler was sitting up in bed, hair disheveled, eyes uneven. He was awake but missing his normal fire. He was there, but not there. Sprawled on the hospital bed among the myriad machines was the shell of Gene Chandler.

An old man had replaced Tommy's dad.

Gene surveyed his family before resting his tired eyes on his wife. "They tell me it was a heart attack."

Helen nodded, stepping forward. "A small one." She grabbed his hand. "You were lucky." A tear escaped her left eye. "This time."

"Quit your bawling," he said, forcing a laugh. He stared at her. "I suppose you're gonna change my diet now? Cut out my red meat and salt? Feed me crap like tofu and kale. Damn rabbit food?"

Helen forced a tight smile.

"For God's sake, Helen," Gene said. "I ain't dead yet. Quit acting like it. You got another forty years before you bury me."

Helen burst into laughter.

"You think I'd let a little heart attack take me out?" A smile escaped his lips. "Heart attacks are for women."

He looked past Helen to Tommy and Brant, motioning them over to the other side of the bed. They obeyed.

"How you boys doing?"

Tommy and Brant nodded. "Okay," they both said, faces blank.

He studied them a minute. "You know I'm not going anywhere just yet. Right?"

They nodded again.

Gene turned to Brant. "You're getting pretty big now, huh?"

A thin smile formed on Brant's lips.

"What are you, thirty now?"

Brant laughed. "Thirteen, dad."

"Thirteen, thirteen," he repeated. "Thirteen going on thirty. Won't be long your mom will let you help out at the store on Saturdays."

Helen squeezed Gene's hand in an unseen signal.

Gene pretended he didn't feel it. Instead, his brow wrinkled, and he said, "Do I have a daughter I don't know about?"

Helen swiveled to Britney.

Helen answered, "This is Britney, Gene. Tommy's girlfriend."

Gene looked from Britney to Tommy and back to Britney. "This is Britney?"

"Yes, dad," Tommy said.

"I expected a girl, not a young woman."

Britney blushed.

"How'd you get a catch like that?" Gene asked Tommy.

Tommy, embarrassed now, said, "Dad."

Gene wiggled his eyebrows, and Tommy hoped Britney hadn't seen it. Tommy still wore his sweats, his basketball uniform underneath. Gene gave him a once-over.

"You came straight from the game?"

"Yes, sir."

"You play?"

Not did you win or how'd you do.

"The last forty-five seconds."

"Forty-five seconds? That's all?"

Tommy swallowed. He knew what was coming, and he didn't want it to happen in front of Britney. His mom sensed it too because she squeezed Gene's hand and said, "Britney told me Tommy had an assist, a steal, and two points."

"You only played forty-five seconds?" Gene repeated as though Helen hadn't spoken. His voice had risen. "You practice every day, sometimes twice a day, go to every game, and you—"

"Gene," Helen interrupted, clearing her throat.

The machines attached to Gene beeped quicker, more insistent.

He continued, "All that time, I work at the store alone while you're spending all your time riding the damn pine?" His voice rose even louder.

"Honey," Helen cooed, patting her husband's hand. "You need to calm down."

"An assist, a steal, and two lousy points. Against the other team's worst players no doubt." He pinned Tommy with his eyes. "This time at the end of the game?"

Tommy nodded, his eyes not leaving his dad's.

"Figures. Forty-five seconds of time that means nothing to the result of the game. Meanwhile, I'm unloading the truck by myself, restocking the store without a single bit of help."

"Steve was there," Tommy said, his voice small.

It was the wrong thing to say.

"Steve?" Gene roared. The machines answered with increased chittering. "Steve? Steve's not my oldest son. In my day, a son helped his father around the store every waking minute. Here I am, busting my ass every day, handing you an opportunity, and you're out skipping around on a basketball court, playing forty-five seconds at the end of a blowout!"

The nurses rushed in and pushed Gene back into his bed, yelling for everyone to leave. Tommy watched his dad fight the nurses until his mom dragged Tommy outside the room.

Tommy shook her off and stalked down the hall, unsure of where he was going. He only knew one thing: each step took him farther from the man who'd given him life, and that was all that mattered. Giving life wasn't enough for his dad; the man wanted to run it too.

"Tommy!" his mom yelled after him.

Tommy almost kept walking, but he stopped. He turned, hands shoved into the shallow pockets of his sweats, and waited for her to catch up. She placed her arms around him as he shook. He closed his eyes.

"Nevermind him," Helen murmured in his ear. "You know how he gets."

"How he gets, mom? He's always like this."

She patted his back, trying to look into his eyes. Helen fished the car keys from her pocketbook.

"Take Britney and Brant home. I'll stay here tonight." She smiled at her older son. "Give Steve a call and ask if he can cover the store. Tell him I'll call him tomorrow."

Tommy nodded and took the keys, shoving his hands back into his sweats. Helen took his face in her hands.

"Mom," Tommy whined, seeing his brother and Britney approaching.

"Shush. If I want to admire my son up close, it's my prerogative."

Tommy tilted his head and looked to the side.

"You're growing up so fast. It wasn't so long ago I was yelling out the window to slow down on your Big Wheel, and now I'm handing you my keys without a second thought."

"Mom," Tommy whined again. "Come on." He tried to pull his face away, but Helen wouldn't relinquish it.

She took a deep breath and sighed. She blinked back tears, then coaxed her son's teenage head down far enough to kiss him on the forehead. She let him go, saying, "It's called a Big Wheel, right?"

"Yes, mom." He smirked, rolling his eyes up.

She reached up and ran her hand through the damp mop on his head. "And we need to get you a haircut soon, or is that how the kids are wearing it now?"

"Mom." He elongated the word into two syllables.

"Okay, okay." She turned to Brant and kissed him on the forehead. She flipped through her pocketbook once more and pulled out a twenty.

The Walk-On

She gave it to Tommy. "Get something to eat before you go home. I had a cake in the oven, but I had to turn it off"—motioning around her—"It might be okay to eat; it might not."

The three teens turned and trudged down the barren halls.

Helen watched them leave, then said after them, "And be careful."

* * *

Tommy pulled the Buick up to the curb and smiled weakly at Britney. "I'll talk to you tomorrow."

She stared at him a second before saying, "Will you walk me to the door?"

Tommy glanced in the back seat. "Brant, close your eyes."

"No," Britney barked. "Walk me to the door." A pause. "Please."

Brant's eyes widened. Tommy huffed, then opened his door and got out. Britney was waiting for him by the time he rounded the car. She took his hand, and they strolled up the cobblestone path.

"I don't want to talk about it," Tommy said as they walked.

"I think you need to."

"What's there to say? Talking about it won't do any good. It won't change anything."

"Tommy, this is what I'm here for." She stopped at the bottom of the steps and turned to him. "This is how it works. You tell me things, and I tell you things. It's called a relationship."

Tommy lowered his head and nudged a rock with his foot. He mumbled, "That's just the way he is, alright? He's never gonna change, and I don't want to talk about it."

Britney took both Tommy's hands in hers and waited until he lifted his eyes. "I need you to confide in me. Even about things that won't change. It's what I want."

"But—"

"Tommy, it's what I want." She paused. "Okay?"

The porch light flicked on, and Tommy cut his eyes at the front door. Britney squeezed his hands, and he turned back to her.

"Okay," he said. "I guess so."

Chapter 8

Greensboro Day was the biggest game Southeast played all year. The Bengals were the most hated and most envied team in the area. As an "elite" private school, they ran a formidable basketball program that boasted a near-hundred percent college recruitment rate. The majority of the players went on to major Division I programs in the ACC, the SEC, and the Big East.

Greensboro Day was hated because they "recruited" the best players from surrounding schools, because they usually won, and because they usually placed high in the State Tournament if they didn't win it outright. But at the most basic level, opposing teams hated Greensboro Day because they were the team to beat.

In the pep talk before the big game, Coach Barrows asked his kids how bad they wanted to beat "those elitist bastards."

"They think they're better than you. They go to a private school; their mommies and daddies pay a butt load of money for the privilege. How does that make you feel?"

Coach Barrows paused for effect, becoming more animated with every sentence.

"When you go out that door and see those pretty-boys strutting around in their shiny little uniforms, going through their fancy lay-up drills, what are you going to do about it? You gonna bow to them, ask them if you can get them a cup of water? Are you?"

Coach Barrows was yelling now.

"You gonna let that bunch of sissy-boys beat you just because they're too good for public school? Well, are you?"

Coach pumped his fists; a chorus of NOs erupted. "Get up! Everybody in here!" Coach extended his arm into the group, his fist clenched.

"Are we gonna win?" he yelled.

"Yeah!" came the response.

"What are we gonna do?"

"Win!"

"I can't hear you!"

"Win! Win! Win!"

It was the same cheer before every game; Coach did it to get the blood flowing. And it worked. The boys stormed out of the locker room with every intent to steamroll over Greensboro Day School, but at halftime, Southeast was down by four, thanks to a last-second shot by Patrick Hart.

During the break, Coach berated his team for not doing enough. According to him, they should be up by fifteen by now. All they had to do was hit their shots.

"Austin, you're letting their center eat you for dinner in the paint. You want me to bring some mustard out for the second half, see if he likes you better that way?"

Coach turned to Jalen Carter. "Jalen, what the hell game are you playing out there? Pattycakes? When somebody shoots"—Coach crouched low and wiggled his behind—"you get in there and box somebody out. Grab that rebound with both hands. Don't tip it around like you're learning to juggle. Block out and use two hands."

Coach pulled the chalkboard over and drew up one of their plays, showing where it wasn't working. "Patrick, when you go around this guy right here? You got to use the pick Miles sets for you. And when you go by him, don't leave any room for your defender ... I want you so close to Miles he thinks he should give you a ring and ask where you wanna go after the game."

This got a few laughs.

Coach shook his head and motioned for a huddle. Everyone stuck a hand in as he said, "Okay, guys. We're here. Can you taste it?"

"I taste mustard," somebody said.

More laughs.

Coach continued, "This game is ours. It's so close. Just sixteen more minutes of good ball, and we can send these boys back to town on a very quiet bus. It all comes down to who wants it the most. That's what you have to ask yourself. How bad do you want it?"

Coach paused and lowered his voice. "How bad do you want it?"

Another pause.

"Go team on three. One-two-three!"

"GO TEAM!"

The huddle broke, and the team sprinted from the locker room. Right into a buzz saw.

Greensboro Day scored the first ten points of the third quarter, a drought only broken by two free throws from Jalen Carter on a questionable foul under the basket.

Southeast roared back on two consecutive steals by Patrick Hart; one was converted into a lay-up, the other an old school three-point play.

The score was tied going into the final minute. Greensboro Day brought the ball down slowly, taking their time. Then the point guard rounded a solid pick at the free throw line, drawing the defenders, and lobbed the ball to their center for an alley-oop dunk that would later be replayed at least four times that night on the two local stations that sent camera crews.

Southeast answered with a three-point shot by Nick Muller, who'd had a relatively quiet night up to that point. The guard sticking to him like glue had signed a Letter of Intent with Clemson.

Then the future Clemson standout took a shot at the other end of the floor that clanged off the rim only to be rebounded and jammed home by the same center who had completed the lob-dunk earlier. The center would be joining Chapel Hill's program in the fall.

The other starters on the Bengals would be attending NC State, Duke, and College of Charleston.

Patrick brought the ball down with ten seconds on the clock; Greensboro Day was up one. Patrick was instantly double-teamed as he rounded a pick set by Miles Flaherty at the top of the key. He dished off to Nick Muller who found Jalen Carter wide open on the block.

Jalen elevated for an easy jumper that skipped off the front of the rim.

The opposing center swatted the ball down court.

The buzzer sounded.

Southeast lost.

Coach Barrows told them they played a great game against the best team they'd see all season. He was proud of them. Secretly, he'd never expected to be in the game at the end. Most of his starters were juniors while Greensboro Day's were mostly seniors: kids being recruited by top tier Division I programs.

The Falcons had played over their heads that night, and everyone knew it. Especially Coach Barrows.

But after he left the locker room, the stale taste of a loss still

The Walk-On

lingered. They were so close. One more basket, or a little better defense, or one less mistake ... and they would have won. It was right there, within reach.

"What the hell, Jalen?" Patrick exploded in the locker room.

Jalen looked up.

Patrick continued, "How'd you miss that shot? You were three feet away! My grandma could have made that shot left-handed."

"Lay off him, Patrick," Austin said.

"Lay off him? What the hell did you do all night? You let their center run all over you. Were you guarding him or holding his hand? You didn't box him out a single time. Hell, you saved him a place near the basket."

Miles spoke up, "The guy had thirty pounds on him, Patrick. Give him a break."

Patrick turned on him. "And you? Do you even *know* what a pick is? You're supposed to square up and knock the other guy on his ass when I go around you. See how that works? You *pick* him off me. But no, you practically asked him how his grades were and if he'd like another cookie."

"Come on, Patrick." It was Nick.

Patrick laughed and turned to his shooting guard. "And just where the hell were you? I scored more points with my left foot than you did all night."

"That's not fair," Tommy blurted out before he could stop himself. When everyone looked at him, he felt the urge to finish. "You barely passed the ball to him. How can he shoot if he doesn't have the ball?"

Patrick squared up at Tommy. "Maybe if your boyfriend would have gotten free from his defender, I'd have gotten him the ball. I guess Miles' picks didn't do him any good either." He laughed and stepped up into

Tommy's face.

"I can't believe you even opened your little mouth. The only time you play is when the coach feels sorry for you. You get my scraps. And that's all you'll ever get, my playing time scraps."

Spittle flew from Patrick's mouth. "Hell, you're so pathetic you give *scrubs* a bad name. You're lower than a scrub. I don't even know why your sorry ass is on this team. You'll never play. You should just quit now, because as long as I'm around, you'll never get in another game."

He laughed, then sneered, "I'll see to that. You can bet on it."

Patrick stormed from the locker room.

The room was quiet. Several of the guys slapped Tommy on the back, telling him not to worry about it.

"You know how Patrick gets," they said. "He can't stand to lose."

But he'd gotten through to Tommy. The words hit home, echoing the very thoughts Tommy had been entertaining all season long. The exact same words his father had said over and over.

Tommy wasn't good enough to play.

He'd always be second or third best. He was wasting his time. It's not like he'd get a basketball scholarship to pay for college. The smartest thing to do would be to quit the team and work at the store, save his money.

Outside, Tommy through his stuff into the Buick.

"You can't quit," Nick said behind him. "There are only a few games left in the season."

"It doesn't matter," Tommy replied, turning around.

"If you quit, he wins."

"He wins anyway, don't you see that? He practically runs the team. Coach caters to him. Whether I quit or not, I'll still get the same amount of playing time."

THE WALK-ON

Nick sighed. "Just stick the rest of the season out. You're not a quitter. If you quit now, that's all anyone will ever remember. In twenty years, at our high school reunion, they'll say, 'Tommy who? Oh, that guy who quit the basketball team?' You wanna be that guy?"

Tommy grinned and opened the car door. His breath formed clouds of mist that dissipated seconds after striking the cold night air. "You're a dick," he said.

"I know," Nick answered, grinning. "But I'm right."

Tommy shook his head. "I just—"

"Go home and sleep on it. At least promise me that. That's all I'm asking. Go sleep on it."

Tommy exhaled and nodded, "Yes, Mom."

Nick smiled, holding his hand out.

Tommy clasped it, and they bumped chests. "Later, man."

"Later ... hey, where was Britney tonight?"

Tommy shrugged. "I think she said something about a test."

Nick nodded and walked away, looking back when he reached his car. "Remember, sleep on it."

Tommy waved him away. "Yeah, yeah." He started the car and sat there a full minute before finding a good song on the radio. He slowly pulled out of the gravel lot and drove home.

Chapter 9

Southeast finished the season winning two of their last three games, with Patrick Hart the star of all three games. Tommy stayed with the team, and true to Patrick's statements, never got in a game again. Gene, relatively healthy, didn't attend a single game, telling Helen, "Why should I go? He doesn't even play. The stockroom isn't going to organize itself."

The world slowly began to get warm and turn green. Flowers popped out of forgotten places and the pleasantness of a North Carolina spring gave way to the beginning of oppressive humidity.

Nick Muller slammed his Jeep's door and raised his arms in the air. He sucked in a loud sniff. "Can you smell it, buddy?"

Tommy threw his towel over his shoulder and regarded his friend with half-lidded eyes. "Smell what?"

"Summer. Women. Freedom." Nick spun around, arms still raised high. "Please tell me you smell it. At least *feel* it."

"I smell my mom's brownies." Tommy pulled a canvas bag out of the Jeep. He reached in and came out with a clear container and peeled the top off. "Yep, chocolate with a peanut butter toffee middle."

Nick came around the Jeep with his hand out. "Gotta start the day right."

Tommy scooped out two brownies and handed one to Nick, then

closed the container and slipped it back in the bag.

Nick cocked his head to peer into the bag. "What all did you bring in there?"

Tommy closed the bag. "Stuff."

"Tell me you got a hidden video camera in there. The hotties are always out in droves the first day the club is open." He licked his lips and rubbed his hands together. "And they'll all be wearing new bikinis."

"Why do you call it a club?"

"Why do you carry your bag like that? Take it off your shoulders and carry it like a man." Nick waited until Tommy complied. "And I call it a club because that's the place's name. See the sign? Says 'swim club.'"

"It's just a pool. A *club* has a sound system and a huge disco ball."

"Okay, Mr. Literal. I don't know why they named it that. Are you ready or what? You need to fix your hair in the side mirror or freshen up your lipstick?"

Tommy started across the pavement without answering. They set up on two chaises in the middle. From there they could see the entrance, the two lifeguard stands, the snack bar, and the entire breadth of the L-shaped pool. The speakers hidden in the surrounding bushes blared Whitesnake's, "Here I Go Again."

"Perfect," Nick said, plopping down and slipping on his shades.

Tommy donned his own shades and got comfortable in his chair, plucking a book from his bag.

The crowd was mostly kids running around under their moms' watchful eyes. There were a few teenage girls there, sunning themselves over to the side. According to Nick, they were early, but that was necessary to get the good seats.

"The real hotties won't show for another hour or so," Nick said. "Then we'll have so much to see our eyes will get tired." Nick looked over. "You know, you can take off your shirt."

"I know."

"Show off both your chest hairs. Girls love that."

"Screw you."

Nick laughed. "What time you gotta be back?"

"I don't. The truck came this morning."

"What's your mom going to do when school starts back?"

Tommy shrugged. "Maybe by then she'll let my dad unload the truck himself. Bribe the truck driver to help or something."

"That's got to be killing your dad."

"Oh yeah. He's hating it. He's so used to not needing help he doesn't know how to accept it."

Nick scoffed. "I've seen that."

"You ain't seen nothing. He *really* yells when there's no one else there."

Nick grunted and nodded. "Look at what just walked in."

Tommy glanced while barely moving his head. Angel Keller had just come in followed by Melody Bruner and Yvonne Winston.

"You know, I gotta say," Nick said as he watched the three girls strut in and skirt across the far side of the pool. They set up just behind one of the lifeguard stations. "You picked a great time to get dumped."

"Gee, thanks. I'll make sure to let Britney know."

"I'm just saying, if you're going to be dumped, the beginning of summer is the perfect time."

"Yeah, well. What you call freedom feels a little crappy to me."

Nick turned to his friend, bottom lip protruding. "Poor widdle baby. You want me to get your bottle woddle?"

"Keep it up."

Nick laughed. "What did she say was the reason? That you had nothing in common? How girly."

"No, she said we only had basketball in common. She said after March Madness was over, we had nothing to talk about."

"That's so stupid."

"I know. I told her we both liked movies. You know what she said? She said, 'No, Tommy, you like movies. I'd much rather read the book.'" Tommy sat up and turned to Nick. "Who'd rather read the book than see the movie?"

"Yeah, I don't get it."

Tommy shrugged. "I guess she's kind of right in a way. I mean, we're in different grades, and we go to different schools. We don't even watch the same TV shows."

"You both liked fooling around, though. Right?"

Tommy didn't answer. The song switched to "Lost in Emotion" by Lisa Lisa and The Cult Jam.

"Come on, man. You're broke up now. You can tell me something. At least tell me her bra size."

Tommy looked up. "Remember what she said about the parachute company?"

"You suck, man."

Tommy laughed. "You talk about your conquests enough for the two of us."

Angel Keller said, "And who have you been conquering lately, Nick?" She'd snuck up on them and stood beside Nick. She wore an aqua blue bikini. Nick turned and tipped his shades forward with his hand. He let out a low whistle. "Hello, Angel. Might I say your appearance today matches your name?"

She smiled. "You might, but it won't get you anywhere."

Tommy raised his left arm in the air and made a *chick-chick* sound as he cocked it down and up. He moved the arm right to left, left to right, staring off in the distance, then said, "Boom!" He whistled like a launching bottle rocket, following something invisible as it spiraled to the ground.

"Funny. Real funny," Nick said. "Some wingman you are."

Tommy winked, and Angel strolled between them, scooted Nick's leg over and sat on the edge of his chaise. She placed her hands in her lap and said, "I heard about you and your girlfriend." Angel looked sad.

Tommy's eyebrows raised. "You heard?"

Angel nodded, her lips thin and tight. "If you ever need someone to talk to, call me." She smiled. "It's a long summer until school starts again."

She patted him on the knee and rose. She gave him a finger wave and adjusted her bikini as she turned to leave.

Nick was sitting up, back straight, and turned to Tommy before Angel got halfway back to her chair. "Dude."

"Dude?"

"She wants her some Tommy sandwich."

Tommy frowned. "You're crazy."

Nick blinked. "You're kidding, right? She was giving off so many signals some of them splashed on me. Look, my leg hairs are still standing up." He pointed, but Tommy didn't look.

Nick shook his head. "You're hopeless. Absolutely hopeless." He swiveled back into his chaise and reclined again. "She practically eye-rapes you, and you stick your head in a book. Sometimes I wonder about you." He held a hand out. "Hit me with a brownie."

Nick's hand remained empty. He turned to find Tommy distracted by the latest visitors to the Southeast Swim Club. Patrick Hart and Laura Novak. Nick closed his eyes and *tsk-tsked*. "Take My Breath Away" by

Berlin surrounded them as Nick humphed.

"Yeah, dude, you're hopeless. Will you ever give up on her?"

"I don't understand what she likes about him."

"Um ... how about good looks, money, and a future? He's not that bad a guy once you get to know him. Really."

"He's an ass."

Nick shrugged. "Some guys got the mojo, some don't. Patrick's problem is that he flaunts his mojo. If I were you, I'd focus on Angel, man. Sure she's not built as curvy, but she's just as hot. Oh, and there's that thing of her wanting to jump your bones."

Tommy broke his gaze and turned to Nick. "I think it's you we should worry about getting laid. That's all you think about."

"We're seventeen, dude. That's what we *should* be thinking about."

"Some of us have other things on our mind."

Nick grunted. "There's plenty of time for that later in life. Right now we're supposed to act young and carefree. Why? Because we *are* young and carefree. Believe me, you'll get the rest of your life to be responsible. This is the only time you can be irresponsible and get away with it." Nick stood up and threw his towel at Tommy. "It's expected of us, for God's sake."

He turned and ran toward the pool with a primal yell. On the edge, he launched into the air and turned a flip before cannon-balling with a huge splash. Kids screamed, mothers frowned, and the lifeguards stood in their stands. They blew their whistles at him as he surfaced, eyes wide, a lopsided smile stretched over his face.

Patrick Hart laughed, then shed his shirt and towel. He sprinted toward the pool screaming, "Cannonball!!" as he sprang into the air. His splash was bigger and Nick gave him a high-five as the lifeguards blew their whistles.

Tommy watched as Laura shook her head and looked around the pool. Their eyes met and she waved at him. He waved back and basked in the vision of her loveliness. She wore a dark striped one-piece that accented her overly-developed curves.

It reminded him of the first time he'd noticed she was no longer a young girl, but instead, a young woman. And as The Steve Miller Band's "Abracadabra" opening notes played over the pool speakers, the memory rushed back as vivid as the very day it happened.

Chapter 10

The Sixth Grade Talent Show at Nathanael Greene was a tradition most kids and parents counted the days up until. As sixth graders, the kids were the "seniors" of the elementary school. And in 1983, innocence was still a fixture in this small country school.

Talking back to teachers was not only unheard of, it hadn't been invented yet. Eleven and twelve-year-olds didn't smoke or sell drugs in the bathroom. And sex was something snickered about in guidance class once a year as Ms. Mathis explained what parts boys and girls had, and how they were used.

The words "penis" or "vagina" could set off a full minute of whispering and snide remarks. Everybody acted as if they already knew everything, but even the cool kids paid attention while pretending not to.

Field Day was another staple of innocence, a full day where kids donned tank tops and suntan lotion, and competed like Olympians in such contests as the long jump, the three-legged race, and the softball throw. A Field Day ribbon was a prized possession to be coveted as much as a good report card.

But the Talent Show was the only day kids could show off that one talent that separated them from everyone else. It was an opportunity to become an individual, to break out of the proverbial pack.

Nicole Simmons showed off the product of private piano lessons, playing the theme to "Arthur." Catherine Coble played a selection of Beethoven on her violin. Terrell Baker banged out Survivor's "Eye of the Tiger" on his drums. Bobby Black and Yvonne Winston performed a raucous skit of Mr. Feeney and Mrs. Causey—the principal and the crabbiest third grade teacher who ever graced the school's classrooms. The skit was well-received by the students and parents, and some of the teachers who hid their smiles behind the mimeographed programs. Mr. Feeney and Mrs. Causey, however, failed to see the humor themselves, but they played along gracefully, forcing laughs at the appropriate times.

Michelle Garrick twirled her baton—complete with red ribbons tied to the ends to simulate flames—to the tune of Toni Basil's "Mickey." She only dropped it twice. Tommy Chandler and Nick Muller performed a magic show that included a real rabbit, and lots of shrieking as the rabbit escaped its hiding place in the box that acted as a stand, and darted into the audience.

But the act that stole the show was performed by none other than Laura Novak, the quiet girl with good grades and long brown hair. Until that day, Laura had been just another girl at Nathanael Greene, although by general consensus, one of the prettiest girls in school. But after that day, Laura Novak was regarded in a completely different manner, by the students, teachers and parents alike.

Unbeknownst to everyone in the school except Laura and her parents, that year had seen Laura begin her "blossom into womanhood," as the guidance counselor so eloquently described the process in her classes. This "blossoming" was to play an important role.

The curtains jerked open to reveal Laura Novak, poised on stage in a modest outfit. From his seat in the front row, Tommy saw Mr. Gruber drop the needle on the record player. The first drum pop from "Abracadabra" exploded from the speakers and Laura launched into her dance routine.

One teacher would describe it later as a cross between ballet and table dancing. Tommy and most of the boys used other adjectives: mesmerizing, amazing, spectacular, and most definitely, sexy.

That one dance of Laura's taught the boys of Nathanael Greene more about sex, and the pubescent changes that happen in young bodies, than a whole year's worth of special classes in Mrs. Mathis' room in the Annex building.

At first, the routine was not unlike most of the other contestants' entries: bland and unspectacular. But there was a subtle shift as Laura began gyrating to moves she'd picked up studying Soul Train on Saturday mornings. It was then that some of the teachers became uncomfortable. Some of the more liberal—and younger—teachers saw nothing untoward in her moves; they clapped to the beat.

But all that changed when Steve Miller sang, "You make me hot, you make me sigh." With those words, Laura ripped off her buttoned-down costume to expose a much more revealing outfit underneath. A person had to be blind at that moment not to notice Laura Novak was no longer a girl, but instead, a "developing" young woman.

And if they hadn't by then, they did when Miller sang, "I feel the magic in your caress." In that one glorious moment, Laura made a move that either advanced the burgeoning women's lib movement or set it back three decades, depending upon whom you asked.

Some of the dads in the audience were said to have been seen blushing after that. And if Mr. Gruber had not been in shock himself, he might have pulled the needle from the record, thus ending the scandalous display, but he was incapacitated on the sidelines.

And for that matter, so was Tommy Chandler.

It was the first time he'd ever looked at Laura in that way. She'd always been pretty, and he'd always liked her more than just a friend, but this was something extra. Something beyond. Not like the ever-present urge to kiss her. It was like that multiplied by a thousand. A million.

More than that. It was indescribable.

He wasn't sure exactly *what* it was, but it was powerful. And he knew one thing for sure, he liked it.

From that night on, in Tommy's mind, all females would have to measure up to the goddess that was Laura Novak.

In the week that followed the Talent Show, there was talk of suspension, but the end of the year was in sight. And since Laura was an honor roll student without so much as a tardy to her name, the controversial decision was made to let the episode slide.

But in the innocent halls of Nathanael Greene Elementary School, history had been made. The day twelve-year-old Laura Novak "danced like a gypsy harlot" in the Sixth Grade Talent Show would be remembered for all eternity. The story was told so many times that people who had not been there could recount the tiniest details, and in later years, would swear on their mother's grave they had indeed been present.

How else would they know about that move she did with the microphone stand that caused Mr. Feeney to choke on his peanuts?

Tommy Chandler was too young to understand the uproar Laura Novak had caused in their small community that day. He was too naive to understand that a thrust of the hips was not simply a thrust of the hips. He was too pure to comprehend the far-reaching and long-lasting implications of Laura's shocking routine.

What Tommy Chandler did understand was that Laura Novak had awoken something primal deep inside him he didn't even know was hidden.

Chapter 11

It wasn't until fourth period lunch on the first day of school in Tommy Chandler's senior year that he heard the news that would forever change the rest of his life.

The morning had been relatively uneventful, everyone going through the familiar motions—learning new locker combinations, finding out-of-the-way classrooms, memorizing the quickest routes, saying hi to everyone they hadn't seen since last June.

But it was over a tray of hot dogs and soggy ketchup-smothered fries that everything changed. Nick Muller plopped his food down in front of Tommy and sat across from him.

"Did you hear?" he asked.

"Hear what?" Tommy replied, biting into his hot dog.

"Patrick's gone."

Nick braced for the outburst that didn't come, then repeated himself.

"Patrick Hart. He's gone."

"Duh, I know who you're talking about. What do you mean by him being gone?"

"I mean he's gone. Transferred. No longer at Southeast."

Tommy paused. "He moved?"

"Did I say he moved? I said he transferred. Now, guess where." Nick was leaning forward, eyes expectant.

Tommy set his hot dog down and said, "Just tell ..." and then it hit him. "Greensboro Day?"

Nick nodded, saying, "You know it."

Tommy studied his tray and poked a few fries.

"I know what you're thinking," Nick said. "And you're welcome."

"What?" Tommy looked up.

"You can thank me with one of your mom's cakes. I'm not picky."

"Thank you for what?"

"A lemon pound cake will do fine. Or maybe one of those cream cheese swirled cakes with cocoa and vanilla pockets."

"Nick! Thank you for what?"

Nick straightened. "For talking you out of quitting last year. Now you'll have the starting spot for sure."

Tommy hesitated. "I wasn't going to play this year."

"But now you will." It was a statement, not a question.

"I ... I don't know."

Nick stuffed a fry in his mouth and talked while he chewed. "I heard Coach was completely pissed when he found out. Turned his desk over and everything."

Tommy didn't respond. He played with his food as Nick talked about how cool the year was going to be now. Lunch continued in a blur for Tommy.

Sixth period for Tommy and Nick this year was gym class. Patrick Hart's defection was the main topic of conversation during dress-out. More than a few sets of eyes turned Tommy's way. Coach blew the whistle in the locker room and told everyone to gather in the gym.

The spread out over the bleachers, clustered together in groups of two and three. When the coach addressed them, he paced back and forth, whistle dangling from his neck, hands clasped behind his back.

"I know this isn't going to matter to *all* of you"—looking down the bleachers where the baseball and football guys sat huddled together—"but I thought I'd go ahead and get this out of the way before a hundred guys come to me."

He paused and took a deep breath, then squared himself up, hands still clasped behind his back. "I know it's been going around—Hell, you probably already know ... Patrick Hart transferred to Greensboro Day." He spit the last part out quickly, trying to appear unaffected, but it was obvious to everyone that he was disgusted. Coach stiffened. "Any questions?"

At first, no one said anything, choosing instead to look around at everyone else. There were a few coughs and sniffs.

"No one?" Coach Barrows asked.

Then Miles Flaherty asked the most obvious question available. "Does this mean Tommy's gonna be the starting point guard?"

Tommy averted his eyes as Coach glanced at him, then back at Miles.

Coach said, "It means that like every other year, each starting position is up for grabs by the best person for the job. That means your position too, Mr. Flaherty." He paused. "Does that answer you?"

Miles nodded. Others joined in.

"Any more?"

Jalen Carter asked, "We got them on the schedule?"

Greensboro Day wasn't in Southeast's division so a game wasn't a given each year.

Coach nodded. "We play at their place this time."

"Good," Nick muttered. A few others uttered the same sentiment.

"What do you think about it, Coach?" Terrell Baker asked.

Coach put his head down and thought for a second before answering.

"Patrick has to do what's right for Patrick."

"You didn't answer the question," Miles said a little too quickly.

Coach Barrows caught his eyes, paused, then said, "I'd be lying if I said I was happy about it." He looked around. "But I'd also be lying if I didn't say I want the best thing for each and every one of you. If that means we're on opposite benches when basketball season comes around, then so be it."

"Well, I'm glad he's gone," Stanley Gattison spoke up. "The guy was a dick."

"Stanley," the coach admonished.

"It's true, Coach. He hurt us as much as he helped us."

There were murmurs of agreement.

"I never liked him," Charlie Madison said. Charlie was a rising Junior who'd played with Patrick on the Junior Varsity team. "I'm with Stanley. Patrick was a dick. We're better off."

Then Jalen Carter said something that made Tommy look up. "Yeah, I'd rather have Tommy run the point any day."

Coach glanced at Tommy but didn't say anything. Talk continued for a few more minutes about the benefits of a team without Patrick Hart before the coach interrupted and said it was time to get started.

They started the new school year with a few miles of cross-country running.

Nick stayed close to Tommy, and eventually, between breaths, he said, "Looks like it's going to be a good year."

Tommy grunted, concentrating on side-stepping exposed roots.

"You know what else I heard?" Nick breathed.

"What?"

"Patrick broke up with Laura."

Tommy stopped. Charlie Madison and Frankie Brown almost ran

him over. Nick slowed down, and Tommy jogged up to him and pulled him off the worn dirt trail.

"What?" he said.

"You heard me. Patrick ended it with Laura."

"You know why?"

"Does it matter?" Nick scrunched his face together. He was breathing hard while Tommy looked like he'd just dressed out. "Have you even been running the same course I have?" Nick asked, looking behind him to some other guys passing them.

"When did they break up?"

Nick shrugged. "I don't know." He knew what was on Tommy's mind. "But I wouldn't wait too long before pouncing. A girl like Laura won't stay single long."

Tommy nodded more out of habit than anything. He was no longer listening. He was thinking how his senior year of school would definitely be one he'd never forget.

Chapter 12

When Helen Chandler asked her son if he was taking anyone to the Homecoming Dance, and he said, "Laura Novak," she immediately raised her eyebrows. "Really?"

She was pulling cookies from the oven and briefly paused, the sugary oatmeal scent filling the room.

"It's no big deal, Mom."

"Whatever you say." She began scooping the cookies onto a cooling rack, barely holding back a smirk. Tommy grabbed one and left before she asked any more questions.

Three days later, after helping unload a truck at the store, Tommy drove his old Buick down Hoopers Road to pick up Laura Novak for the Homecoming Dance. It was their first date! He wore charcoal dress slacks, a crisp white button-down shirt, and a skinny blue tie. He'd also splashed himself with some British Sterling cologne.

He rang the doorbell and waited, butterflies dueling in his stomach. Laura's mom answered the door, her smile radiating a warmth that took him off guard.

"Well, hello," she said. "You must be Tommy."

"Yes, ma'am."

"Come on in before you catch a chill." She waved him in and closed the door behind him. She pointed him to the living room and said to make himself at home.

Tommy smiled and sat on the edge of the cream leather couch, making sure to keep his posture correct. This was the most nervous he'd ever been on a date. It was as if all other dates had been warm-ups for this one moment. This was his time.

Nick had offered to double-date with the girl he'd asked, Michelle Garrick, but Tommy wanted Laura all to himself on their first date.

Ms. Novak asked if Tommy would like something to drink, and he declined. He was too nervous to eat or drink yet.

"You're Gene Chandler's boy, aren't you?"

Tommy nodded.

"I went to school with your father," she said, sitting in an overstuffed beige-patterned chair. She crossed her legs. "I can see a lot of him in you."

Tommy didn't know how to respond to that. He never did. "It's the eyes," he said. "People say we have the same eyes."

Ms. Novak squinted. "It's more than that. The chin too. Possibly the nose."

Tommy nodded.

"Did you know your father was the class clown?"

Tommy's head tilted like he hadn't heard her correctly, "What?"

"He was a funny one, Gene was. Always cutting up and playing practical jokes." She smiled, and for the first time since Tommy had walked in, he saw where Laura inherited her beauty from.

Ms. Novak continued, "We had this one teacher, Ms. Jessup. Never forgot her. She was a mean one." A laugh. "She'd let us eat in class, but as payment, she'd walk around and take any food she wanted. Just swipe it right off your desk."

Ms. Novak shook her head, a smile still leaking from her mouth.

"Then one day, your dad brought some chocolate chip cookies. He left them on the edge of the desk, and Mrs. Jessup strolled by and snatched two of them from the pile without so much as a word."

She giggled. "The principal had to call in a substitute teacher for half that day and the whole next one. We heard Ms. Jessup had spent more time on the toilet then off it." Ms. Novak uncrossed her legs and leaned forward, her voice bubbling. "Your dad had mixed in two whole packages of laxatives into those cookies."

When Tommy's mouth dropped open, Ms. Novak slapped her knee and rocked back in her chair. Tommy was floored. His dad did that? Surely she must be mistaken. Tommy tried to remember seeing his dad laugh at anything. He couldn't.

"Did they find out he did it?" Tommy finally asked.

Ms. Novak nodded. "He got suspended a week, but I heard secretly the principal thought it was the best gag in the world. In fact, the way I heard it, Mr. Bellamy talked about it for years."

"Bellamy?" There was a Mr. Bellamy who came into the store at least once a week. He was old enough to have been the principal then—he used a cane now—and he and Tommy's dad usually talked for hours every time they saw each other. Could he be the same Mr. Bellamy?

"Your father was also quite the athlete. Started on the basketball team if I remember correctly."

His dad played basketball on the school team? Tommy was almost eighteen years old and had never once heard his dad talk about playing basketball.

"In fact," Ms. Novak continued, "I heard he got a few offers from colleges."

Tommy's mouth parted. Hid dad? College?

"Mom, are you boring Tommy with old stories?" Laura had popped into the room.

Tommy rose to greet her, and the dueling butterflies returned. Tommy had wondered if he was overdressed—after all, it was only the Homecoming Dance—but when he saw Laura, he felt inadequate.

She wore a sleek black dress that stopped just above her knees. It hugged her figure without being too tight and managed to appear respectable and sexy at the same time. Tommy was in the middle of his growth spurt, and because Laura wore black pumps—they saw eye to eye.

Laura had curled her hair enough to give it some body, and as she turned her head, it bounced and shimmered like a Prell shampoo commercial. She wore minimal make-up that accented her face without overpowering it, and her eyes sparkled like pools of honey.

"Hey," Tommy said, aware his voice wavered.

Laura smiled. "You clean up well. Mom tell you how she went to school with your dad?"

Tommy nodded.

"She tell you the laxative story too?"

A smile eased from Tommy's lips as he glanced at Ms. Novak.

Laura shook her head, then tugged her dress. "I hope this is okay?"

Tommy swallowed. "You ... you look perfect."

"Great! Now, let's go before Mom starts another story."

Laura grabbed a light jacket, and they walked out into a cool October night, Ms. Novak telling them to have a good time and not to be too late. As Tommy started his car, the Billy Ocean song, "Get Outta My Dreams, Get Into My Car," erupted from the speakers. He smiled inwardly at the irony.

They ate dinner at TK Tripps and talked about the new class they had in common, Trigonometry. They covered topics from the new president to Saturday Night Live to what movies they loved.

"By night's end, I predict me and her will interface," Tommy said.

Laura paused, her forkful of seafood linguine suspended in front of her. "Easy. Sixteen Candles." She bit her lip and looked up, then said, "This is all wrong. I don't know what it is. But when I kiss you, it's like I'm kissing ... my brother. I guess that doesn't make any sense, does it?"

Tommy laughed. "Back to the Future. Pick a hard one next time." He sipped his tea and fired back, "*This is an incredibly romantic moment, and you're ruining it for me!*"

Laura shook her head. "Too easy. Ducky: Pretty in Pink." She paused. "You keep using that word. I do not think it means what you think it means."

Tommy was laughing so hard by the time she finished, tea shot out his nose. He replied in the best little boy voice he had, "*They're kissing again. Do we have to read the kissing parts?*"

"I can't compete with you physically, and you're no match for my brains."

"You mean you wish to surrender to me? Very well, I accept."

"And wuv, tru wuv, will fowow you foweva ... "

"There's a shortage of perfect breasts in this world. It would be a pity to damage yours."

They both froze at the utterance of Tommy's last words. The assault of *The Princess Bride* quotes had sped into such a frenzy that they both spit them out without thinking. Tommy's face reddened as amusement crept onto Laura's face.

"I ... uh ... I didn't mean ... uh ..." Tommy stuttered.

Laura laughed and shook her head. "Don't worry about it. They're out there." She glanced down at her chest and wiggled her shoulders. "Especially tonight."

The dress she wore exposed enough cleavage to make Tommy blush and look away when Laura raised her head. She bit back another smile and changed the subject.

"So, I've applied to a couple of colleges," Laura said.

"Oh yeah? Which ones?"

"East Carolina, Appalachian State, Wake Forest, and Hollins."

"That's quite a range."

"Mom says I've got to be prepared. I'm pretty sure I'll get in at least one of those."

Tommy smiled. "You'll get in all of them." Tommy couldn't stop looking at Laura. He had to keep pinching himself during dinner to remind himself he wasn't dreaming.

They ate in silence for a while.

"Whatever happened with that girl you dated?" Laura asked. "What was her name? Britney?"

Tommy almost swallowed a shrimp whole. He chewed and washed it down with his tea.

"Britney?"

"That's her name, isn't it?"

"Yeah, uh ... well ..."

"Oh, never mind. It's none of my business."

"No, that's alright." Tommy wiped his mouth and sat up straighter. "She, uh ... dumped me because we didn't have enough in common."

Laura's head tilted. "Didn't you go out for almost the whole year?"

Tommy nodded. "Yeah, I guess so."

"She was pretty."

"You're prettier." Tommy said it before he knew what he was doing. He turned over a scallop in the following silence.

"So," he finally said, clearing his throat. "What happened to you and

Patrick?"

Without even looking up from her plate, Laura answered, "Patrick's an ass."

"Oh, I didn't mean to—"

Laura laughed and raised her face. "Sorry, it's a reflex."

Tommy stabbed a shrimp with his fork and twisted it in the white sauce. "I gotta ask." He looked up. "What did you ever see in him?"

"Patrick?" Laura smiled thinly and set her silverware down. "When we were younger, he was different. You know?"

"Not really," Tommy said.

"He was ... I don't know ... innocent."

"Patrick? Innocent?" Tommy shook his head. "I don't think so."

Laura laughed. "He was. Before his parents got divorced."

Tommy scrunched his face together. "Your parents got divorced, and you didn't turn into an ass."

"That's because my dad is an electrician."

Tommy frowned. "I don't get it."

"Patrick's dad is a big-wig in the furniture industry. He's one of the guys that makes the Furniture Market happen, so everybody thinks he's a god. And so he acts like one, bossing everyone around like his word is the final say."

"What's that have to do with Patrick?"

"When Patrick's mom and dad got divorced, his mom was forced to leave. His dad had an affair, and still, his mom got kicked out. Then his dad sued for custody and won, because he plays golf with half the judges in the county. Plus, he gives a lot of money to politicians, so nobody wants to cross him. He gets his way. There's even been a rumor he might run for office one day."

Laura took a sip of her drink. "Anyway, ever since the divorce,

Patrick changed. He became more like his dad every day, telling instead of asking, expecting everyone to fall in line with his views and do what he wants without question."

Laura paused. "His dad essentially turned him into a younger version of himself."

Tommy studied Laura. "You feel sorry for Patrick, don't you?"

Laura looked up from her plate and took a breath. "Not anymore. It's just sad. If his parents hadn't gotten divorced ... who knows." She shrugged her shoulders.

"Well, I still think he's a dick."

They shared a smile and finished dinner a little more at ease, spreading into topics like the upcoming basketball season and TV shows they both liked to watch: "The Wonder Years." "The Cosby Show." "Family Ties." "Cheers."

It was the most perfect first date he thought he'd ever had, and it was just getting started.

Chapter 13

Tommy parked the Buick in the school's gravel lot. It was officially Tommy's car now after his mom had told him in front of his dad that it was high time she get something different, and there was no reason to trade in the Buick because trade-ins were where the dealerships got you. "And besides," she said. "A young man needs his freedom." She winked as she tossed him the keys.

He opened the car door for Laura and helped her out with an extended arm. Laura thanked him and entwined an arm in his. They entered the school gym like they were arriving at an opera house. Tommy was floating.

Laura patted Tommy's arm and said she was going to go say hi to Angel, she'd find him again in a few minutes. Tommy caught a glimpse of Nick with a girl he didn't recognize and said okay.

Nick bowed, saying, "The king has arrived," when Tommy approached.

Tommy straightened his right arm and tapped Nick's shoulder. "You may rise."

"I still can't believe it," Nick said, looking at his friend as he straightened. "You did it. You finally asked her out. And to the Homecoming Dance no less."

Tommy nodded, absorbing the moment.

THE WALK-ON

The girl beside Nick punched him and introduced herself as Renee. Nick gave her a "what?" shrug and quizzed Tommy about the night so far. What happened when he picked her up? Where'd they eat? What'd they talk about?

After ten minutes, Tommy held up his hands and said, "Enough." He left and found Laura chatting with Angel Keller and Kim Fleming.

"Wow, Tommy," Angel said. "Love the tie." She ran her hand down it. "Makes you look older." She flashed her eyes at him.

Tommy blushed, and the girls laughed.

"Same old Tommy," Laura said.

The night was going well. The gym, normally a bland, boxy concrete prison, had been decorated in black and white streamers. Multicolored spotlights filled the gym with the warmth a dance floor deserves, and a huge, mirrored ball hung from the ceiling, twirling and creating a sense of movement even during the slow songs. Somehow, yards of sheer tapestry had been hung from the rafters, billowing outward from the center, so that the gym—and the night—took on an ethereal feel.

An hour after their arrival, Laura convinced Tommy to join her on the dance floor. Tommy had no clue what to do so he followed Laura's lead. It was a fast song—"Never Gonna Give You Up" by Rick Astley. Tommy felt like he was flailing to the beat instead of dancing, but Laura was laughing and looked like she was having a good time so he went with it.

A slow song came on next—"Hold On To The Night" by Richard Marx—and Tommy begged off. He wasn't ready for a slow dance yet and convinced Laura into coming along with him to the punch table.

As they sipped and watched others, Laura said, "Thank you so much for asking me to come tonight. I wasn't going to come."

"Why not?"

"I don't know." She shrugged. "Just didn't feel like it."

"Well, I'm glad you came too."

Laura smiled and placed a hand on Tommy's arm. "I haven't had this much fun in a while. It's so much better than staying home and feeling sorry for myself."

The opening line to Tommy Tutone's "867-5309 (Jenny)" filled the gym—*Jenny, Jenny, who can I turn to?*— and Laura's eyes lit up. "I love this song!" She grabbed Tommy's hand and yanked him onto the floor. He was barely able to set his cup down.

They danced with the energy that only afforded the young, and lost themselves in the song. The rhythm moved their bodies for them, and the electricity followed them through the next two songs.

A slow song began—"Kiss On My List" by Hall and Oates—and Tommy bit back his fear. He held out his hand and smiled, sweat trickling down both their faces. Laura returned the smile and moved her body into his. They danced in tandem, Tommy's hands resting delicately on Laura's waist, Laura's arms draped over Tommy's shoulders.

And a memory flooded Tommy like a tidal wave ...

* * *

February 14, 1981. The Nathanael Greene Valentine's Dance. It was a bitterly cold night, and as students came through the glass doors in the front of the gym, they shed their heavy coats like caterpillars shed their cocoons.

Kids of all ages searched for friends, dressed in their Sunday best, chattering away with nervous energy. The gym was no longer a gym. Everything was decorated in pinks and reds. The place was covered in streamers and paper swirlies. Huge hearts of sturdy construction paper were taped to the walls at varying heights and angles—they were cut out and glue-glittered by Mrs. Grayson's first grade class.

Lights flickered and danced across the building so that anyone driving by the place that night would have no question about the party inside.

But the Valentine's Dance was not just any party or dance. It was *the* dance: a magical night where boys screwed up the courage to ask for the hand of girls they secretly admired. And the girls would smile and giggle, gathered in the protection of groups, until one by one, they were separated from the group.

"I dare you to ask Laura," Nick Muller said to Tommy Chandler.

Laura's best friend, Angel Keller, stood beside her, both of them laughing and swinging to the beat.

They were all in fourth grade.

"You ask her," Tommy said. He was leaning against the wall, his left leg bent at the knee so he could place his foot on the wall. He had his thumbs locked into the belt loop of his new corduroys. It was how he'd seen The Fonz stand.

"I'm not the one who likes her," Nick answered. "You do."

Tommy ran a hand through his slicked-back hair, trying to look relaxed and uncaring. But inside, his heart was beating faster than the song reverberating around the gym, "Funkytown."

Tommy sniffed and pushed off the wall. "Tell you what, I dare you to ask Angel Keller to dance. You do that, and I'll ask Laura."

Nick squinted his eyes. "Next song."

Tommy held his hand out, and they did their special shake. It was a done deal now; there was no turning back.

Nick held the handshake and pulled Tommy closer. "Even if it's a slow song."

Tommy's breath caught. "Deal."

They squeezed each other's hand, tighter and tighter, eyes locked and unblinking, until "Funkytown" ended, and the next song began.

"Kiss On My List" by Hall and Oates.

They broke, and Nick led the way.

Laura and Angel were watching couples switch from fast to slow dancing, smiling, and pointing at friends, when Nick approached. The girls turned, eyes alight, mouths upturned.

Nick bee-lined for Angel and choked out, "May I have this dance?" He extended his trembling hand.

Angel's smile faltered and she glanced at Tommy. "Okay," she said.

They left and Tommy swiveled toward Laura.

"Hey," he said.

"Hey," Laura responded.

Tommy shuffled and rocked some. "Having a good time?" Unsure what to do with his hands, he placed them in his corduroys.

"Yeah." Laura smiled and glanced out on the dance floor.

Tommy was dying. He'd heard the saying about ripping off the Band-Aid, but it was a lot more difficult when it was your Band-Aid. He sucked in a breath and said, "So, you wanna …" He nodded toward the sea of kids swaying to the music.

Laura smiled. "Yeah."

She reached for his hand and he took it. They walked to the dance floor, and when Tommy turned to her, Laura stepped into his space. They looked around, and Laura shrugged. They copied the dancers on either side; one arm out with hands clasped together, the other placed lightly on the waist of the partner.

Forward and left, back and right, turn, forward and left, back and right, turn.

THE WALK-ON

Tommy got the hang of it, then braved a look into Laura's eyes. They held him, her smile natural and unforced. Tommy's heart slammed against the confines of his ribcage, pumping so hard he had trouble hearing the beat of the music.

He looked to his left at one point and saw Nick and Angel. Nick was looking at Angel; Angel was looking at Tommy and Laura.

Forward and left. Turn. Back and right. Turn.

Your kiss is on my list of the best things in life.

Tommy looked back at Laura and realized he no longer felt his feet. This was the most perfect part of his life ever, and he never wanted it to end. He wanted so badly to kiss Laura Novak because like the song said, her kiss was on his list.

Forward and left. Turn. Back and right. Turn.

* * *

They danced to the beat half-speed, the music lolling them into a hypnotic rhythm. Tommy returned from his memory with a singular thought in his mind. He'd made up his mind to finally fulfill the urge he'd felt almost eight years previous. As the song continued, he pulled them closer and closer.

And when the time felt right, Tommy leaned in and kissed Laura on the lips. His heart was skipping and thumping so loud the music disappeared. It was the perfect moment on a perfect night.

But Laura jerked away, her eyes wide. "No, Tommy. I ... no ... it's not ..." She trailed off, her face pained.

They'd stopped dancing. The world had frozen in time. Tommy couldn't breathe.

Laura looked as if she might cry. "Oh Tommy. I didn't mean ..."

She broke away and pushed through the dancing couples. Tommy watched her leave, mouth slack, face reddening. The world was spinning again, but going the wrong way. This wasn't happening. It couldn't be happening.

Tommy felt eyes on him and turned to find dancing couples halted in various positions, staring at him. Humiliation enveloped him, seeping through his pores into his very soul.

He tried to run after Laura, to catch her, to apologize. It was all his fault. He needed to tell her. It was nothing she did wrong. She couldn't have. She was perfect. He was wrong. He was to blame.

But by the time he fought his way through the crowd, she was nowhere to be seen. There were just sets of eyes watching him no matter which way he turned. He ran out the back; he needed fresh air. Now.

There were couples mulling around in the cool night, guys with their arms around girls. They glanced at Tommy and returned to their hushed conversations and cigarettes.

Tommy shoved his hands into his pockets and—head turned down—shuffled over to the football field. He climbed to the middle of the concrete bleachers and plopped down, the cold seeping through his slacks. It was weird, being there without lights or people. He lowered his head into his hands and replayed the night's events.

Had he read the signals wrong? Did she not ... was it not a date? A real date? Was it only two friends going to a dance together? Is that the way it was? The way it would always be?

Tommy tortured himself, running it through his mind over and over. The way Laura pulled back: surprised, disappointed, sorrowed. Now he'd ruined their friendship. There was no going back to the way things were. There never was.

"Tommy?"

Tommy lifted his head and realized he'd been crying. He wiped his face and sniffed. "Angel?"

Angel Keller click-clacked up the bleachers, her coat wrapped around the slinky blue dress she wore that night. She carried something in her right hand and held it out; it was his jacket. He smiled as he took it and slipped it on. He said nothing, returning to his pity party of one as he stared down at the bleachers.

After a minute of silence, Angel sat and said, "I saw what happened."

Tommy nodded, not making eye contact. He slumped forward, suddenly feeling drained.

Angel placed a hand on Tommy's back, and he closed his eyes. She rubbed him, and he broke into heaving sobs. Angel pulled him close and wrapped an arm around him. Tommy lowered his head to Angel's shoulder and tried to breathe normally. He wiped his face.

Tommy looked up into Angel's face and said, "Is my make-up running?"

Angel laughed, and Tommy smiled, still sniffling. "Now I've got a headache," he said, looking down and shaking his head. "Ugh."

Angel lifted Tommy's chin with a trembling hand and kissed him. Their lips met and slowly parted. Tommy tasted the saltiness of his own tears and then the licorice of Angel's mouth.

They kissed with passion and emotion, tongues swirling playfully, only coming up for air when Angel leaned forward and nuzzled his neck. Her nose was cold, but he didn't pull away. The warmth of her lips held him immobile as their softness kissed him repeatedly. He returned the favor and sucked in the heavy vanilla scent surrounding her.

Then they held each other silently.

"This place is eerie when it's empty," Angel finally said.

"I was thinking the same thing."

Angel glanced up at Tommy, eyes moist, lips full. "Let's go somewhere else," she said. The look in her eyes was unmistakable. It was more than how a friend looked at you. Way more.

Tommy nodded.

Chapter 14

Nick finished tying his shoes and closed his locker. He and Tommy were the last two players left after practice. Nick had challenged Tommy to a one-on-one game and lost 9-10.

Nick dried his hair with his towel and began combing it in the mirror over the sinks. "So you haven't talked to Laura since the dance?"

Tommy got his last shoe on and said, "She hasn't talked to me either."

"And you've got math together?"

"Yeah."

Nick shook his head. "I don't know how you do it, man. You're the only guy I know who can strike out and get lucky in the same night."

Tommy glanced around. "Come on, man."

"Nobody's here. Quit freaking." Nick laughed. "Angel's a hell of a catch, you know."

"She's nice."

"Nice?"

"You know what I mean."

"No, I don't. Half the guys in school would give their left nut to have Angel Keller on their arm, and to you, she's *nice*." Nick said the last word as if it had cooties.

"Alright. She's beautiful and smart and kisses good ... what do you want from me? I don't like to talk about stuff like that so can you drop it?"

Nick held his hands up. "Your wish is my command."

Tommy threw his wet towel at Nick, but Nick ducked. It landed at the coach's feet. Both boys looked up. "Hey, Coach," Tommy said.

Coach nodded. "Tommy, when you get ready, I want to see you in my office." Coach disappeared behind his door.

Nick glimpsed at Tommy. "Ooooh. Somebody's in trouble."

Tommy fidgeted with his socks. "What do you think it's about?"

Nick shrugged and shoved his comb into his back pocket. "Probably wants to know what kind of underwear Angel wears."

Tommy sprang after Nick, but Nick was quicker. He scooted out the gym door, and Tommy returned to his locker. He gathered the top to his sweats, his keys and wallet, then knocked on the coach's door.

"Enter."

"Hey, Coach," Tommy said as he loped in, trying to sound upbeat and carefree.

Coach Barrows nodded for Tommy to take a seat, and he leaned back in his own chair, fingers steepled across his chest.

"How's your year going so far?" he asked.

Tommy cleared his throat. "Uh, fine, sir."

"Keeping your grades up?"

"Yes, sir." Tommy had a B average so far.

"Good." Coach looked down at his fingers, then back at Tommy. "We've had, what, six practices so far?"

"Seven, sir."

Coach tilted his head. "What's your assessment of the team so far?"

"How do you mean?" Tommy swallowed.

"I mean, who do you think our starting five should be? We play a tough schedule this year, and we're gonna need some tough guys we can count on."

"Uh, well ..." Tommy thought for a second. "I think we're gonna have to move Jalen to center. He's the biggest guy we've got, and he lifted a lot of weights this summer. And, uh, I guess we'd have Miles and Terrell as forwards. Miles would stay the '4' man. And, of course, Nick would be the shooting guard ..."

Coach waited a second before saying, "And at the point?"

Tommy dreaded this moment. He knew this was why Coach had called him into his office. He felt a sweat about to break out and hoped it wouldn't show.

Everybody was so certain Tommy would take over the point, but Tommy knew it wasn't a given, especially with Charlie Madison coming up from Junior Varsity.

Charlie could handle the ball like college players. He could shoot the lights out, and he was only about three inches shorter than Tommy. That made Charlie quicker and almost moved Tommy out of contention for the position altogether.

Whoever heard of a 6-1 point guard in high school? That kind of height usually got you relocated to forward, and he knew that's what the coach was going to talk to him about.

"Tommy," Coach said. "Who do you think should start at the point position?"

Tommy swallowed, looking down at his knees. "I don't know, Coach."

"Tommy. Look at me a second." Tommy raised his head. "It's going to be you, Tommy."

Tommy blinked twice and cocked his head. "Me, Coach?"

Coach frowned. "Yes, of course, you." He paused. "You think I ought to let Charlie start at point? You think that's best?"

Tommy shrugged and realized he'd looked away again so he turned back to Coach. He knew his sweating had to be showing now.

Coach Barrows ticked off his fingers as he talked. "One, Charlie can only dribble with his right hand. He tries to go left, and he might as well serve the damn ball up with a pat of butter. Two, you've got a few inches on him. Three, Charlie's assist-to-turnover ratio is bass-ackwards. He gives the ball away to the other team more than he does ours. Four, you can see the whole court. Hell, you actually look at the court when you bring the ball down, not the ball itself. Five, you make better decisions with the ball, which, I guess is really part of the assist-to-turnover ratio thing, but it's important, so there it is. Six, your first thought is to find the open man and not to shoot. I've got to get that out of Charlie or move him to shooting guard. Seven, and this is most important, the guys respect you when you have the ball, and do you know why?"

Tommy shook his head.

"Because of numbers one through six. And when your team respects you, they will follow you into battle with confidence." Coach paused. "Don't let anyone tell you different"—Coach pointed out his door—"that court out there is a battlefield. Every time you step on the hardwood, you go to war."

Coach lowered his arm and made a fist. "And confidence wins wars. You want to beat an opponent, you step on the court knowing you're gonna win." Coach pounded his fist on the desk. "That's who I want taking my team to war, Tommy. I want someone who's going to step on that court knowing he's already won, and he just has to take his team through the motions to prove it to everyone else."

Coach Barrows sniffed and leaned back in his chair. "Can you do that, Tommy? Can you lead these guys through every game, and teach

Charlie how to lead? Teach him what you know so every once in a while I can give you a breather and not worry if we're going to lose ten points in the half a minute you're on the bench?"

Tommy was sitting up straight now, fully alert. "Yes, sir."

"Yes, sir what?"

"Yes, sir. I can lead this team."

"You can lead this team where? To McDonald's?"

Tommy smirked. "To victory, sir. I can lead this team to victory."

Coach stared at him for a few seconds. "Okay, now get out of here before you make me cry with all this Disney bullshit." A smile crossed his lips, and he began shifting papers around.

Tommy left the office, his blood pumping wildly. He was jazzed. He was stoked. He was going to be the starting point guard. It was a dream come true.

Nick was waiting at Tommy's Buick. "What'd he say?"

A grin escaped Tommy's mouth before he said, "He's gonna start me at point guard this year."

"Duh. That all he said?"

Tommy scratched his forehead. "Yeah. I guess so. He gave me a pep talk, but that was the gist."

"That you're gonna start? That's all?" Nick rolled his eyes. "Everybody already knew that. I thought it was going to be something good."

Chapter 15

The All-Star Lanes bowling alley was a holdover from the time of dark dungarees, greased hair, and poodle skirts. It had made it through the sexual revolution and disco age virtually unscathed, with the only major updates being the addition of arcade games and black lights.

Tommy Chandler wiped the fourteen-pound ball down and stuck his fingers through the finger holes. He picked it up, squared himself, steadied it in both hands, launched down the alley, swung, and released.

The bowling ball bounced once with a soft thud and sped toward the pins with a slight spin. It struck the first pin head-on and plowed through the middle, taking out pins as if they were trailers in the path of a tornado.

"Oooh. A split," Nick Muller said, laughing and pointing down the lane. "No chance."

Angel Keller hopped up and—standing on tiptoes—kissed Tommy on the mouth, wishing him luck. Nick whistled and his date, Trisha Jackson, goosed him in the leg.

Tommy retrieved his ball from the chute, steadied, and rolled it down the lane. The shot was much gentler than the first one and hit the two pins on the right.

"Missed one," Nick said, hopping up. He scooted up beside Tommy and pointed with one eye closed. "Right there. See that one? On the left?

Missed that one."

"Thanks, I never saw that one." Tommy turned to the girls. "Have you met my sidekick, Captain Obvious? Next, he'll demonstrate the dance that's made him so popular in such faraway places as Raleigh and Charlotte."

Tommy flourished his arm and stepped aside as Nick launched into a modified Pee-Wee-Herman/Walk-Like-An-Egyptian dance.

The girls squealed and clapped. The old couple in the next lane stared for a moment, then went back to their own game.

"All I've got to say, ladies and gentlemen," Nick began as he held his hand up like it contained an imaginary microphone, "is that I'm glad our boy Tommy knows how to handle a different kind of ball." He switched the microphone to an imaginary cigar and began flicking it near his mouth. "And I'm not talking about that kind of ball either."

Tommy rolled his eyes. "You are such a douche."

"How many games have you guys won this year?" Trisha asked.

"We're seven and one, babe, and leading our division. And this guy right here"—pointing at Tommy—"is the reason why."

Tommy had sat beside Angel and was shaking his head. Nick continued, "Don't let his false modesty fool you. He's averaging ten assists and two steals a game, not to mention, what, six points?"

Tommy shrugged and picked at the blister the bowling ball was producing. "Something like that."

"Ladies and gentlemen of the court," Nick said, extending his arm. "I present to you, the shyest point guard in the history of the game ... until he gets on the court."

Angel wrapped herself around Tommy's right arm as Trisha asked, "What's he like on the court?"

"An animal with fangs and claws"—Nick miming fangs and claws—

"yelling at us like we're his red-headed step-kids."

"I do not."

"No, of course not. You're directing a ballet out there. You're as soft and gentle as a newborn kitten." Nick shook his head. "Not."

"I don't yell at you guys."

Nick laughed. "I don't know what you call it then. Talking really, really loud?"

"I don't yell," Tommy's voice lowered.

"You yell, but you don't scream. We don't mind yelling. Keeps us in line." Nick laughed again. "It's alright, bud. When the coach yells, we look up. When you yell, we listen."

Nick picked his ball up and bowled. When the ball struck just to the right of the first pin, Nick cocked his fist and pumped, twisting around in place. The ball collided with the rest of the pins and sent them flying. "Steeeeee-rike!"

Nick strutted back to his seat beside his date and patted her butt as she stood for her turn. "We are totally killing you guys."

Later that night, after they tired of bowling, the group split into couples and parted ways. Tommy was taking Angel home when she suggested they detour to The Rock.

"We've only got thirty minutes before you have to be home," Tommy said.

"I can be a little late every once in a while," she said, placing her hand on his.

So Tommy drove to The Rock. There were three vehicles there already, and he parked in the farthest corner where they would have privacy. They climbed in the back seat and held each other.

Angel kissed Tommy and said, "I'm lucky to have you."

"Me too." He returned the kiss.

"I think it's cute how you yell on the court."

"Do I really yell?"

Angel nodded.

"I try not to."

Angel touched Tommy's cheek. "It's because of your dad, isn't it?"

Tommy loosened his grip and turned toward her. "What do you mean?"

"You don't want to be like him."

"No. Not really. Not in that way."

Angel kissed him lightly on the lips and shivered. She snuggled closer, and Tommy tightened his hold again.

Angel ran a hand over Tommy's chest and slipped it inside his shirt. She kissed his neck and nibbled his ear. Her hand moved lower as her tongue took Tommy's earlobe into her mouth.

Tommy squirmed. "We don't have time for this."

"Just for a little while."

"It's too chilly."

"We'll heat it up."

Tommy pulled her hand away. "I thought you just wanted to snuggle?"

Angel lowered her eyes, the playfulness sucked out of them. "I thought maybe we could—"

"I'm not in the mood tonight, alright?"

Angel pulled back. "What's wrong?"

"Nothing's wrong. I just got—"

"You're never ever in the mood, Tommy. Am I not pretty enough?"

Tommy looked at her. "You're beautiful."

"Then why don't you want me?"

"Angel ..."

"We haven't gone all the way but twice since that first night." Angel placed Tommy's hand on her breast. "Do these not turn you on?"

"Angel ..."

"Because they've never gotten any complaints before."

"I just ... I'm not in the mood tonight, okay?" He pulled his hand away. Tommy didn't understand why he wasn't in the mood. He liked Angel. He thought she was hot. Any guy would kill to be with her, but for some reason he couldn't figure out, he just wasn't feeling it. And that bothered him.

Angel huffed and leaned back in the seat, pulling away from him. Tommy sighed and said, "Don't be mad."

"I'm not mad."

"You look mad."

Angel twisted toward Tommy. "I'm pretty damn hot. You know that?"

"Angel. Don't be mad."

"You know how many guys would kill to have sex with me?"

"Angel."

"I just don't understand you, Tommy. Sometimes I don't get you at all."

Tommy fiddled with his jeans. He looked up at her. "If you really want to that bad, I guess we could—"

"Oh hell, no. Not now," Angel spit out. She squared herself forward in the seat. "Take me home."

Chapter 16

The first thing Gene Chandler did when he stomped into the house was yell, "When's supper gonna be ready?" Helen was in the kitchen and yelled back that it would be ten minutes and to get washed up. Gene grumbled and stalked to their bathroom.

Tommy heard the entire exchange from his room and went to the kitchen to see if there was anything he could do to help. "You're a dear," his mom said. "You could set the table for me and pour the tea."

Gene walked into the kitchen a few minutes later—he'd been getting around without his cane a few weeks at that point—and sat at the table. Helen was finishing up the gravy and told Tommy to get his brother, supper was ready.

Dinner conversation that night was sparse. Gene informed everyone he'd begun carrying a new kind of bread, a potato bread with little oat pieces on top. Brant shared how he'd aced a history test. Tommy said they had Page High School coming up this week.

"No basketball at the table," Gene said.

"But it's what I have going on, and that's what mom asked," Tommy said, holding a forkful of Salisbury steak in front of him.

"No basketball at the table. I'm not gonna repeat myself."

"You just did," said Brant, a smile lifting his lips.

Gene shot Brant a dangerous look, and Brant lowered his head back to his plate of food, still smiling. After a few minutes of eating in silence, Helen said to Tommy, "Well, I for one would love to hear about your basketball."

When Gene raised his eyes to hers, her face was impassive. She turned to Tommy and smiled, "Tell me about your last game."

Tommy waited until his dad had gone back to eating and told her how he'd gotten three steals and ten assists. He didn't score as much that game, but they won by fifteen so it didn't matter.

"You'll score more next game, honey," Helen said.

"It's not about scoring for a point guard, Mom. It's about controlling the team and leading them. Scoring is secondary. My job is to make it possible for the other guys to score."

"Oh," she said. "So you had a good game?"

"Yeah, it was pretty good."

"Then that's all that matters."

"As a matter of fact," Tommy said, putting down his fork and wiping his mouth. "Coach says I might even be able to play in college."

The statement was met with silence at first. Then Gene cleared his throat and said in a steady voice, "We've had this discussion."

Gene Chandler never went to college. It wasn't a question of money. It was about principle. People went to college to get a career, and if you've already got a store to run and bring in money, why waste money on learning something you'll never need to know?

Tommy had heard it all before.

You got products from your distributor, marked them up, stuck the price on, and people paid you. What could college teach you about that? Why pay thousands of dollars to learn something you already know?

If something doesn't sell, mark it down, get rid of it, and try something else. "There," Tommy's dad had told him. "Pay me twenty thousand, and I'll print you out a certificate."

"That's not the only reason you go to college, Dad," Tommy had replied.

His dad had trudged over to the fridge and pulled out a six-pack. "Since you already owe me twenty grand, I'll throw in some free beer. If you're good, I'll get you a subscription to Playboy. Maybe they'll cover the girls of the ACC again, and you can get the whole college experience."

Gene lumbered from the kitchen, and that discussion had ended.

This time Tommy was prepared.

"We haven't had *this* discussion before," Tommy said, sitting up straighter. He'd been waiting to broach the subject again ever since the coach mentioned college.

"I ain't paying for college. End of discussion. Happy now?"

"But if I get a scholarship to play basketball, you don't have to pay for anything."

Gene humphed. "Have any colleges actually contacted your coach?"

Tommy shifted in his seat. "I don't think so."

"Then it doesn't matter, does it? End of discussion." Gene resumed eating.

Helen had been watching the interchange without talking. She said to Tommy, "Did the coach say there was a good chance of getting a scholarship?" From the moment Tommy was born, she'd hoped he would go to college. No one in their families had ever been. Tommy would be the first.

Tommy turned to her. "Coach called me into his office and told me. Said I'd come a long way in the past two years, and if I kept it up, I might get to play college ball."

Gene grunted. "You wouldn't play for anyone good so what's the point?"

"Gene!" Helen exploded.

"I mean, what's the point if you're not playing in the ACC?"

"The point is to get a free education," Helen responded.

Gene shoveled mashed potatoes and gravy into his mouth.

"Coach said I could probably play at a small school like Guilford or Greensboro College."

Gene scoffed. "They're Division Three."

"So?"

Gene looked Tommy in the eyes. "So Division One is the only level allowed to offer athletic scholarships. Division Two and Three, you still have to pay for school."

Tommy didn't know that. He pushed peas around his plate imagining them as tiny green basketballs. It didn't seem like a fair rule for small schools or the guys that played for them.

Tommy's mom changed the subject to what the boys wanted for Christmas. Tommy was going to ask for a new leather basketball, one like the guys in college used in their games, but now he didn't feel like it. He mentioned maybe some new games for their Nintendo or maybe a new tape deck for his car.

Helen had baked a chocolate chip sour cream cake for dessert, but Tommy ate without really tasting it. He tried to smile and join in the conversation about their cousin Sharon's new baby, but it was difficult.

The biggest dream he'd ever had, to go to college, had just been dashed. All he wanted to do was curl up in bed and go to sleep forever.

Chapter 17

Miles threw a huge party during Christmas break just before school was supposed to start back up. The team had won its three games during the break, despite Tommy's lackluster performances.

He'd only dished out two assists the first game, then combined for a whopping five points the other two games, all from the free throw line. His only saving grace was zero turnovers. The one thing Tommy did without fail was protect the ball.

The whole team showed up to the party with their girlfriends. Then other friends dropped in, and in no time it felt like the whole school was there.

Other than idle chatting during class, Tommy hadn't talked with Laura since the Homecoming Dance. Laura and Angel were best friends, and since Tommy and Angel were dating, he saw no reason to bring up the incident. If there was any talking to be done, he was sure Laura and Angel had done it.

Tommy had his arm around Angel when Laura walked through the front door. They were on the couch and Guns N' Roses was blasting on the stereo.

Although he told himself Laura would probably show up, it still threw him off balance when she strolled into the house with Melody Bruner and shrugged off her coat. She wore a purple dress that looked so new she had to have gotten it for Christmas.

Tommy had given Angel a pair of gold and emerald earrings for Christmas. She wore them that night with her hair up in a banana clip so everyone could see them. She had given him a new Swatch he wore for her benefit as much as his. As soon as someone noticed her new earrings, Angel liked to immediately point to Tommy's Swatch and tell how they swapped gifts.

Angel was busy telling Catherine Coble the whole story when Laura showed up. Tommy watched her look around the room, smile, and wave at people. The rumor going around was that she'd sworn boys off for the rest of the year.

Miles' older brother, Jamie, was home from Carolina during the break and had gotten a keg for the party. He was out on the patio doling out beer when Tommy excused himself to get a refill.

Tommy and Nick had pulled the classic switcheroo on their parents. Each one got permission to stay over at the other's house, and they both planned on getting drunk and crashing at Miles' place. The Flahertys were down in Florida for a week visiting Miles' grandparents.

Tommy planned on getting way smashed, and the night was still young.

He snatched an extra cup of beer from Jamie and walked over to Laura. He'd had two beers already—the third was in his hand—and the liquid courage was flowing through him in a big way.

"Got you a beer," Tommy said, holding out the extra cup.

"Oh, hey, Tommy." She looked down and took the beer. "Thanks."

"No problem." He leaned against the wall and tilted his head up. He sniffed. "So what you been up to lately?"

Laura shrugged and looked around. "Just school." She sipped the beer.

"You get anything good for Christmas?"

"Clothes." Laura ran her hands over her dress.

Tommy nodded. "Looks good on you."

Laura smiled and said thanks. Tommy looked away.

What was he doing? He suddenly felt foolish, talking to Laura. The memory of the failed kiss at the Homecoming Dance came rushing back to him, and he felt as if everyone was staring at them.

"So look," he said, "I wanna apologize about the dance."

Laura held her free hand up. "Don't worry about it. No big deal."

"You know. I just thought that ... you know ... we were on a date ..."

"I know, Tommy. I'm sorry. I'd just broken up with Patrick, and I thought going with you, well ..."

"It would be safe," Tommy finished her thought, looking into her eyes.

Laura pursed her lips and frowned. "Yeah, I just didn't ... at that time ... I wasn't looking at anyone like that, you know?" She shuffled her feet. "I just wanted to be myself ... and we were having such a good time ..."

"And I ruined it."

"No, you didn't."

Tommy laughed.

Laura smiled. "Okay, maybe a little. The moment, you know. It was nice to just be with someone and not have all that other stuff."

Tommy nodded. He felt the opposite, how nice it was to be with someone he felt that "other stuff" for. It was then, as he gazed into her honey-flecked eyes that he realized he still felt that way.

"So," he said, clearing his throat, "I just wanted to say I'm sorry ... I'll let you mingle .. I just wanted to, you know, make things right, I guess."

She placed a hand on Tommy's arm and said, "Things were never wrong between us, Tommy."

Tommy nodded and backed away, then went to find Angel. He finished his beer before he made it back to the couch, and went to get another refill.

On his way, Tommy was high-fived by Jalen Carter and Terrell Baker. "There he is!" shouted Jalen. "There's the man!"

Terrell held up his cup in a salute. "Fifteen points and twelve assists! You're the man!"

Tommy smiled and saluted with his empty cup.

"Northeast didn't know what hit them, but we do!" Jalen continued. "We call him Tornado Tommy!"

Terrell downed his beer. "'Cause when he comes through your defense, all he leaves behind are twisted bodies!"

Tommy laughed. "You guys are crazy." And being generous. Northeast was the game before his current slump had set in.

Jalen belched. "We're still working on it. But we're gonna make sure the nickname sticks."

Tommy winked. "Right. If you remember it after tonight."

Tommy encountered two more high-fives and a chest-bump before he made it to the back patio.

Nick was hanging out at the keg talking about Carolina with Jamie.

"And there's a Mexican restaurant on Franklin that's awesome," Jamie said. "Can't miss that."

Nick nodded at Tommy. "Jamie's filling me in on all the cool places to go at Carolina." Nick had already sent off his application and hoped to hear back for early admissions. "He stays in the Granville Towers."

"Where you going, Tommy?" Jamie asked.

Tommy held his empty cup out to be refilled. "I don't know. I was hoping to play somewhere."

"Oh yeah? Any coaches been in contact with you?"

Tommy looked up. "No. Should there be?"

Jamie searched his face. "Usually. A lot of times, they've got a bead on you when you're a junior."

"Well. I'm not hoping to play somewhere like Carolina. I thought maybe a small school like App State or East Carolina."

Jamie sucked in through his teeth. "I was talking about the small schools. Schools like Carolina and Duke starting looking at you in JV."

"Oh." Tommy's cup was full, and he threw back a gulp. "I didn't know."

"What you need to do is get some tape of you playing. Put it together and send copies to schools you want to see you." Jamie began filling Jalen Carter's cup. "Your coach tapes the games, right? Make you a highlight reel and send it out."

Tommy nodded and wished somebody had told him this before half the season was gone. His mind was cranking when the noise back inside the house grew. But something was off, it wasn't the good kind of noise you heard around a keg stand. Something was up.

He walked back inside with the guys and followed the noise, now realizing it was someone yelling. Tommy broke through the crowd to find Patrick Hart yelling at Laura Novak.

"So I ask you for space, and you can't wait to get drunk somewhere?" Patrick was yelling.

"You didn't ask for space. You said you wanted to see other people," Laura responded, her voice steely and steady.

Patrick held his hand up and looked away, slurring his words. "I don't want to hear it, slut. I know you. Not one week after I took you to Harrison's and told you I wanted to be with just you, you're seen making out with Tommy Fucking Chandler at the Homecoming Dance. Tommy Fucking Chandler?"

"We didn't make out. We kissed. And it's none of your damn business because I said no to you. I didn't want to see you then, and I don't want to see you now. And guess what? I don't want to ever see you again." Laura's eyes had turned wild, her face red.

"You're lucky. I'm gonna give you one last chance on the Hart train. See if you're worthy." Patrick thrust his hips forward as two strange guys behind him laughed. He belched and said, "Let's go somewhere private where we can talk this out." He grabbed Laura's arm and yanked.

Laura shrieked and tried to pull free, but his grip was like iron. Tommy stepped forward to say something, but Miles beat him to it.

"Come on, Patrick. Don't bring that stuff in here."

Patrick held his other hand up. "Stay out of it, Miles. This ain't got nothing to do with you."

"But you're at my house, man. I'm just saying ..."

"Don't worry. We were about to leave this shithole."

Patrick yanked Laura again like she was a Cabbage Patch doll. She cried out and tried to pry his fingers from her arm. This time Tommy stepped out to within a foot of Patrick, blocking the way. He said, "Let her go."

Patrick stopped and sneered as Laura struggled to free herself. "Well, well, well. Little Tommy Chandler." But Tommy wasn't little anymore. He was eye to eye with Patrick. "I ain't here for you tonight, but don't you worry"—he winked—"you'll get your turn."

Calm and collected, his anger building below his emotionless facade, Tommy repeated, "Let her go."

Patrick laughed. "What are you gonna do, Tommy?"

"Let her go." Tommy repeated the words, again with the same coolness, not blinking a single time and not taking his eyes off Patrick. "She said she doesn't want to see you."

Another laugh. "You gonna make me let her go? That what you're gonna do? Puh-leaze." He turned with a big smile to his new friends who smiled back at him. It was obvious the two guys were members of Patrick's new basketball team. They were at least 6'4" and as wide as linebackers.

Patrick swiveled back around to Tommy. He slurred, "You can't even tie your shoes without somebody drawing you up a play." His goons laughed. "Think you're a big boy now? Gonna take up for your slutty girlfriend?"

Tommy glanced into Laura's eyes. They were a mixture of fear and anger. Tommy said to Patrick, "Laura's not my girlfriend. She's just a friend."

Patrick laughed so hard Tommy could smell the alcohol on his breath. "Tommy," he said, "I'm giving you one more chance to back the hell out of my way before I lay you out."

Tommy remained still, clenching his fists, his eyes boring down into Patrick's.

"Let her go, Patrick," Miles said.

"Yeah," Nick and Jalen chimed in.

Several members of the basketball team had surrounded the intruders from Greensboro Day. Patrick's friends no longer had cocky expressions on their faces. One of them tapped Patrick's shoulder and said, "Come on, man. Let's blow this place."

Patrick looked around him. He sneered and tossed Laura to the side. She fell to the couch, rubbing her arm as she sat up. He said to Tommy, "Fine. You can have my sloppy seconds like you always do. A second-rate girl and a second-rate basketball team"—looking around at the guys—"They're all yours." He laughed. "That's all somebody like you will ever get, sloppy-fucking-seconds."

Patrick lunged forward to poke Tommy in the chest, but Tommy reacted by throwing a roundhouse right that connected flush with the left side of Patrick's face. His goons stepped forward but held their ground. They were outnumbered and surrounded.

Patrick staggered to the left and came up with his eyes blazing. He screamed and swung at Tommy, although he was slow and off-balance. Tommy pulled back and Patrick missed.

Tommy's left hand connected square on Patrick's nose. Patrick's head snapped back, and he stumbled into his goons. They kept him from falling down, but he shook them off and stood on his own. He felt his nose and came away with blood.

Patrick viewed his red-stained hand with surprise, his eyes widening. He glared at Tommy and screamed, "You're dead! You hear me? You're a dead man!"

He held his nose and pushed his way through the crowd and the front door, his new teammates right behind him.

Chapter 18

Southeast destroyed Ragsdale at the next game, 64-42. The Falcons were now 12-1, and it looked like nothing could stop them. Of course, they hadn't played perennial power, Greensboro Day School, and if anyone could stop Southeast from going to State, they would. Greensboro Day was undefeated.

After the game, Tommy found Angel in the parking lot waiting for him. "Want to go for victory tacos?"

Angel shrugged. "Sure."

Tommy drove them to Taco Bell. They ordered and sat. Tommy began opening and squirting hot sauce onto his tacos while Angel did the same thing to her taco pizza.

"You don't look happy," Tommy said. "We just won a big game. It's customary to be in a good mood, hence the idea behind"—he threw up imaginary quotes—"Victory Tacos."

Tommy laughed, but Angel didn't. Instead, she offered a thin smile.

"What's wrong?" he asked. "You look like your tape collection just got stolen."

Tommy took a huge bite of his taco.

"I think it would be best if we broke up," Angel finally said. She had placed her hands in her lap and sat there waiting for his reaction.

Tommy set his taco down. "What? Why?"

Angel glanced around the restaurant. There was another high school couple in the far corner and an older man in a jeans jacket seated at the window, eating and watching cars cruise by.

"I just think it would be best."

"That's ... that's not a good answer."

Angel looked down at her food, then pushed it away. "Because you don't really love me."

Tommy frowned. "Sure I do. I always tell you I love you."

"No, you always repeat it after I say it."

"You mean, you're upset because I don't say 'I love you' first?"

"That's just part of it, Tommy." Angel sighed. "I never feel like you're really with me. Do you understand? It's like you're going through the motions."

"Going through the motions?"

"Like your heart's not really in it. In our relationship." A tear trickled down Angel's cheek. She wiped it with a paper napkin. "I didn't want to do this here."

"Angel, I love you. I really do. Tell me what I'm not doing, and I'll start doing it. I promise."

Angel was shaking her head. "That's just it, Tommy. It's not just one thing. It's everything." She sniffed and wiped her eyes, make-up smearing. "I love you so much, Tommy, and I have for a long time, but you've never seen it."

Tommy drew his face together. "I don't get it."

Angel smiled sadly. "I know. That's what makes this a little bit easier. You don't know how hopeless you are. You're not even conscious of it."

"Now you're not making any sense at all."

"Not to you I'm not, and that's kind of the point." Angel took a deep breath and steadied herself. "Tommy, you've never really been single in your heart. You've never been available, and I've had too much of a crush to see it. Or I wouldn't accept it. Whichever."

Tommy sipped his Mountain Dew. "You're talking crazy. I love you, Angel. I know I do, and you can't tell me I don't."

Angel exhaled. "Oh Tommy, I know you believe that, and I have no doubt you love me as much as you can." She paused. "But you're not *in love* with me. And that's what I need. What I deserve."

"So now you're admitting I love you? I don't understand."

"I know, I know. If you did understand, it wouldn't be true." She wiped her eyes, laughing. "I thought I was already all cried out, but I still have some in me."

Tommy slumped back in his seat, face drawn. "You've been thinking about this a while, huh?"

Angel nodded.

"You really want to break up."

"I *need* to break up, but I don't *want* to."

"But, I love you, and you said you love me too. I don't get it."

"I do love you, Tommy. But you can't give me all of you, and that's what I want. All of you." She shook her head. "Tommy, I'll never be the love of your life. I want that, to be someone's Juliet. Someone's Juliet they can't live without. I need it. I deserve it." She paused. "You don't have room in your life for another Juliet."

Tommy scrunched his face and started to say something but didn't. He just looked at Angel as she ate her burrito. She held it delicately, as if it were a musical instrument, with her right pinkie slightly raised.

They sat in silence, absorbing the moment, nibbling on their food and thinking to themselves. "Every Rose Has Its Thorn" dribbled out of the drop ceiling. Tommy went to the bathroom. They refilled their Cokes and drove back to the school.

"So this it?" Tommy said when he'd parked and turned off the car.

"It's for the best. It really is."

"You sound more like you're convincing yourself instead of me."

Angel smiled. "I am."

"Then let's—"

"No, Tommy. Don't. Please." She placed on hand on his. "I will always love you, and it would kill me if we couldn't part friends."

"Of course we'll be friends. That's stupid."

"Tommy Chandler. You're a very special person. Don't you ever settle."

"I wasn't."

Angel shook her head. "You're not there yet, but you will be. Just promise me you won't settle. Ever."

Tommy tilted his head. "I don't—"

"Just promise me. Say it."

"I promise."

Angel leaned toward Tommy and kissed him. It was a long kiss that not even salty tears interrupted, tears from both of them. When they parted, Angel scrambled from the car and closed the door. She didn't look back at him until she had turned the ignition on in her own car.

She smiled the way a character does at the end of a movie when no one knows what's going to happen to her, but somewhere inside, you feel she's going to be okay, things will work themselves out.

But for now, Tommy felt empty and confused.

Chapter 19

The weather was the main topic on everyone's mind at the store, and Mrs. Lineberry chattered on about how crazy it was non-stop. She was on crutches because she had twisted her ankle when she slipped on the ice a week earlier. A freak snowstorm had blitzed the area; then dissipated just as fast. Now the temperature was back up to sixty, and the only evidence of the storm was left behind in shadowed areas that never received direct sunlight, the corners and crevices highlighted in dirty white.

Tommy took Mrs. Lineberry's bags to her car. He nodded and said yes repeatedly, allowing her to carry the discussion until she was safely on her way. He made a note to himself to never marry a woman who could have an entire conversation by herself.

Grant Gardner's dad came into the store next. He bought two quarts of oil and a loaf of bread. "Having a good year aren't you, Tommy?" he said at checkout.

"How do you mean?" Tommy asked.

"Basketball. Y'all are undefeated, right?"

Tommy smiled. "We lost a game early on, but that's the only one."

Mr. Gardner nodded. "Got a big one coming up, don't you?" His son Grant played on the JV team so Mr. Gardner kept up with both teams.

"Yeah. Greensboro Day will be tough, but I think we can take them."

"I hear that kid, the Hart kid that used to go to Southeast, is being recruited by Duke. Got a couple other kids on that team, one of them's going to State, another one to Virginia Tech."

"Yes, sir." Tommy wondered if Mr. Gardner knew he wasn't helping.

"You gonna play anywhere?" he asked as Tommy bagged the oil and a Snickers Mr. Gardner added at the last moment.

Tommy smiled and glanced toward the back to see if his dad was still in the office. "Got a couple prospects," he said. "Ain't made up my mind yet."

"Any hint where?"

"If I told you, I'd have to kill you." Tommy held his hand up like a gun and fired.

Mr. Gardner shook his head. "I understand. I understand."

But Tommy wondered if he did. Did he know Tommy's dad thought college was a waste of time and money?

The truth was, Tommy did indeed have a few prospects. With the help of his mom, he'd applied to four in-state colleges: Appalachian State, Western Carolina, UNC Wilmington, and finally, UNC Greensboro, where if it came down to a case of money, he could attend while still living at home.

They weren't basketball prospects because to Tommy's knowledge, no programs were interested in him. But to him, basketball was merely a means to an end, the end being a college education.

There was a rumor that college coaches would be at the Southeast-Greensboro Day game, and Tommy held the smallest bit of hope that he could show up Patrick Hart. If Hart was going to Duke, and Tommy could shut him down or hold him to a few points, the coaches might look at Tommy too.

It made him want to go shoot some ball. He worked for another hour before he went to his dad to ask if he could leave early. When his dad finally nodded, Tommy yelled thanks as he flew out the door.

He drove home and called Nick to meet him at the school's outside court. Nick was tied up helping his dad take down all the Christmas decorations, but he said he'd be there as soon as he could. Tommy changed and drove straight to the school, planning on working on his dribbling and free throws until Nick showed.

Tommy found four orange cones around a hole in the side parking lot. He parked and dragged the cones to the court behind the gym, then set them up in a line down the middle of the blacktop.

He began with his left hand, dribbling around the cones as fast as he could, weaving in and out, then launching into the air for a left-handed lay-up. He turned and drove right-handed toward the other end of the court, weaving around the cones, finishing with a right-handed lay-up.

After about ten trips, he switched to crossover drills, changing dribbling hands after rounding each cone. Next came drills he made up where at each cone, he went between his legs or behind his back, "fancy" stuff he'd been practicing so much it was now as natural as a crossover dribble.

"Hey, hey ... if it isn't the little prick who blind-sided me."

Tommy turned to find Patrick Hart and the two goons he'd brought to Miles' party. "He thinks he's a real basketball player," Patrick said to his friends. He smiled at Tommy. "We just happened to be driving by, and I thought I recognized that piece of shit car of yours."

Tommy quit dribbling and held the ball against his right hip. "What do you want, Patrick?"

"Got up a good sweat, do you? Getting ready for our game this week?" Patrick and his friends strolled onto the court, still ambling toward Tommy.

"I always practice in my spare time," Tommy said, shifting his feet.

"Well, you need to. Of course, it ain't gonna help when you play us." Patrick laughed and his two friends joined him. They walked right up to Tommy and spread out.

Tommy, now understanding the danger he was in, started dribbling and backing up. "If y'all would excuse me, I've got some more drills to run before the guys show up."

"Guys?" Patrick said, looking up at his goons with a smile. "I don't see any guys around here but us. We'll play with you."

"Don't worry. They'll be here any minute." Tommy was still backing up, dribbling. Patrick and the goons matched his pace. Tommy continued, "I'd say you could join us, but we'll already have three on three."

Patrick looked behind him. "Seems to me they're late. Really late, because by the looks of it, you've been out here a while." He sneered. "Makes me wonder if anybody's coming at all."

"Oh, they'll be here. Any second now. I showed up early to do my drills, just like at a game."

"You know, guys?" Patrick said, still walking toward Tommy. "It's just occurred to me that maybe Tommy here is making the whole thing up. The part about the other guys. I don't think he wants to play with us. What do you think?"

The guy on the left, with short dark hair and black eyes, said, "I think you're right, Patrick." He was the biggest of the three.

The other goon grunted.

Tommy knew he couldn't make it to his car before they'd get him. Even if he did, he couldn't get it started and moving in time. He could take off and maybe outrun them as he circled the school, then get to his car and get out of there before they caught him.

He studied the two big guys; they didn't look like they would make it halfway around before having to stop for a breather. But Patrick was quick, maybe quicker than him.

Tommy weighed his options. It didn't look as though he had any choice. They weren't going to be stalled until Nick showed up. How many damn decorations did he have to take down anyway?

Tommy continued to dribble and back up, but pavement was becoming a premium. It was now or never.

Tommy tapped the ball against his right hip and smiled. He raised his left hand, looked behind the guys and yelled, "Hey, Nick!"

The two goons turned to look, and Patrick grinned, his eyes locking on Tommy's. Tommy cocked his arm and rocketed the ball at Patrick, then turned and sprinted for his life.

But Patrick was ready, deflecting the ball and launching into pursuit in the same motion.

Tommy built a lead at first, but Patrick closed it after the first turn. On a straightaway, Patrick was too quick. It was just before the next corner that Patrick tripped him up.

Tommy went head-long into a metal pole supporting a covered walkway. He twisted at the last second, and instead of ramming it with his forehead, he connected it with his shoulder. The pain shot down his body to his toes.

He tried to scramble up, but when he put weight on his left shoulder, it gave way with a searing bolt of pain. By then Patrick stood over him, saying, "Where you going, Tommy? I thought we were gonna play a little ball."

Patrick's first kick struck Tommy's side so hard he almost threw up.

Patrick's goons finally arrived, wheezing and bending over at the waist. The dark-haired guy lunged forward and delivered a kick to

Tommy's gut that doubled him over into a fetal ball. The guy yelled something about making him run.

Tommy couldn't breathe and felt like he might never suck in oxygen ever again. He tried, but the air wouldn't come. It was as if his lungs had been ripped from his body, sandbags left in their place.

Patrick was laughing and said, "Pick him up."

The goons lifted Tommy by his armpits. His shoulder screamed with pain, and he still couldn't breathe. He was trying to suck in a much-needed breath when Patrick threw an uppercut that snapped his head back so hard the world went fuzzy.

"Son of a bitch!" Patrick yelled, waving his hand. "The movies don't tell you how much that hurts your hand." He hopped around shaking his hand and mumbling.

Tommy felt the blood flowing down his chin. He tried to wrest himself free, but it was like he was trapped in quicksand. Every move he made drained his energy, and he sunk farther into the darkness, swallowed by the silence.

He took another shot to the gut, but there was no breath in him to knock out. He wasn't even sure he was trying to breathe anymore. Tommy welcomed the darkness and the numbness it promised.

"Lower him to his knees," Patrick said.

Tommy opened his eyes in time to see Patrick's size twelve Air Jordans kick him in the face. This time his head snapped so far he thought it touched his back. The darkness hastened, his face already numb.

Tommy heard laughing as he dropped to the ground. He heard the goon that hadn't spoken say they might ought to go.

And that's when he heard a shout from the direction of the basketball court. Tommy squinted through a swollen left eye.

Someone was running toward them, an aluminum bat in his hand, yelling at the top of his lungs. Daylight touched Tommy as his three attackers moved away from him. Tommy could tell by the way the guy ran it was Nick. Tommy wanted to reach out to him.

Patrick laughed as Nick approached. "He got what he deserved," Patrick said, "He sucker-punched me the other night."

Nick swung at him, and Patrick backed away, holding his hands out, saying, "Hey, I ain't got no problem with you, Nick."

Nick swung again, catching Patrick's shirt but nothing underneath it. "You got a problem with me now," he yelled, swinging again. "I wonder how much playing time you'll get with two crushed kneecaps?" Nick swung low.

Patrick jumped back, arms outstretched. "Hey, hey! Watch it. That one was close."

"That's the point." Nick extended as he swung, catching Patrick's hip.

Patrick yelped, and his goons took a step forward. Nick held the bat up, saying, "Go ahead. Who wants to be the first to end his basketball career today?"

"Come on, Patrick. Let's go," one of them said.

Patrick nodded. "Sure, okay." He pointed at Nick. "I owe you one now, pal." Still rubbing his hip.

"But Tommy owes you about a dozen. I'll be there when he collects. You can try to pay me back then."

Patrick and his friends backed away, then turned and left. One of the goons kept checking over his shoulder until they rounded the corner of the school building.

Nick dropped the bat and fell to his knees over Tommy. "You alright, buddy?"

Tommy swallowed. "You swing like a girl."

Nick laughed and looked into Tommy's good eye. "You're gonna look like Karl Malden now." He pointed to Tommy's busted nose.

"It'll add character," Tommy wheezed. "I was too good-looking anyway."

"Well, he sure didn't hit your sense of humor. Maybe I should go get him to finish the job."

Tommy tried to sit up, but it was too much. He winced and draped an arm over his midsection. "Ow. If my funny bone's right here, he got it."

Nick helped Tommy upright and propped him against the same pole he'd hit with his shoulder earlier. "You think you can stand?" Nick asked.

"Probably. They didn't hit my legs, just my face and my gut." Tommy pulled in a long breath, wincing. "Got a couple ribs."

"Well, the sooner we get ice on you, the better off you'll be. You're starting to look like the Elephant Man."

"So does this mean you don't want to play some ball today?"

Nick laughed, shifting his head. "You always got jokes."

Tommy spit out some blood. "I just got one question. Where the hell were you?"

"Taking down Christmas decorations."

"The whole time? You know, I'm not trying to make you feel guilty or anything, but if your dad wasn't Clark Griswald, I might still be my same cute, lovable self."

"Tell me about it," Nick said. "He bought some more crap off Eckerd's clearance bin the other day and stuck it in the attic for next year."

Nick finally dragged Tommy to his feet, and as they rounded the corner of the school, Tommy said, "You know what I keep thinking about?" He didn't wait for an answer. "How much my mom's gonna freak out."

Nick nodded. "Yep. She's totally gonna freak."

"Hey, what made you come around back with your bat?"

"You kidding me? I drive up, see Patrick's car and your car and the basketball off in the grass. I remembered the party the other night, and put two and two together."

Tommy coughed and spit out more blood. "Well, I'll give you one thing. You may swing like a girl, but you're a smart girl."

"I could drop you right here. You know that, right?"

"Yeah, you could, but then who'd feed you the ball when you're open?"

* * *

That night, Helen Chandler reacted just as Tommy thought she would. She fawned over him, applying ice and cold compresses, and insisted he go to the emergency room, despite Tommy's assertion he was alright. When she called Gene to tell him where they'd be, Gene rushed home to inspect the damage himself.

He barreled through the kitchen door and took the bag of frozen peas off Tommy's bloody face.

Tommy kept his eyes down.

Gene turned to Nick. "Who did this?"

"Don't worry about it, Dad," Tommy rasped.

Gene fixed his stare on Nick. "I asked you a question."

"P-Patrick Hart," Nick stammered. Then he added, "And two other guys."

Gene's face hardened. "Why?"

Nick looked at Tommy.

"Why?" Gene roared.

Nick snapped his head back to Gene. "Because Tommy flattened him the other night at a party."

Helen's eyes perked up as she looked at her son.

"Why?" Gene asked, face impassive.

As Nick turned toward Tommy, Gene took a step toward him. Nick snapped his attention back to Gene. "Because Patrick was hurting Laura."

Gene swiveled toward Tommy. "The girl you took to the Homecoming Dance?"

Tommy stared at his feet.

"I'm asking you a question, boy."

Tommy raised his head. "Yes."

Gene glared at Tommy, and Tommy lowered his gaze again. Gene pursed his lips and turned toward Helen. "Patrick Hart. That Vance's boy?"

Helen hesitated. "What are you gonna do, Gene?"

Gene shoved his hand in his pocket and pulled out his car keys. "I'm gonna go do something I should have done a long time ago." He moved toward the door.

"No, Dad!" Tommy yelled.

Gene stopped and twisted his head, his brow creased into angry lines. "What did you just say?"

In a lower voice, Tommy said, "No. It's not your fight." He winced and held his chest. "It's mine."

Gene studied his son with stony eyes. He jingled his keys and relaxed a fraction. "He get your ribs too?"

Tommy nodded.

Gene fiddled with his keys a moment more, glanced at Helen, then back at Tommy. He exhaled and said, "Well, you coming or not?"

THE WALK-ON

Tommy frowned. "Where?"

Gene shook his head. "X-rays cost enough. I ain't paying for no damn ambulance, too." He motioned with his hand and raised his eyebrows. "Let's go. I don't have all night."

Chapter 20

The grapefruit of flesh over Tommy's eye had shrunk to the size of a golf ball by game day. His ribs were bruised but not cracked. His left eye was black and blue, but that wasn't the worst. What hurt him most was the shoulder that had rammed into the pole. The doctor said it was probably a partial dislocation and to be careful.

Tommy looked at the doctor and said, "I'm always careful; can't you tell?"

The doctor didn't laugh. He had the personality of a wet coat.

Earlier that week, Nick had wanted Tommy to go to the coach at Greensboro Day and tell him three of his players had assaulted him. "They'll get suspended for sure," he said.

Tommy shook his head. "No. You really want to beat Greensboro Day that way? Without three of their starters?"

"Sure, why not?"

"It would be an empty victory, that's why."

"Geez, why you gotta always do everything the hard way?"

"Because it's usually the right way."

"Man, twenty years from now, all anyone will remember is that we beat Greensboro Day in our senior year."

Tommy shook his head again. "We'd know, Nick. We'd know."

On game day, Tommy was bruised and not pretty to look at, but he

THE WALK-ON 139

was ready. Nick helped him tape his ribs in the locker room before the other guys started showing up. He'd been exempt from the practices that week on the strict promise that he'd rest and be ready for the game.

When his dad had wanted him to help unload a truck, his mom put her foot down. Her son was recuperating, and Gene could get someone else to help. Gene even tried the "If he's well enough to play basketball" argument, but Helen would have none of that. Tommy was to rest and that was that.

So Tommy rested his body and watched basketball. He caught practice from the bleachers, scrutinized ACC games on TV, and taped games on ESPN from around the nation. If he couldn't play basketball, he could sure as heck study it.

"You ready?" Miles asked. He was the first player in the locker room after Tommy and Nick.

Tommy nodded, face passive.

Terrell Baker and Stanley Gattison showed next, then Paul Geary and Charlie Madison. Charlie was amazed at how sickly the black eye had gotten, more purple than black.

Jalen Carter and Frankie Brown came in next, and Jalen made a joke about blacking Tommy's other eye and calling him Raccoon from now on. The guys all knew who'd beat up Tommy, and at first, they'd wanted to pay Patrick a visit after practice one night. But Tommy talked them out of it.

"Let's punish him on the court," Tommy said.

Everyone vowed to save a hard foul just for Patrick.

Coach Barrows strode into the locker room once all the guys had arrived. He looked at Tommy first, reading his face. "You ready?"

"Yeah, Coach."

"Charlie's ready to pick up a few more minutes, so when you're out there, take it easy and just remember the basics. Patrick"—Coach usually called the other teams by their positions, but even to him, this game was personal—"is quick so don't try for so many steals. You'll just put more strain on your ribs than you need and get nothing out of it."

To the others, he said, "That goes for everyone. This is the best team we'll face this year. It's not like we'll be playing Southern Alamance where there's just one or two real players on the team. Every one of these guys can play." He paused and smiled. "Just like us."

This got an uproar from the players. Coach motioned for them to quiet.

"Jalen, you're gonna have your hands full with their big guy, Callaway. He's got you by a few inches so you've got to focus on boxing him out. You other guys collapse on him when he gets the ball. Double or triple-team him and make him earn his points the hard way. I don't want Callaway dipping into double-digit points or rebounds tonight."

Coached pointed at Miles Flaherty. "Miles, you're gonna be on Kiebler. We've gone over this in practice. He's got that little fake when you come at him too hard, so watch out for that. He'll get you out of your shoes and go around you if you're not careful."

To Terrell Baker, he said, "You got Smithey. He loves the three-pointer so you'll have to step out on him. He's gonna shoot it, but for God's sake, make him shoot it with your fat hands in his face. I don't want him getting open shots. Pretend he's another guard instead of a small forward. They're gonna set picks galore to get him open, and you gotta do everything in your power to fight around them and put the pressure on."

Coach took a breath and turned to Nick. "Folsom is quick. They'll pop him out for long-distance shots from another zip code, and he's got the range to knock them down. You gotta stick to him like stink on shit."

This got a laugh from everyone because the one thing the coach didn't do was cuss, even when the guys were screwing up royally.

"They're gonna set a lot of picks for him, too, and all of you need to be prepared to switch on those picks. Talk to each other. I don't want to see them getting no easy back door lay-ups on simple picks."

Coach Barrows shuffled over to Tommy and lowered to a squat. "You sure you're up for this? It would be the toughest game of your life if you were healthy. It's gonna be even tougher stitched together like Frankenstein."

The guys chortled, and Tommy said, "I'm ready, Coach. I want this game."

Coach looked into Tommy's eyes for a moment, squinted, then rose to his feet. He shuffled to the front of the room, ignoring the mobile chalkboard he usually drew on before games. When he turned, his face was stony.

"Guys," he said, his voice low and even. "I want this game more than all the other games this year put together. I've never said that before, and I've never meant it as I do right now. I. Want. This. Game."

There was silence for a few seconds, then Coach threw his hand out. "Everybody huddle!" The team hopped up and crowded in, everyone shoving a hand in the circle. Tommy winced from the bodies pressing against him.

"Who's the best team!" Coach shouted.

"The Falcons!" came the reply in unison.

"Who are we?"

"The Falcons!" Louder.

"And who's gonna win?"

"The Falcons!" The team shouted at the tops of their lungs.

Chapter 21

During warm-up drills, Tommy blocked out the pain that wracked his body. Nick's dad had a stash of pain pills he used when he suffered from kidney stones, and Nick had smuggled one out for Tommy, giving it to him when they first got into the locker room. Tommy was still waiting for it to kick in.

Tommy sunk a lay-up and jogged to the back of the line behind Nick.

"Maybe you should've gotten me two," he said.

"No. One's enough. Just wait. You'll see."

By the time they were huddling before tip-off, Tommy was smiling at Nick and nodding. "See?" Nick said.

And Tommy did. Not only was there no pain, but he was also surrounded by a warm fuzzy aura that protected him, enveloped him in a sense of invulnerability and euphoria. Not so much he couldn't think, but rather, just enough so that his pain dulled and actually allowed him to think about something other than the pain itself.

"You check them out?" Nick said, cocking his head to the opposite end of the court.

"Yeah, I see them." Tommy glanced over his shoulder.

The two goons that had helped Patrick were warming up. Their names were on their uniforms. The big guy with the dark eyes and hair was named Kiebler, the other Smithey.

"What do you wanna do?" Nick asked.

Tommy paused and looked his friend in the eyes. "Win."

In the huddle, Coach said, "Okay guys. We're here. I've already said everything in practice and the locker room that needed saying. All but the most important thing." He paused and smiled. "Have fun. This is a game, and you play a game because it's fun. It's fun to pop that three or make that amazing pass or grab that impossible rebound. But you know what's the most fun about this game?"

He waited. "Anyone?" The guys were quiet.

Coach nodded his head. "Scoring more points than the other team."

Everyone laughed, even the coach. He stuck his hand out. "Go Falcons on three. One-two-three!"

"Go Falcons!"

Jalen lost the tip as Brenden Callaway out-jumped him, which Tommy had anticipated. Callaway had knocked it to Patrick, but Tommy's quick thinking put the ball in his hands instead as he cut the pass off.

Tommy weaved left, then right, dribbling around the Bengals' William Smithey. Terrell Baker broke away from Smithey and took off parallel with Tommy toward their basket. The only thing between Tommy and the basket was Greensboro Day player, DeSean Kiebler, one of the goons.

Tommy gave a thumbs-up to Terrell, then went right, drawing Kiebler from the basket. Tommy elevated ten feet away from the basket, just close enough Kiebler had to come for him instead of camping out.

It was what Tommy hoped he'd do.

Even though it wasn't a play they ever drew up, Terrell knew what to do. Tommy had told him with a simple hand gesture.

Terrell leapt a split second after Tommy released the ball, caught the alley-oop pass a foot from the rim, and still rising, slammed the ball through the rim.

The home crowd erupted in a gym-shaking cheer that set the tone for the game. The Falcons were here to play.

After Southeast scored the first eight points, stopping Greensboro Day with their solid defense, the game settled into a normal rhythm.

Tommy, without his full mobility, held his own, but he had difficulty going left and gave the ball up once to Patrick. Nick was having the game of his life, firing threes like they were second nature.

Tommy looked up once into the bleachers, and his mom smiled. But his dad wasn't there. It was the biggest game of Tommy's life, and Gene Chandler was at home watching UNC versus Duke on Channel 2.

Southeast built a twelve-point lead by the end of the first quarter on almost flawless execution. But Greensboro Day was a team chocked full of college talent. They would not be beaten so easily.

The Bengals came out of the second quarter with a vengeance, led by Patrick and the big guy, Callaway. Then, once Southeast began collapsing inside to stop the juggernaut center, the perimeter show heated up. Smithey and Folsom rained threes like Coach had promised, and Southeast's lead dissolved.

At the half, despite the Falcons' best efforts, they only led by two, 46-44.

Tommy said to Nick as they entered the locker room, "This game has flown by."

"Yeah."—Nick shaking his head—"I can't believe we let them back in it."

Coach Barrows interrupted, saying to everyone in the locker room, "We didn't let this team back in the game." He looked around. "They were never out of it. We started the game strong and knocked their breath out, but they began playing the game I warned you about. The game I told you they had."

He pointed at Jalen. "Callaway down below." Pointed at Terrell and Nick. "Smithey and Folsom outside."

Coach shook his head. "We gotta fight around these picks. We can't let them get open shots like that. Y'all are playing good, probably your best game all year, but it's gonna take a little more to win. And I can't do it for you. You gotta find that inside yourself, that extra half-step, that extra speed. Anticipate on defense. Get in front of them. They ran all over you that second quarter. They might as well have been playing our JV team for all it mattered."

Coach squatted and lowered his voice. "Forget that stuff I said before the game. We gave them fun in the first half. Fun got us a two-point lead. Fun got the crowd in it early."

He paused and met the eyes of every player. "Forget having fun. You've already had it. Right now, I want you to fight! Fight for every point. Fight for every possession." Coach's voice was rising with each sentence now. "Fight for every loose ball. Fight for every steal."

He stood, his voice still rising. "Fight for every second you're on that court! Fight for every fan in those stands who came to see you win! Fight for your teammates who are out there fighting for you! But more than anything, guys, more than anything else, you gotta fight for yourself!"

He was shouting now.

"Fight for your dignity! Fight for your respect! Fight like it's the last game of your life!"

He paused, his voice echoing through the room. He swept the room with his eyes, and in a raspy, almost-whisper, he said, "Fight for the win ... Fight for the win ... Fight for the win."

He extended an arm; the team scrambled to the huddle.

"What are we gonna do?" Coach said.

"Fight for the win!"

"I can't hear you."

"Fight for the win!" Louder.

Coach shook his head. "I don't feel it."

"Fight for the win!" they shouted, then broke and ran out to the floor.

Coach grabbed Tommy and waited until the team left. He said to Tommy, "You alright?"

"Yeah, Coach."

"You're playing sluggish. You know there's college coaches out there, right?"

"Yeah."

"I know you're in pain. I can put Charlie in some."

"No, Coach," Tommy said quickly. "I want this one."

Coach nodded. "Okay. Go show me how much you want it."

Waiting for the ball to be inbounded, Patrick said to Tommy, "You guys were lucky in the first half."

Tommy said nothing, didn't even look at Patrick.

"The shiner makes you look older," Patrick goaded, laughing under his breath just loud enough for Tommy to hear. "We're gonna beat you worse than you got beat the other day."

Greensboro Day scored six straight points before Tommy found Nick for an open three. Down by one. As they headed down the court, Tommy yelled for the guys to quit messing around and play defense.

And they did.

Terrell Baker stole a pass intended for William Smithey and chunked it down the court to a sprinting Tommy Chandler. Tommy went up for a quick lay-in, and Patrick Hart clobbered him, barely getting his hand on the ball.

Tommy turned a three-sixty in mid-air with a partial somersault, landing awkwardly. He laid there a second, pain racking his body. The pain pill was wearing off.

The crowd hushed as the ref came over and said, "You alright, son?"

"Did I make it?" Tommy asked from the floor.

The ref smiled. "No, but you're gonna be fine."

Nick arrived and helped Tommy to his feet. Tommy shook it off, took a few deep breaths, and sank both free throws.

Coach Barrows called a timeout and asked Tommy if he could still play.

"I just dropped two in the basket."

Coach nodded and said, "Okay. You guys keep up the intensity of that last trip. Keep the defense tight. Keep trying to push the ball inside." As they broke, he added, "And use your picks!"

As the team walked out to the court, Nick said, "Alright everyone, time for Operation Foulfest."

Everybody but Tommy nodded. Tommy said, "Wait, what's that?"

"Don't you worry about it. Just do us a favor; the next few times Patrick tries to drive by you, let him."

"What?"

"Just do it," Jalen Carter said, his eyes steady, face impassive.

The next three times Patrick tried to drive, Tommy put forth a token effort to stop him, and let him by. Patrick paid for it.

First, it was Jalen Carter who railroaded Patrick with a hard forearm. Then on the next drive, Miles Flaherty pulled off his man and flattened Patrick to his back. Terrell finished the trifecta with a brutal foul that left Patrick slow to get up from the hardwood.

Terrell's man, Smithey got up in Terrell's face, yelling, "Why don't you try that on someone your own size?"

Terrell bumped him back. "Don't worry. I got more where that came from."

The ref jumped between them and pushed them apart. "You boys save it for the court. I'd hate to have you out of the game."

Terrell threw his hands up. "No problem here."

"Lay off my guy," Smithey barked to Terrell. To the ref, he said, "They're killing him inside."

Terrell smiled. "He shouldn't come into the paint without his bodyguards protecting him."

Smithey's eyes flashed recognition, and Terrell added, "The odds are even now. I'd tell your boy to stay out of our paint unless he wants to end up with his pretty face swollen too."

Patrick didn't try to drive again, even when the lane appeared wide open. Instead, he began drilling shots from the outside.

By the end of the third quarter, the score was 63-59, Greensboro Day.

Coach Barrows told the guys to run the press after their first basket. "I want to trap them at half court and get that ball. But no fouls. If they break the press, I want to see everyone sprinting back. They better not get an easy two." Then he drew up a play to begin the final quarter.

On the inbounds pass, Tommy used a pick set by Nick to get free, and Jalen tossed him the ball. Nick broke for the basket as Terrell set him a pick, and Tommy launched a pass. Nick caught it, dribbled twice and tossed it up for a Miles Flaherty alley-oop dunk.

The crowd went crazy as the team set up in their 1-3-1 press. The pass came in to Patrick; Tommy and Miles trapped him in the corner. Patrick panicked and threw a quick pass that Nick easily intercepted, then bounce-passed to a breaking Tommy. Tommy rose against Greensboro Day's big man, Brenden Callaway, faked a lay-up, brought the ball down low and held it until he reached the other side of the basket. A split second before he landed, Tommy heaved the ball up and stuck a spin on it. It touched the top of the backboard once and dropped through the rim.

The crowd erupted in cheers.

Tie ball game.

Tommy landed, wincing. His ribs were bothering him badly now, the pain pill definitely having worn off.

Greensboro Day pounded the ball inside the next two possessions, rebuilding a four point lead. Nick broke free for a three that clanked off the back of the rim, but Jalen was there for a quick put-back.

On the other side of the court, DeSean Kiebler set a pick that held back Terrell. Smithey drained a trey. This time Nick answered to keep the margin at two points. Greensboro Day tried to get the ball to Callaway again, but Jalen was ready, playing perfect deny-defense. He tipped the ball to Miles, who saw Tommy break down-court, and delivered a pass that explained why he was also the school's starting quarterback.

Tommy caught the pass with his right hand over his head, took two steps, and laid the ball in with ease. His left hand never even touched the ball.

Tie game again.

Great defense on both sides kept the teams from scoring for a full minute until Terrell Baker stepped for a surprise three-pointer, his first of the season. The coach shrugged and laughed as they ran back on defense. Ryan Folsom immediately answered with a three that the closest ref overruled, indicating Folsom's foot was on the line.

Greensboro Day's coach yelled and screamed, coming out onto the court. The ref that made the call, an overweight balding guy who looked more at home in a recliner with a beer and remote than he did on the court, motioned the coach to back off and return to the bench.

But the coach persisted, getting in the ref's pinched face and yelling until finally, the ref turned to the scorekeeper and signaled a technical foul, teeing him up without a morsel of emotion.

Coach Barrows put Tommy on the line, and Tommy glanced at the scoreboard. Two point lead, fifty-eight seconds, and a chance to go up by four with the ball back.

They couldn't lose.

The ref tossed the ball to Tommy and blew the whistle. The gym grew quiet except for the section behind the Greensboro Day bench. Parents and friends of players screamed while Tommy sucked in a breath and took a dribble.

His breath caught. The pain pill had run its course. Tommy felt like his chest was crushed in a vise. He took another breath and knew he should tell the coach to let someone else shoot the free throws.

But this was his game. His game now, to win or lose.

Chapter 22

Tommy Chandler looked up into the stands as time slowed. He saw his mom, Angel Keller, Laura Novak. They were all cheering him on. Even his little brother was there making a fool of himself with a painted face and foam #1-hand.

The only person missing was his dad.

He sucked in another breath and tried to block the pain crackling throughout his body. It was like the pain pill had never existed, like he'd just gotten kicked in the ribs a few minutes ago. He exhaled slowly and looked up at the rim.

It was his game now. It was up to him.

He took another dribble, bent at the knees, brought the ball over his head, and in the same fluid motion, released it toward the basket. The ball was dead-on straight with perfect rotation. It clanged against the front of the rim, bounced once, and hit the floor.

Greensboro Day's bench and fans erupted in cheers and applause. Tommy lowered his head and backed away from the line. He shook his hands and stretched to his feet.

The pain. No, he told himself, block it out. It's crunch time. Now or never. This is the situation you dreamed of every night. The big game on the line, the ball in your hand. Suck it up!

Tommy stepped back up to the line, and the ref bounced him the ball. Dribble, breathe, no pain. Dribble, breathe, no pain.

The second shot was long—Tommy had overcompensated—and it bounced twice on the back of the rim before veering off to the side.

Tommy Chandler, a ninety-three percent free throw shooter, had just missed two consecutive free throws that could have clinched the biggest game of the year.

Coach Barrows called a time out.

The first thing he said was, "Don't worry about it. We got the ball and a two point lead." To everyone now, he said, "We hold it until you get an open shot. Run that time down, then play the best defense of your lives. No fouls ... no fouls."

The horn sounded and the teams took the court.

Jalen threw the ball to Tommy, and as he brought the ball down, Patrick shadowed him, talking to him the whole way. "You didn't think you were actually gonna win, did you, Tommy? ... Hey, Tommy, there's no way you walk away from here tonight anything but a loser, because that's what you are, a loser ... You'll always be second-best anytime I'm around, Tommy. Always."

The entire time, Patrick was reaching for the ball, darting his hands out for it. Tommy dribbled, crossing over, between his legs, keeping the ball protected at all times. He saw the trap coming before it happened, saw Ryan Folsom twitching to head his way as soon as he stepped across the half-court line.

But Tommy's time was up. His internal clock told him the ten seconds he had to get the ball over half court was almost gone. As he stepped over the line, he sped up and went sideways, drawing Folsom toward him even more.

Tommy faked a pass down low to get Patrick in the air. It left Nick open for the pass that Tommy wanted to throw all along. Nick caught it and dribbled until Smithey pulled off Terrell to come trap him with Folsom, who was scrambling back. Nick bounce-passed to Terrell.

Terrell immediately got rid of the ball, knowing like everyone else he shouldn't have the ball in his hands as one of the worst free throw shooters on the team. He threw a quick pass to Tommy just as Tommy cut for the basket.

Tommy feinted left to throw Kiebler off, then faked a pass to Jalen to rock Callaway back on his heels. Then it was there like a spotlight had been turned on: a wide-open lane. With Patrick close on his heels, Tommy drove and launched into the air. But Callaway had recovered and fought around the screen Jalen had set once he saw what Tommy was doing.

Tommy switched the ball to his left hand and laid it up, but Callaway tipped it at the last second. The ball deflected off the backboard and into Kiebler's hands.

Kiebler two-handed an outlet pass to Folsom at the right hash, who tossed it down court to a speeding Patrick Hart. Patrick caught the ball one-handed, took three dribbles, and rose into the air for an old-fashioned finger roll.

Nick caught him on the dribble and went for the ball, but Patrick had too much of a lead. Nick raked Patrick's chest, and the whistle blew. The ball tapped the backboard and dropped through the hoop.

Patrick pumped his fist and yelled with the Greensboro Day fans. His team ran down the court and congratulated him. On his way to the free throw line, Patrick got in Tommy's face. "That's how you make a lay-up, loser."

Despite the noise that rocked the gym, Patrick swished his free throw to give Greensboro Day a one-point lead, 74-73. Patrick bowed to the spectators on both sides of the gym, drawing derisive jeers and boos.

Coach Barrows called his last timeout. He drew up a play and said to take the first open shot. "Don't worry about the time. Get the open shot, then play defense."

Thirty-two seconds on the clock.

Southeast ran the play to perfection. Tommy skirted a pick set by Terrell at the top of the key and passed to Nick, who'd come out of the paint and around behind a Jalen Carter screen. Nick drilled the shot with sixteen seconds to go.

65-64, Southeast.

Greensboro Day called a timeout.

Coach Barrows congratulated his team then got serious. "How many times have I said what wins games?"

Nick answered, "Defense."

"Right. Defense. And right now, defense is the only thing that can win this game. You've done everything right up until this point. You've played the best game of your lives, but if you don't stop them now, stop them this one time, it's all for nothing."

Coach grabbed Nick's arm. "No stupid fouls. Got it?" He looked at everyone. "Got it? If they're gonna be shooting the ball, it's not gonna be from the line with nobody in their face. Play them close and stay in their grill. I wanna know what each of them ate at pre-game. Jalen, deny Callaway like your life depends on it. Be prepared for some kind of alley-oop pass from Patrick. That's the kind of thing they'd do."

The buzzer sounded, and the refs blew their whistles.

"Defense. Get your hands up." Coach placed his hands in front of himself like a mime. "And no fouls."

The team took their places on the court.

Patrick brought the ball down, Tommy closely shadowing him,

sidestepping like a crab, arms out in ready position. Patrick talked the whole way like time wasn't ticking down.

"You guys actually think you're gonna win. How pathetic. And you know what's worse? I'm gonna make the winning shot right over you. I'm gonna fake left, then go right. You remember that move?"

Tommy tried to block Patrick out, focus on his mid-section. He'd learned to never follow the ball; follow the mid-section because it didn't matter where the ball went, if middle didn't move, neither did the guy.

"You ready to lose? You ain't got no game. Remember, I'm gonna fake left, then go right. You ready?"

Then Patrick did it; he faked left and drove right with a quickness Tommy was ready for. But as Tommy slid to his left to stay with Patrick, his ribs groaned in defiance. He tried to ignore it, but his body couldn't. The bruises were on the very muscles he needed to twist.

Patrick gained a half-step on Tommy which was all he needed. That half-step left Tommy reeling and unable to recover in time to defend the ten-foot jump shot Patrick took.

The ball swished through the basket as the horn sounded.

Greensboro Day won 76-75.

Tommy stared at the basket, oblivious to the cheering and celebrating exploding around him. Patrick had done it again. Against Tommy again.

Southeast lost. Greensboro Day won. Patrick won. Again.

He felt his team patting him on the back, consoling him, telling him they'd get them next time. Don't worry about it.

It was only Southeast's second loss of the year, but it was the hardest loss of the season. The win was within their grasps, but it was not to be.

When they shook hands after the game, Patrick shot Tommy a half-smile-half-sneer, and Tommy felt the full pressure of defeat.

He had wanted this game so badly, not for his team, but for himself.

To prove he had what it takes. To prove he could play at the next level. To prove he could beat Patrick.

The locker room was quiet. Tommy yanked his jersey off, and for the first time, the guys saw the tape around his mid-section. Tommy tore the tape off as far as he could but had to get Nick to help him. When first bits of black and blue became visible, the guys stared, speechless.

Tommy held his breath as Nick ripped off the last of the tape, exhaling as the pain spread like lightning. He collapsed on the bench, clenching his fists until the pain subsided.

"Damn, Tommy." It was Jalen Carter, standing over him. "I didn't know."

The blues and purples and blacks that mottled Tommy's chest and sides were bright and pronounced against his pale skin. They were deep and screamed in anguish.

Tommy looked at Charlie Madison. "I should have told Coach to put you in. I had no business thinking I could play like this."

Charlie shook his head, stealing glances at Tommy's swollen chest. "Even at my best, I couldn't have played as good as you did tonight." Charlie motioned at Tommy. "And you were ..."

Tommy felt the pity being thrust at him, but it didn't console him. Didn't make him feel any better. The bottom line was that they'd lost. Tommy'd had several chances to win the game, and he didn't. That was what mattered.

Not moral victories. There was no such thing as a moral victory in his mind.

Tommy shrugged on his sweats and left, skipping his shower. He wanted no more pity. No more sympathy. No more basketball.

Not tonight.

Not for a while.

Chapter 23

Summer was in full blast with the sixth straight ninety-plus degree day in a row, and the store was selling ice cream as fast as Tommy could keep it stocked. The dairy truck usually came once a week, but Tommy called for an extra trip during the heat wave.

July Fourth cleaned them out, and the following heat wave did the same. Tommy was waiting on the truck to arrive when Laura Novak walked through the door, the brass bell on the door announcing her presence.

They had not spoken since the party except for small stuff in school. *You ready for the test? You coming in on Senior Skip Day? You playing hooky during the GGO?* Inconsequential conversations.

But those times, there'd been other people around. Now, they were alone.

"Hey, Tommy," Laura said as the door shut behind her. "You're not closed yet, are you?"

Tommy looked up from the inventory books, his normal customer-smile replaced with hesitation, his skin turning instantly clammy.

"Hey, Laura," he said, his voice faltering almost as if he'd asked a question. "No, not yet. How's it going?"

"Good. You?"

"Alright."

She paused at the counter, half-smiling, her eyes communicating an unsaid thought. She looked down. "Got anything new?"

Tommy thumbed at the green ledger. "Got some new ice creams. Got a new honey wheat bread, too."

"Oh, cool." She hesitated again. "So, you catch *When Harry Met Sally* yet?"

"No," Tommy answered. "I did finally see *Dead Poets Society*, though."

Laura broke into a huge smile. "Wasn't it great!"

"Oh yeah, I liked everything about it except what happened to the roommate."

"Neil? Yeah, it's sad he killed himself. But I think he had to for the movie to work."

"Well, he shouldn't have. He should have fought back harder. He gave up."

Laura grinned. "We can't all be Tommy Chandler."

Tommy looked up. "What do you mean?"

"Nothing. I just heard you're going to college even though your dad said no."

"Oh, yeah, that," he said. "UNCG. Thought I'd live at home the first year or two, maybe get an apartment in town later, one near the school. I don't know. Where are you going?"

"I got a scholarship to Hollins."

"In Roanoke?"

"Yeah."

Tommy nodded. "Cool." He thumbed at the ledger pages.

Mr. Varner came in stinking of sweat and cigarettes. He made eye contact, then bee-lined for the beer cooler.

"You still have cat food?" Laura asked.

"Yeah. In the back, on the right." Tommy pointed.

Laura smiled and drifted off as Mr. Varner snatched a six-pack of Bud out of the cooler and plopped it on the counter. Tommy rang him up and charged him for the twenty dollars of gas he'd pumped.

Mr. Varner left, and Laura returned with a bag of tuna-flavored Cat Chow. She set it down and looked around. "What's that smell?"

"That was Mr. Varner. He did it before he left, I swear."

Laura laughed. "No. It's something sweet."

"Oh." Tommy's ears reddened. He reached under the counter and pulled out an open Tupperware container. "It's my mom's cranberry lemon muffins."

Laura leaned forward and sniffed. "Oh wow, those smell wonderful!"

"You want one?" Tommy held the container out.

"Oh, no. I couldn't." She held a hand up in front of her.

"No, really. If you don't take a muffin, I'll be forced to eat one in front of you."

Laura grinned. "If you're gonna twist my arm."

Tommy returned the grin as Laura grabbed the closest muffin. Tommy snatched one and returned the container to the shelf below the counter, pulling out some napkins in the same motion. He came out from behind the counter and flipped the OPEN sign around on the door so it said CLOSED. He turned off some of the outside lights and went to the drink cooler.

"Whatcha want?" he asked, pulling out a Mountain Dew for himself.

"Oh, I couldn't."

"My treat. I insist."

"Oh, okay then, uh ... Diet Coke?"

Tommy grabbed her drink and let the cooler door close. He set the Diet Coke on the counter and leaned back against the register as he unscrewed his Mountain Dew.

"Mmm. This is really good!" Laura said after taking her first bite of the muffin.

"Yeah. Mom's always experimenting. I'm surprised I'm not three hundred pounds."

Laura smiled and twisted open her Diet Coke.

After a moment of nibbling and sipping, Laura said, "The team had a good season."

"Yeah, we did alright."

"You played great."

"Yeah, I guess," Tommy snorted. "Except for one game. The one that mattered."

"You mean the Greensboro Day game?"

"Yeah." Tommy crossed his legs the other way, looking at his feet.

Mr. Caldwell came through the front door, the bell dinging in frustration. "You open or closed?" he said, looking around. "The CLOSED sign's up, but I saw you in here. I just need a quart of oil."

Tommy set his muffin down and motioned with his head. "Come on and get it."

Tommy waited on Mr. Caldwell to pick out a quart of 10W-40 and rang him up. Tommy followed him to the door, told him to have a good night, and locked it behind him. He grabbed his muffin and drink, then snatched the Tupperware of muffins. "Come on. I want to show you something"

"I ..." Laura began, but Tommy was already walking away. She wrapped the muffin in her napkin and followed him. She thought he was going to the back office, but he stepped out the back door and began climbing some metal stairs attached to the wall of the store.

When Laura got to the top, she paused, mouth open. There were two

Adirondack chairs with fluffy cushions, a corrugated metal side table and flower pots everywhere, pots of all sizes and shapes filled with plants. She stepped onto the roof, and Tommy motioned for her to sit down.

She did, still looking around. "I had no idea this was up here."

"Yeah. I don't think Mom and Dad do either."

Laura looked at Tommy sideways. "Your dad doesn't know there's an oasis on the roof of his store?"

"Oasis?" Tommy laughed. "I like that. Here I've been calling it 'The Roof Top,' and all along, it's been 'The Oasis.' No wonder you got a scholarship."

Laura leaned back and propped her feet up. "Comfortable."

"Can you believe somebody set those beside our dumpster to throw away? The legs were broken; all they needed were reinforcing."

Laura sipped her Diet Coke and asked, "Where'd all the plants come from?"

"Cuttings from stuff around the house. Seeds, bulbs, you know."

"Cuttings and seeds? You grew all those from cuttings and seeds? There's gotta be like thirty or forty pots up here." Laura looked all around the roof.

"Yeah. It's not that hard. Just takes time."

"Where'd you get the pots?"

"Most of them are cracked or chipped. You'd be surprised what people call trash." Tommy reclined and shifted to get comfortable. "If you lean back, no matter where you look, you can't see this ugly roof."

Laura scrunched her face, then leaned back and looked around. "You're right!"

The only view, other than the plants and purpling sky, was the wheat field and woods behind the store. A breeze wafted through the air, rustling the roof plants and rippling through the field. Most of the roof plants were green, but there were smatterings of color throughout: variegated hostas, creeping phlox, multi-colored zinnias, lavender, and lots of plants Tommy couldn't remember the names to right off hand.

"This is pretty amazing, Tommy," Laura said.

"Yeah, it is. It's where I like to come and think." He sipped his drink. "I make all my important decisions up here. You know, where to go to school, what to major in, when to get a haircut."

Laura giggled and nibbled on her muffin. She sighed. "This is so perfect up here. I'd stay up here all day."

"And now it has a proper name."

Laura turned to Tommy, and he said, "The Oasis." She laughed.

They sipped their drinks and snacked on cranberry lemon muffins. The breeze stirred the plants, and the sun set to the west, lighting up the cloudy sky in shades of reds and purples. The temperature was leveling off as the sun raced to the horizon.

"Tommy," Laura began. "I never really got a chance to thank you for what you did at the party."

"The party?"

"The one with Patrick ... where you ... you know."

"Clocked him?"

Laura chuckled. "That's one way to put it."

Tommy waved his muffin at her. "No problem. Believe me, it was my pleasure. I'd been wanting to do that for a long time."

"He's such an ass."

"A big ass."

"So arrogant. So pompous. So full of himself like he's the only guy in the world." Laura sat up. "He thinks money will buy him everything. Tried to buy me with money and gifts. Wanted to show me off like a hood ornament." She clenched her fists. "God, he's so vain and selfish. So greedy. So arrogant. Did I already say arrogant? I think I did."

Laura, who up to that moment had been calm and composed, spilled into a rant that left her flustered and excited. Tommy leaned toward her, a concerned look on his face. He said, "Quit holding back. Tell me how you really feel."

Laura did a double-take and melted into a grin. Tommy laughed, and she shook her head. "I'm sorry," she said.

"Hey," Tommy replied. "I totally agree. You're not saying anything that people don't already know. You know he got a basketball scholarship to Duke?"

"Figures." She grinned, then growled in a high-pitched whine. "He just seems to always get everything he wants. It's infuriating."

Tommy sipped his Mountain Dew. "Not true."

"What do you mean?"

Tommy turned to look into Laura's eyes. "He didn't get you."

Laura smirked. "Yeah. There's that."

The breeze was warm, and the night approached quicker now. The sky bled its color into darkness. Stars appeared and vanished behind clouds.

"Did Patrick ..." Laura said. "I mean, I heard a rumor that after that party ..." She winced, unsure of how to ask the question.

Tommy nodded and took a bite of muffin. "Yeah. Patrick did it. With two of his teammates."

Laura frowned and brought her knees to her chest, still looking at him. She wrapped her arms around her legs. "He did it because of what happened at the party."

Tommy stared at the field. "Yeah."

"I ... I ... never thought ... I'm so sorry." Laura averted her eyes.

"Everybody was talking about it."

Tommy shrugged. "It happened. I still think it was worth it just to punch him one good time."

"Two times." Laura held up two fingers and grinned. "You punched him twice."

Tommy laughed, remembering. "Yeah, twice."

How could Tommy tell Laura that he'd take a million such beatings for her? He'd defend her and rush to her aid without a second thought. There was no need for her to be sorry. He was happy to save her. It was what he lived for. He loved her and always would.

Instead, he said, "Don't worry about it."

"But you lost the big game because of it. I heard one of the guys talking about what you looked like in the locker room afterward. He said your chest was like a huge eggplant."

Tommy laughed. "That's about right."

"You must have been in such pain."

Tommy shrugged. "It's part of the game. You play through the pain."

Laura paused. "Well, I just wanted to say I'm sorry. I didn't know how to ... I mean ..."

"Really, Laura. Don't worry about it. I've already forgotten about it. It's no big deal. Water under the bridge and all that."

Laura reached over and placed her hand on Tommy's bare arm. They looked into each other's eyes. "Thank you, again," Laura said.

Tommy shrugged. "Yeah, no problem."

Laura's hand slid away as Tommy sipped his drink. The trail of her fingertips burned into his skin, and he wanted to reach out to her, wanted to take her hand in his, to confess his love for her.

But that wasn't their relationship. This small bubble of time in "The Oasis" wasn't real life. It was an instance where the world slowed to a halt, and an indelible memory formed from the haphazard luck of coincidence. Tommy knew that this night, this very moment, would forever stain the fabric of his mind, because Laura Novak was the essence of perfection, and like perfection, she was also unattainable.

There was a certain sweetness in knowing that such a woman existed. But there was also heartache in knowing she could never be his.

Chapter 24

Financial aid was the ticket. It was the only way Tommy could attend UNC Greensboro. He looked after the store part-time and went to college full-time. Even with living at home, the tuition ran almost a grand, and once you added the price of books and other assorted unseen costs, each semester cost fifteen hundred minimum.

And Tommy wasn't even counting the insurance and gas for his aging car. Those didn't figure into school costs. He couldn't have done it without student loans.

Gene Chandler held firm on his promise of not paying for college. Why should his boy get a degree to run the store? It was a preposterous idea, and he'd have nothing of it. A business degree—Tommy had declared his major within two weeks—to run a simple general store?

There was no discussion about school at the few meals Tommy ate at home. Not even his mother would broach the subject until his dad was in the living room watching TV.

Nick Muller had gone to Carolina as he'd always dreamed. So had Angel Keller. Laura, of course, attended Hollins.

Jalen Carter was recruited by App State and went on a full basketball scholarship. Miles Flaherty did the same at Winthrop. Tommy had not even received a nibble from a single Division I college. He refused to go to a college away from home because his student loans would be overwhelming, so playing for either of the two Division III schools that contacted him was out of the question. They were private colleges anyway, and the tuition would have held him hostage for the next twenty years.

UNCG had a nationally recognized business school, and he could save money by living at home. It was a no-brainer.

UNCG was a Division II college with an enrollment just shy of twelve thousand, and the school had a two-to-one female-to-male ratio. Not a small college, but not a large one—UNC Chapel Hill was twice that size—it was a fit that Tommy liked.

Then one day he went to the gym to play some ball during the recreational hours it was open. A flyer caught his eye.

Walk-on Tryouts. For the men's basketball team.

With his course load and duties at the store, there was no way he had time to play college basketball. Not with two-a-day practices and games and weight training. No way.

But it wasn't like he'd make the team anyway.

What was the harm in trying?

He showed up early for tryouts and began stretching. Since high school, he'd grown another few inches and topped out now at 6'3." He felt tall and lanky as he walked the campus, but in the gym now, he felt at home. Normal size.

Most of the guys showing up were his size or a little taller. Some a little shorter. Those would be his competition; other guards. What was he thinking? There was probably room for one or two walk-ons on a college basketball team. Everyone else was recruited. The big guys had the best chance. Not him.

Besides, he knew most of these guys from playing against them in high school or during rec time in the gym. They were good.

Tommy was on floor stretching out his hamstrings when he was shaken from his thoughts.

"Thanks for coming out."

Tommy looked up to see a man about his size and probably in his late twenties wearing a blue and gold warm-up suit. The UNCG logo was embroidered over the left breast.

"Yeah," Tommy stood and shook the man's outstretched hand.

"Name's Coach Fulton. I'm an assistant coach. I do recruitment and strength training."

"Tommy Chandler."

"Tommy Chandler?" Coach Fulton squinted. "You played locally ... Southern?"

"Southeast."

"Yeah, Southeast. I thought you looked familiar."

Tommy's brain clicked. "You've seen me play?"

"A couple times. Tough game against Greensboro Day last year."

Tommy shuffled his feet. "Yeah. Let that one get away."

"You played a helluva game if I remember correctly. Showed some impressive stuff against a kid who went to Duke."

"Didn't feel too impressive."

Coach Fulton leveled a gaze at him. "You've grown since then."

"A little bit."

Coach Fulton nodded. "Well, I didn't want to interrupt your stretching. I'll let you get back to it. I just wanted to introduce myself. Good luck today."

"Thanks."

Tommy watched as Coach Fulton strode over to another coach wearing the same sweats. They talked for a minute; the other coach kept looking over Coach Fulton's shoulder at Tommy.

Tommy returned to stretching and took a few laps around the court before one of the coaches blew his whistle and called everyone over. Dribbling and shooting stopped as hopeful players gathered in a U around the coach. It was eerily quiet in the huge gym until he spoke.

"I'm Coach Denton, but you can call me Coach D. Tryouts will be held for two days." He looked around, making eye contact with all the boys. "After today, I'll post a list outside the gym of all players I want to return tomorrow. If you're not on the list, I want to thank you ahead of time for coming out and giving me your best."

He cleared his throat and paused. His voice was raspy from hours of yelling during practices. It was a trait of coaches everywhere.

"To my right are two other coaches that will be helping me out today. They'll be working with each of you personally throughout practices, running drills, and assessing your skills and abilities."

He smiled. "It's not necessary to make every shot or to be perfect." Everyone chuckled. "But it is important to do your best. Give a hundred and ten percent at all times." Coach D. nodded to his coaches.

The tall coach stepped forward. "I'm Coach Slater, and I'll need all the big guys down at this end of the court." He pointed and almost half the group shuffled away. Tommy counted: twelve guys were trying out for guard positions.

The first coach stepped forward. "I'm Coach Fulton, and for my knowledge only, how many of you consider yourself a point guard?" He raised his hand, and so did Tommy and five others. "And the rest of you consider yourself shooting guards?" Four of them nodded.

Coach Fulton looked at the other two. "Three-men?" They nodded.

For almost four hours, Coach Fulton had the guards run drills. Dribbling, passing, shooting, diving for the ball, defense.

Tommy was given the ball, "trapped" in the corner by two defenders, and told to get the ball to his "teammate" under the goal. The first time he was able to dribble around them. The next time he split the defenders in a textbook move before passing the ball. The third time, he immediately jumped and passed the ball over the defenders' heads.

Tommy was one of the tallest players on the guard side of the gym. It was easy for him to play over his defenders.

When he was stuck on defense, he got his hand on the ball twice, once knocking it out of bounds and once recovering the tap in his hands.

They ran three-on-three fast-break drills, sometimes with Tommy leading the way, other times with him on the wing.

They did wind sprints and suicide drills, and followed them up immediately with shooting and defensive drills. The coaches tested for skills and endurance. They tested for defensive smarts and ball smarts. And they tested for heart.

Coach D. flitted between the big guys and guards, issuing drills he wanted to see, watching with interest. He carried a clipboard and made notes, occasionally asking for names from drill participants.

By the time the four hours were up, coaches and players alike were breathing hard and grabbing their shorts. Tommy was dripping with sweat.

Tommy barely slept that night. He thought he'd done well, but so had a lot of other guys. The coaches thanked everyone again and said they'd have a list up in the morning of those they wanted to see tomorrow.

Before his eight o'clock class, Tommy took a detour by the gym. It had to be posted already, right?

Tommy's name was third on a list of six!

Only six guys out of more than twenty. And he was one of them.

At that afternoon's tryout, the coaches gathered the six standouts in a line and asked them all their qualifications. Like Tommy, all had started for their high school teams. One was playing for a Division III college in Virginia but transferred to be closer to home.

They ran more of the same drills as the day before, this time under the watchful eye of each coach. The coaches shouted directions and corrections, asking why somebody did this or somebody did that.

If Tommy thought the first day was tiring, the second day was ridiculous. Practice only lasted two hours, but it was more intense with little downtime.

When Coach D. dismissed them, he told them he'd have a list up by the next morning. If there were no names, that would be listed also. If anyone made the team, they were to report for practice at four sharp.

Tommy raced through dinner that night, wolfing down his mom's lasagna and chocolate chip cheesecake without savoring either. His mind was still on the court. He shrugged off the usual conversation and went straight to his homework.

But the strategy didn't work. All he could think about was the list outside the gym. It occurred to him that the coaches might post the paper before they left that night. And then he could think of nothing else.

"I left something at school," Tommy said on his way out the door.

"It's almost ten," his mom replied.

"I gotta get it," he said, shrugging on his jacket.

Tommy parked as close to the gym as he could, flipping on his blinkers. He wasn't in a real parking space, and he hoped the campus police didn't give him a ticket for the thirty seconds he'd be there. He ran up the walk to the front door of the gym and scanned the bulletin board. Nothing.

He stalked back to his car.

Halfway there he heard his name. "Chandler?" Tommy turned.

It was Coach Fulton. He'd just popped outside the door. He had a piece of paper in his hand.

"Yeah," Tommy said.

"What are you doing here at this time of night?"

"I was just ... I thought maybe you might post the sheet tonight."

"We said we'd post it in the morning."

"I know." Tommy glanced at his shoes. "I couldn't think about anything else."

"I see." Coach Fulton crossed his arms, the paper in his right hand dangling like a flag at half-mast. "How do you think you did?"

The question caught Tommy by surprise. "Pretty good, I guess. I was tired enough." Coach Fulton laughed.

"You think you should make the team?" the coach asked.

"I don't know. But it doesn't matter what I think, huh?"

There was a moment of silence.

"Well, come on over here and look at the sheet so you can sleep tonight."

Tommy jogged up the walk and took the paper from him. He squinted in the halogen lights protruding from the gym. There was only one name.

In twelve-point Helvetica, it read, "Thomas Chandler."

Tommy whooped and pumped his fist. Coach Fulton smiled and held his hand out. Tommy shook it with force.

Coach Fulton laughed. "Okay, okay," he said. "Now just so you know, we expect a lot, even from a walk-on. Every practice, every drill, every game, you give everything you got. You get treated like everyone else on the team."

"Yes, sir, Coach. Yes, sir!"

Coach Fulton chuckled. "Okay, go home and get some rest."

Tommy turned, and the coach said, "Wait, one question." Tommy looked at him. "When we looked back to the tape of that game you had against Greensboro Day last year, we saw something. It was why we didn't try to recruit you." He paused as if trying to figure out how to ask his question. "You had quite a shiner that game and looked to be playing injured."

Tommy nodded, waiting.

"How'd you get that way?"

Tommy scrunched his face up. "I got in a fight."

"Yeah. That much we could tell. We're not looking for that here, you understand? That's the quickest way to get kicked off the team."

"Yes, sir. It didn't happen on the court. The fight, I mean."

Coach Fulton nodded. "Between you and me, what was it over?"

Tommy wanted to tell Coach the whole story, about Patrick and Laura, and how he'd been ganged up on, but he didn't want to sound like a whiner. Finally, he said, "A girl."

Coach Fulton smiled. "Isn't it always?" He paused. "You know what else we noticed when we watched the tape?" Tommy shook his head. "Even playing hurt like you were, your shoulder and face and ribs"—Tommy's eyes widened, and Coach paused—"Yeah, we could tell all that. We're pretty good at what we do. But you know what we noticed more than anything when we reviewed that game?"

Tommy shook his head again.

"The trust your team had in you."

Tommy nodded.

"That's what we're looking for, Tommy. Leaders. Anybody can dribble and shoot and play defense. You saw that these last two days. But a point guard has to be a leader, and at this level, a good leader makes a difference. A *great* leader, however, one with the respect and attention of his team, one who commands the best from his teammates ...

that's the leader who takes his team beyond their own expectations."

Tommy nodded, memorizing his words.

"That's what we see in you, Tommy. That's what we hope you have. Not just leadership, but that special leadership." Coach Fulton paused and smiled. "Now go on home and try to get some sleep."

Tommy called Nick in Chapel Hill as soon as he got home. They talked for an hour until Nick said he had a French exam first thing in the morning. He begged off the phone, and Tommy laid awake half the night before he finally fell asleep.

He didn't tell his dad the news for another week.

Chapter 25

Tommy's freshman year flew by. The first game was against the Campbell Camels, UNCG's most hated rival. Tommy was warming up with his team when he saw his old girlfriend, Britney, behind the UNCG bench. She didn't seem surprised to see him.

It wasn't until after the game that they got a chance to speak. She was waiting for him outside the locker room. Several of the guys gave low whistles as they passed the couple. They knew she was the coach's daughter.

After the first day of tryouts, Britney said, her dad had asked if Tommy was the same kid she dated in high school. Britney said he was, and he was never mentioned again.

She couldn't believe Tommy didn't know Coach D was her dad. She swore she'd told him while they were dating. Didn't he ever listen?

They hung out a few times after the Campbell game, not dating because Britney said she didn't want to go there again. They made out some, but each time Britney stopped it before it went too far.

Christmas came and went, and Spring Break approached. Tommy met up with Nick, and they spent most of the week in Myrtle Beach, despite objections from Tommy's dad. Gene expected him to work, but Helen overrode her husband, telling Tommy to go be a kid while he still could.

Tommy "hung out" with four different girls, including Britney, careful to keep each relationship at arm's length. The last thing he wanted was another distraction.

School, basketball, and the store were enough to keep him busy.

Despite the relationship with the coach's daughter, Tommy rarely saw Coach D. outside the gym. The man lived in the gym.

The relationship also didn't garner him any favoritism; Tommy only played in games that were blow-outs, and only in the last minute or two of those. But still, he learned a lot in the time he was on the court and off. College basketball was a different game, much faster and more physical.

Big guys were really big, and wide. It was like playing Greensboro Day every single game instead of once a year.

UNCG was in the middle of an unprecedented transition from Division III to Division I, the entire process was to take five years. They were in the Division III Dixie Conference until 1988, when they shifted to Division II. According to the plan submitted and approved by the NCAA, they would become a full-fledged Division I athletic program in 1991.

Bumper stickers floated around campus that sported the slogan: *Division I in 91*. Tommy even stuck one on his ailing Buick.

If Tommy continued with the team, if he was allowed to walk-on to the team next year and again in 1991, he would finally be playing basketball for a Division I program. He wondered what his dad would say then.

But the reality of the situation hit him. Division I meant recruits with talent that played at another level. Tommy probably wouldn't make the team; he couldn't hang with those guys. Tommy saw the proverbial writing on the wall.

During their current Division II years, UNCG was an independent school without a conference. So after the regular season, there was no conference tournament. Basketball was done.

The week following the final game, Tommy visited Coach D.'s office.

"Hey, Coach, you got a minute?" Tommy asked after he'd stuck his head in.

"Sure, Tommy," he said, lowering a stack of papers onto his desk and removing his reading glasses. "What's on your mind?"

Tommy sat in the fake-leather side chair in front of Coach D.'s desk. He took in a breath and tried to sit up straight. "Well, I just wanted to thank you for the chance to play this year. I learned a lot."

"You're welcome, Tommy. The team was better with you on it."

Tommy paused. "But I hardly played."

"When you played, you played well. And you gave Roddy a helluva time in practice. You made him work hard, which transferred over to the games. He became a better point guard because he had to face you in practice."

Tommy was confused.

Coach D. sighed and continued, "Sometimes a player's role on the team is behind the scenes. Roddy has a lot of talent, but he's never had to face a 6-3 point guard with your quickness and skills. He's got tons of experience, but playing against you day in and day out made him elevate his game, literally. He had to learn how to get around someone with a reach beyond his, and when he wanted a jumper, he had to pull one quick before you got a hand up."

"I see," said Tommy.

Coach D. leaned back and steepled his hands. Tommy thought of Coach Barrows and almost laughed; it must be a thing all coaches do, like yelling and losing their voices.

"Tommy," Coach began, "Let me ask you something. Did you learn anything from Roddy?"

Tommy scrunched his eyebrows together. "What do you mean?"

"Well, I matched you against him in practices for two reasons. He needed to play against someone your size, and you needed to play against someone with Roddy's experience and abilities. Did you notice how well Roddy could see the floor? Did you notice how, even against somebody your size, he was able to get a shot up?"

"Yeah," Tommy said, rubbing his shoes together. "No matter what I did, he beat me."

"He was always one step ahead because he has experience. It's why he started for us, his ability to out-think his opponent. Talent is only half the equation, Tommy. What you do with it is the other half."

Tommy nodded.

"So what is it you came to see me for? I feel like I took over there." Coach D. laughed.

Tommy smiled. "Well ... I've been doing some thinking. You know, about us going to Division I in two more years?" Coach nodded. "What do you think my chances are of playing then?"

Coach D. sniffed and straightened in his chair. "I'll be honest, Tommy, I don't know what two years from now is going to look like. D-1 recruits, even though they'll be freshmen, will be at a different level than the team we have now." He was shaking his head. "I don't know what the team will be like or"—looking Tommy in the eyes—"what kind of point guard we'll get. If we get one."

Coach D. cleared his throat. "What I can tell you for sure, is that I need you next year. Roddy didn't know this, but he was grooming you for the starting point guard position after he graduates in May. Next year, Tommy, this will be your team. Flores has nowhere the talent you do, and I've been keeping an eye on you, I think you're still growing. You're probably 6-4 now, or you will be by the time next season begins."

Tommy's mouth dropped open, and Coach D. pursed his lips.

He continued, "But I can't make any promises about the year after that. I can tell you we're looking at a few point guards, and we're going to offer at least one of them. It's the way this game works."

Tommy didn't know what to say. He had come to the coach's office to tell him he was quitting, he wouldn't be returning next year. But now, he was being told that as a sophomore walk-on, he was being given the keys to the team.

The Spartans would be *his* team to run.

Chapter 26

During the following summer, Tommy focused on two things: working at the store and working on his basketball game. He measured himself multiple times, and the coach was right. By the time school began in the Fall of 1990, he had grown another inch. He was now 6-4.

Tommy, as part of his basketball regimen, had spent a lot of time lifting weights to increase his strength. Where once his frame had been thin and wiry, he was now solid and strong. He'd added fifteen pounds of muscle without sacrificing his quickness, working with Coach Fulton every other week to refine his routine.

He'd left his freshman year at UNCG a boy and returned a young man. Every time he'd played ball with Nick during the summer, he'd beaten him. Soundly. Nick said it was as if he was playing somebody different.

Something had changed in Tommy. He'd grown in more ways than just height. He'd gained confidence he never knew he had. He stood tall when he walked, he looked people directly in the eyes when they approached. He wanted to experience the whole world, not just sneak through it with an idea of what it should be.

Tommy embraced the unexpected, looked forward to it, reveled in its challenge. The world was full of opportunity, and this was going to be his best year yet.

He felt it.

Early in his sophomore year, Tommy met a girl who captured his heart at first sight. He was jogging to the gym, meeting his team there for an unofficial practice, when he glanced over at the tennis courts. Something made him pause and watch.

Or rather, someone.

She was tall, lithe, with long blonde hair pulled into a ponytail. She glided across the tennis court as though it was covered in ice, the racket merely an extension of her arm rather than an instrument used to control the ball.

Tommy sat on the brick wall above the sunken courts and watched in awe. She used her entire body when she served, every muscle performing a function like a perfect synchronized machine. When she lunged for a shot, it was as graceful as ballet. And that was the attraction, Tommy realized. While her opponent was playing tennis, this goddess was performing a complicated dance but making it appear simple and smooth.

"Why don't you take a picture? It'll last longer."

Tommy blinked and recovered. "I would if I had a camera."

The girl had stopped playing and was toweling her face off, looking up at him. She wore a tennis skirt that revealed lean, muscular legs, and a blue and gold UNCG t-shirt spotted with sweat. She smiled at him and walked over, squirting a water bottle into her mouth.

"I know you, don't I?" she said.

Tommy grinned. "I thought that was the guy's line."

The girl smiled back. "But I'm not just dropping a line. I'm serious. Do we have a class together? Psych maybe?"

"I know that's right."

"Huh?"

Tommy shook his head. "What I mean is ... I'd definitely know if you were in one of my classes. I wouldn't be able to look at the professor."

She raised her eyebrows. "Now that's a line."

"I'm not just dropping a line. I'm being serious."

This made her laugh. "In that case, my name's Leigh Ann." She held her hand out and Tommy thought it odd to shake a girl's hand the first time he met her.

He turned her hand over and leaned forward to kiss it, but doing so caused him to lose his balance on the wall. Suddenly he was falling. Onto the girl.

She screeched and tried to catch him, but Tommy bowled her over, landing on his feet and clutching her body just before she hit the ground. He pulled Leigh Ann up and steadied her on her feet, but it was difficult. She was laughing hysterically.

He apologized and asked if she was okay. Leigh Ann chortled out a yes. Her laugh was hypnotizing, child-like in its enthusiasm, but womanly in its depth. Her laugh made him want to laugh too, so despite his embarrassment, he joined her.

They had just met, and already, they were laughing giddily, Tommy's hands grasped firmly around Leigh Ann's arms. To a stranger, they might appear to be old friends or comfortable lovers.

For Tommy, it emboldened him like never before. Leigh Ann's very presence made him heady.

"May I kiss you?" he said after the laughter subsided into grins. He stared deep into her blue eyes and willed her to feel the electricity flowing through his body, to experience the same light-headedness she gave him.

"Getting a little ahead of yourself aren't you?" she said, the right side of her mouth rising into a half-smile.

"No, not really. I feel like I've already lost too much time."

Leigh Ann raised her eyebrows, her expression playful. "You're a smooth one. I'm gonna have to watch out for you."

Tommy had no idea where all this stuff was coming from. It wasn't like him. Leigh Ann was having an effect on him he hadn't felt in a long time. Time stopped and sped up simultaneously.

"Tommy!" The yell came from the bridge to the gym. He knew the voice before he turned. It was Brian Cassidy, the starting power forward on the team. Tommy turned as Brian said, "You coming?"

"I'll be there in a minute!" Tommy yelled back.

Brian was with Lamar Johnston and DeJuan Flores. They were making faces at him, giving him thumbs up. He turned back to Leigh Ann.

"I'm hurt," she said. "You weren't just here to watch me."

He moved closer to her. "And yet you caught my attention."

Leigh Ann cocked an eyebrow, "C'est vrai."

Whistles erupted behind him, and Tommy shook his head. "Listen, I've got to go."

She smiled. "At least now I know my stalker's name. Tommy. And I also know where I've seen you before."

"Oh?"

"On the basketball court."

He nodded. "Well, on the bench, anyways." He hesitated, distracted by the catcalls from the guys. "Are you out here much?"

Leigh Ann nodded. "I'm on the tennis team."

"Can I ... can I call you?"

She squinted her face, finally saying, "No." Then, "But why don't you come by after your practice?" She motioned to the dorm above them, just across the one-way street. "Bailey. Tell the desk to call me.

Leigh Ann Pearson. Maybe if you're nice, I'll let you go that party on Kenilworth with me tonight."

Tommy felt as if he was filled with helium. "Okay," he said. "Count on it."

He turned to go, and she said, "Wait."

Tommy looked back at her. She said, "You're forgetting something."

Before he could respond, Leigh Ann stood on her tiptoes and kissed Tommy lightly on the lips. She pulled away with a wink. "That'll give 'em something to talk about." She laughed as she waved at the guys over his shoulder—now quiet with surprised expressions—and pushed Tommy toward them.

"Don't make me wait too long," she said, then grabbed her racket and bounced up the steps toward her dorm.

Chapter 27

Leigh Ann couldn't come to Thanksgiving that year, but she had already made plans to hang around Greensboro during Christmas break. Her family in Ohio was flying out to California to see her grandparents, and Leigh Ann wasn't going this year.

She was more than happy to spend the holidays with Tommy's family.

Every Christmas Eve, Tommy and his family gathered with his mom's side, the Vogles. There could be as many as thirty to forty crammed into his grandparent's house any given year, and this year was no exception.

The men in the family naturally gravitated toward Leigh Ann the way men do toward every leggy blonde. Leigh Ann was used to the attention and took it in stride. But she also had a personable genuineness that didn't automatically repel other women who might be jealous of her beauty and the attention it garnered.

She answered questions like a game show contestant:

"Why'd you come all the way down here from Ohio to go to school?"

"They gave me a tennis scholarship."

"Are you planning on going pro when you graduate?"

A laugh. "I'm not nearly that good, no matter what Tommy says."

"What are you majoring in?"

"Psychology, and then I plan on going to school for international law so I can travel."

"You're going to be a lawyer?" Eyes widening.

"A traveling lawyer. Don't forget that part. I'm going to see the whole world and get paid to do it."

Tommy's aunts were heard later talking about how cute they looked together. The adjectives for Leigh Ann spanned from *stunning* to *hot* to *so well-mannered.*

They had the usual spread of food as was common at Vogle Holidays: a cornucopia of meats and vegetables, casseroles and starches, biscuits and desserts. This year, Tommy's mom brought peppermint chocolate bars, a seven-flavor pound cake so moist it didn't need to stay covered, and what she called coffee cup torte, a coffee-hazelnut-flavored torte already portioned out in festive red and green paper coffee cups.

Leigh Ann insisted on bringing something, despite Tommy's assurances that there would be more than enough food. At Tommy's house, she transferred her store-bought brownies into a large container and pushed red and green M&M's into the brownie tops.

"At least they're festive," she said, shrugging.

Helen Chandler said it was very creative and resourceful, and the brownies would fit in beautifully.

Christmas Eve at the Vogle's was a not-to-be-missed event. Family members may occasionally take vacations over Thanksgiving, but never over Christmas. That was unheard of, like serving store-bought sweet tea or making instant mashed potatoes.

The "adult" TV in the living room was always set to the station that played Christmas music and aired a fireplace with a real crackling fire. Every once in a while, you'd see someone stoke the fire and add a log or two.

While the women readied the food, the men caught up on the year, sometimes declaring intentions for the next year.

The conversation lulled until Steve spoke up, "Me and Rhonda are thinking of going to Scandinavia this summer."

"Why the hell would you go there?" Gene asked.

"She's got family in Norway. They just came over on the boat two generations ago. Plus, have you seen pictures of the fjords? We don't have anything like that here."

"Well, you won't catch me going nowhere that don't speak English," Gene said. He took a sip of his coffee as if that ended the conversation.

The talk eventually steered itself toward sports and in particular, ACC basketball. Speculations were made on who would win the regular season this year. The consensus was between Carolina and Duke although Bill put in a vote for his alma mater, NC State. The comment brought a chuckle from everyone.

Tommy's grandfather Howard said. "I saw in the paper where Wake played UNCG the other day and guess whose name I saw?"

Gene Chandler sipped his tea and studied the logs burning in the TV fireplace.

"I saw that too," Steve said, smiling.

His grandfather continued. "Wake won by twelve, but our own Tommy Chandler scored eight points, dished out seven assists, and even stole the ball twice."

"Wake's pretty good this year."

"And I read where UNCG gave them a fight until the very end. It was a four-point game until they had to start fouling. Oh yeah, I almost forgot, Tommy had five rebounds, too."

A moment of silence passed, and Gene looked at Howard. "I don't care what you say, Howard. I still think Carolina will sweep the ACC this year."

Eventually, dinner was called, and a feast of Southern proportions was served. Everything from turkey and homemade biscuits to sweet potato pie. After the clean-up, it was time for gifts.

Every year there were gag gifts from Santa interspersed with the real gifts. Some were re-gifted each year, like the infamous reindeer poo. No one remembered the first year it had been introduced.

It was a big deal that Brant received the reindeer poo. It was more than just a simple gag gift; it was a rite of passage. Receiving it meant that you were now part of the club. You may not be old enough to vote or drink, but according to the men of the family, you were now a peer.

Brant beamed as he held up the reindeer poo for all to see. Laughs and quick quips were hurled his way as necks craned to see his face turn pink.

Then Brant opened his second Santa present. Inside was a Playboy, the cover model posed in a skimpy piece of lingerie, a sultry look emanating from her pouty face. Brant's eyes widened, and he glanced around.

"Whatcha got there, Brant?" Uncle Andrew asked, a grin already showing on his face.

Brant thumbed through the book, his embarrassment melting into mirth. He held the book up, cover closed, and displayed it for all to see. Heads turned all around the living room. Giggles and gasps were abundant.

"Y'all wanna see the centerfold?" he asked, and without waiting for the women to object, he thumbed through the book to a page he'd picked out.

It was just enough time for his mom's eyes to almost pop out of their sockets. "Brant! Don't you dare ..." She trailed off as Brant held the book open. Everyone erupted into laughter.

Uncle Andrew had taped the cover of a Playboy over an issue of Southern Living, September 1990. The centerfold Brant opened to was an ad for National Geographic. There, in full glory and taking up both pages, was a large photo of an even larger elephant. A naked elephant.

When the laughter broke for a moment, Brant added, "She's a little big for my tastes." More laughter.

"Hey, Mom!" Brant held the book open to a colorful photo of a triple-layer chocolate fudge cake. "They've even got stuff in here for you." Everyone laughed as Helen shooed her hand at him and shook her head.

It was rare for a boyfriend or girlfriend to receive a gag gift their first Christmas at the Vogles', but it wasn't unheard of. As Leigh Ann opened her gift from Santa, all attention was turned toward her.

She pulled out a 4-pack of C batteries and held them up. "And there's a note here," she said, smiling as she read it to herself. She looked up. "It says, 'Toy not included.'"

Laughter all around.

Then she sucked in her breath loudly, adding, "It's nice and all, but my toy actually takes D batteries."

Eyes widened. Men chuckled under their breaths and women remained silent, unsure how to respond to such a brash statement. Tommy's cousins laughed out loud, shaking their heads at the gall and forwardness of this new girlfriend of Tommy's. But most surprising was that Maw Maw Vogle laughed the hardest of everyone.

Leigh Ann reddened and turned to Tommy. In a lowered voice, she said, "Too much, huh?"

Tommy was grinning. "Possibly."

"I just figured with the Playboy thing ..."

"Yeah, doesn't matter. You're branded now."

"Branded?"

Tommy kissed her neck. "Now you're my dirty girlfriend."

Leigh Ann pushed him away, giggling.

Tommy laughed. "Just wait till next year. There's no telling what you'll get. Crotchless underwear, whips and chains ... you'll see ... you're fair game now. I can't protect you."

Leigh Ann raised her left brow. "I don't need your protection, Tommy Chandler. I can dish out as good as I get." She looked around. "Which uncle can take the best joke?"

Tommy didn't hesitate. "Uncle Andrew. He's the biggest prankster. Mom says it's because he's always been stuck in a house full of women. Two sisters and now three daughters. She says he never really grew up."

"Good," Leigh Ann stated, a crooked smile forming. "Next year he'll get my toy. There'll be a note inside that says I needed to get a bigger one. And I'll leave the batteries in ... type up a note that says 'Batteries Included.'"

Tommy rolled his eyes and laughed. "You'll be declaring war. You know that, right?"

"Hey, I've got three older brothers. I can handle it."

Tommy kissed her on the lips this time. "I've no doubt."

The next morning, Tommy's immediate family exchanged gifts. Tommy, Brant, and their mom had gone in on a large gift for their dad. A computer.

"What do I need a computer for?"

"For the store," was the answer.

"I don't need a computer at the store," was the immediate response.

"Dad," Tommy said. "It's the twentieth century. The business should be kept on a computer instead of a big green book with a bunch of lines.

You can spit reports out to tell you what's selling, what products have the best profit margins. All kinds of stuff to make running the business easier, like inventory management and your banking."

"I already know which products sell the best. And as far as when I need to order something, it's when I run out of it. Don't need a computer for that. Never will." He scowled.

"Gene." A single word from Helen said all she needed to say. It was the deadpan inflection that communicated the rest.

"What?" he replied. "I don't need none of that fancy stuff."

Tommy pleaded, "Dad, when it comes to tax time, all you have to do is print out your totals. You don't need to spend a week combing through ledgers, checking and re-checking your math."

Gene shook his head and pushed the box aside. "You start putting stuff in that contraption, and you lose your feel for the business."

"But how nice would it be to hit a single button and get a printout of everything that sold for the week? Then, without doing anything else, you know how much of what to order to replenish the shelves."

Gene was still shaking his head. This was a man who still didn't completely trust microwaves because he couldn't see the food cooking. ATM cards were also not to be trusted. When Gene Chandler needed money, he wrote a check for cash or went to the bank itself during business hours. Dealt directly with a teller.

No, sir. Tommy's dad didn't want anything to do with no fancy computer and no fancy schooling. He knew how to run his business already and that was that.

Merry Christmas.

Chapter 28

March Madness had begun. NCAA college basketball ruled the airwaves, and it seemed as if it was the only thing on TV. UNCG's final season as a Division II program was done and gone. They finished with a respectable 13-9 record, most of the wins coming against Division II or Division III opponents: Longwood, Guilford College, Wingate.

But at the store, Tommy wasn't a point guard. He was still just Tommy. He swept the floors, restocked the shelves, ran the cash register, cleaned up spills, and unloaded trucks. The work wasn't glamorous, but it was honest and necessary.

Tommy had the NCAA tourney games playing on the thirteen-inch color TV over the register, turned up loud enough he could hear the action as he dusted in the back of the store. His dad came out of the back to the register.

"You seen my marker?" he yelled, scrounging around the shelves.

"No," Tommy yelled back.

"I just had it."

Tommy came up front, holding a package. "Well, I've not seen it." He held the package out. "What's this?"

Gene looked over. "A shammy."

Tommy shook it. "You know we've got ten of them back there?"

"Yeah, so?"

"As long as I can remember, we've always had ten of them back there, taking up space. I go to dust, and they're all covered, always."

"What's your point?" Gene rifled through the shoebox under the counter where they stuck found items. Matchbooks, lighters, buttons, change, half-used pens. Tommy had no idea why his dad actually kept the box. No one ever asked for that stuff.

"My point is that I've never known one to sell. You got this product on your shelves that isn't selling. It's taking up space that could be used for something that sells. Why don't you cut the price in half, put it up front here, and get rid of it?"

"Cut the price in half?" Gene shook his head, flabbergasted. "I'd lose all my profit. You're wasting your damn money on that college education. They're teaching you all wrong."

"No. You're the one wasting your money. If you sold all ten of these for a ten percent loss, then put something comparably priced on the shelf with a normal forty percent mark-up, you'd only need to sell three to have made a profit. Those shammies have been back there for at least a dozen years."

"But when they sell, they'll make me money."

"You're looking at it all wrong, Dad." Tommy dropped the shammy on the counter. "You're thinking of a product that doesn't sell as simply one not making you money. A product that isn't selling is actually *losing* you money every day it doesn't sell."

Gene rolled his eyes and threw the shoebox back under the counter. "What the hell are you talking about?"

"Inventory turnover."

"Oh, for God's sake, Tommy."

"No, Dad, hear me out. For that ten dollars you have tied up in shammies, you also have shelf space tied up. Think of that space as rental property. Right now, you got a deadbeat tenant that hasn't paid a dime in ten years, but—"

"This is the dumbest thing I've ever heard."

"You could evict him, lose a bit of money now, and put a tenant in that pays you every month. The first month, you'll have made more money in that space than a whole ten years combined. And you'll make up for the money you lost the month you had to short sell the shammies on clearance."

Gene was shaking his head. "Do me a favor. Leave that college crap at college. Don't bring it in my store."

"Come on, Dad. Try it with one product. Just one. I got an even better idea. It's gonna be nice outside soon. Spring is on its way." Tommy held a finger up. "Stay here a minute."

Tommy disappeared into the back of the store and came back a minute later. He set five items on the counter: an orange mop bucket, a bottle of green Palmolive, a bottle of Armor-All, a container of Turtle Wax, and a shammy. He said, "Sell this as a Car Wash Special." He put the soap, Armor-All, Turtle Wax, and shammy in the mop bucket, hanging the shammy over the side, and said, "There, put a sign on it that says 'Car Wash Special, 10% off,' and it'll sell. You'll make money on every item instead of losing on one, and more than that, you'll move five items at once."

Gene rolled his eyes.

"Do it this one time. Leave it here on the counter or somewhere up front. If this bucket of stuff doesn't sell in a week, I'll buy it all myself at full price. How about that?"

Gene's lips curled slowly into a smile, then he squinted. "And what do you get out of it?"

"What do you mean?"

"If you win?"

Tommy hadn't thought of it that way. It was always a competition with his dad. It could never just be a simple change or suggestion. "Okay," Tommy said, "If I'm right, you finally take your computer out of the box and let me set it up."

"Aw, come on."

"What's the matter, Dad? Afraid you'll lose and accidentally make money?" Tommy couldn't hide the sarcasm in his voice.

Gene stuck his hand out, a hard expression clouding over his face. The one thing Gene Chandler couldn't take was being called a chicken. He was worse than Marty McFly.

Tommy shook his dad's hand, then grabbed an index card and pulled the marker out from where it was stuck over Gene's ear. Tommy drew a Starburst on the card and filled in the words, "Car Wash Special, 10% off!!" He taped it to the bucket and slid it to the edge of the register.

Gene grabbed the marker from Tommy's hand, mumbling something about being a smart-ass, and lumbered back to his office.

Three customers later, Tommy sold the bucket of items to Mrs. Atwater, a pretty older lady who laughed and said her husband, Fred, would have no excuse not to wash the car now. Tommy called his dad out front after telling Mrs. Atwater the special was Gene's idea.

Gene Chandler, a scowl hidden beneath a fake smile, stood there and nodded while Mrs. Atwater told him how the bucket was such a great idea, and maybe he should do some kind of Spring Cleaning Special, too. Gene nodded again and told her to have a nice day. "Tell Fred I said hello and not to let you work him so hard."

Tommy didn't gloat, didn't say a word, as Mrs. Atwater strode out the front door with her new bucket in tow. Instead, he went to the back of the store and returned with three more buckets of cleaning items to sell, slid two of them under the counter and reattached the sign to the bucket he left on the counter.

Then he looked at his dad and said, "I'll go make a place for that computer."

Chapter 29

Nick Muller dropped by the store later the same day. He'd come home from Chapel Hill that weekend. Carolina was playing at seven that night, and he and Tommy had plans to go to Buffalo's, gorge themselves on wings, and yell at the TV with everyone else.

They took Nick's Jeep, Nick saying how he missed the old girl. "I drive to school and that's it. Once I'm there, I walk everywhere. We used to be so close." He patted the dashboard.

"Well, my old girl's about to die," Tommy said. "I drive her too much."

"Shoot, a basketball star like you ... your old man should get you a new car."

"Heh. Basketball star, right. To him, it's not basketball unless it's ACC."

"Are you kidding?"

"Nope."

Nick shook his head. "I don't understand. You had a great year, and he won't even acknowledge you're playing at a level he never dreamed of."

"It's just the way he is." Tommy shrugged. "How do you know how good a year I had, anyway?" Tommy picked at his seat, part of the cushion coming off in his hand.

"Hey! Careful. She's delicate."

"You need seat covers."

"I haven't found any that match."

"Nick. It's a Jeep Wrangler. Even camo seat covers would match."

Nick turned onto Battleground Avenue.

"My mom saved all the write-ups in the paper," Nick said.

"What?"

"Write-ups of your games. She sent them to me."

Tommy turned to his friend. "You're kidding me."

"Nope. By my calculations, you averaged around 12.5 points per game, 7.3 assists, 3.6 steals, 6.2 rebounds."

Tommy laughed hard and looked back out at the road. "You have way too much time on your hands."

"My dad went to a few games."

"Yeah, I saw him there."

"He said you could play at a bigger school."

"Yeah, sure. You trying to blow my head up?"

"I'm just saying. You thought of trying to transfer? Based on the season you just had, you might could get in at an ACC school."

Tommy scrunched his face and glanced at Nick. "You're joking, right?"

"Actually, no."

Tommy humphed. "You know what? I wouldn't even if I could."

"Wouldn't what?"

"Transfer. Coach D. gave me my chance. I couldn't do that to him."

"But, man, to play at a Division I school. That's big."

"We'll be D-I next year."

"You know what I mean. An established program. And you majoring in business? After you graduate, you could walk in anywhere and get a job, having played at State or somewhere, and be a leg up over normal guys."

Tommy laughed. "Normal guys. That's good."

"You know what I mean."

Nick pulled into the parking lot. It was full so they parked in the back.

"Nah. I like UNCG. It's a small school with the perks of a big school. And there, I'm not just another number."

"I hear they have one helluva women's tennis team."

Tommy chuckled, and Nick followed with his own laugh.

"That they do," Tommy said. "That they do."

"I can't believe she's giving you the night off."

"Hey. She's cool. She's a jock and totally understands the concept of guy's time."

They hopped out and went inside.

Sucking down his first Coke, Nick said, "You know something I really like about UNCG? Every time I step on campus, there's this vibe. You know?"

Nick nodded. "I feel the same thing at Chapel Hill."

"Yeah, it's like I've come home."

"Geez." Nick took a sip. "We sound like a commercial."

"No, really. Imagine twenty years from now." The bartender set two more Cokes down in front of them as Tommy continued, "We'll be sipping beer instead of soda, reminiscing about the good ole days. These days right here. Hell, maybe even this moment right now."

Nick laughed. "So we'll be talking about this day, where we were talking about that day when we'd be talking about now?"

"Something like that."

"Dude." Nick put his hand out and lowered Tommy's drink hand.

"You're cut off. No more caffeine."

"I'm serious. You hear old people talk about the good ole days. These are our good ole days, Nick. How deep is that?"

Nick shook his head. "Too deep to be sober."

Chapter 30

The hostess sat Tommy and Leigh Ann at a booth on the far side of the restaurant. Tommy ordered the crab dip as Leigh Ann looked at him funny. The waitress left, and Leigh Ann said, "Alright. What are we celebrating? The school year almost being over?"

"What do you mean?" Tommy feigned innocence.

"We both have huge papers due in a few days but instead of working on them, we're at the Village Tavern. You had me dress up. And you just ordered an appetizer." Leigh Ann tilted her head. "We never get appetizers."

"The crab dip here is awesome."

"Tommy, don't play dumb with me. Spill."

"Spill?"

"Spill. Now." Leigh Ann sat back in the booth and crossed her arms.

"Spill? I'm still trying to figure out how I got mixed up with a gangster."

Leigh Ann tightened her lips and said, "Spill now, or I'll get Vinny to visit you late one night and introduce his best friend, first name of Louisville."

Tommy smiled. "See, that's what I love about you. Your subtlety."

"Tommy."

"Okay, okay." Tommy raised his hands.

The waitress interrupted them with their drinks. She told them the specials, and Tommy said they still needed a minute. She left and Leigh Ann said, "Well?"

"Should I get a steak after crab dip, or go with tuna because it's seafood also?"

"Tommy."

"What? This is a difficult decision. Maybe I should get the seafood pasta instead."

"If you don't tell me your big news in three seconds, you're gonna have to order something you can suck through a straw."

"Such hostility."

Leigh Ann's eyes flashed, then drew up halfway.

Tommy laughed. "Okay. Well, you know the coach called me in this morning?"

"No, but go ahead."

"I told you about it this morning."

"Whatever. Continue."

Tommy took a breath and once again took in Leigh Ann's beauty. He had talked her into wearing a dress for the night. "Pretend we're going to a formal," he told her. She wore a navy blue number that plunged her neckline just low enough to garner her a few lurid looks. When he'd picked her up, he made her turn repeatedly. Not only did he never see his tomboy girlfriend in a dress, he didn't even know she owned a pair of heels. The shoes showed off her tennis legs so well she'd received lavish attention from the moment they entered the restaurant.

Leigh Ann's hair was up, as it usually was, but this time in a chignon. He knew that's what it was because she told him. She didn't need makeup, but the little she wore accented her deep blue eyes and rosy cheeks.

"Tommy?"

"Sorry." He shook his head. "I was just soaking in your presence."

She tilted her head slightly and raised her eyebrows.

"So I went to the coach's office today, and he started out talking about this year. Things we did right and things we did wrong. Places we improved and places we didn't."

When Tommy had told his mom the news that afternoon, she hugged and kissed him until he had to literally push her away. He said he still hadn't told Leigh Ann. He wanted to take her somewhere nice. Helen suggested the Village Tavern and said he should dress up. She picked out one of his dad's ties—admonishing Tommy's thin ties—a paisley design with lots of reds and tans.

Tommy fingered the tie as he talked. "So then he switched to talking about the recruits he had coming in. Division I recruits. Some great talent, he said. A couple of steals because he said they'd get immediate playing time. If they'd gone to a bigger program, they knew they'd probably have to wait a few years before they could shine."

Leigh Ann was rapt, leaning forward in the booth now.

"Then he looked at me and said he had a scholarship left over. Wanted to know if I'd like it."

Leigh Ann blinked a few times, and then it struck her. She jumped out of the booth, knocking the table and almost spilling their drinks, and rushed to hug Tommy. Other diners watched with smiles as Leigh Ann smothered Tommy with kisses, Tommy laughing and trying unsuccessfully to push her away.

The waitress returned as Leigh Ann settled back into her side of the booth. "Did you just get engaged?!" The waitress was looking for evidence on Leigh Ann's hand.

Tommy's eyes opened fully, and he looked up. "Uh. No."

Leigh Ann laughed and shook her head, beaming. "He just got a basketball scholarship."

"Oh yeah?" The waitress turned to Tommy. "Where to?"

"UNCG."

The waitress frowned. "They have a basketball team?"

Tommy laughed. Half the kids on campus had the same question.

"Yeah," Leigh Ann said, turning her attention toward Tommy. "They do now."

Chapter 31

The exhilaration lasted through most of the following summer, even when Tommy's Buick, nicknamed "The Tank," finally died, and he bought his Uncle Andrew's used Honda Accord. Uncle Andrew was going through his mid-life crisis, or so Aunt Louise said, "On account of him never really growing up," and he came home one day with a candy red Mazda Miata.

"You look foolish in that thing," Aunt Louise had told him.

"I don't care," he said. "I've always wanted a sports car."

Aunt Louise told Helen, "He puts the top down and drives around like he's seventeen again, only now he doesn't have a full head of hair." She leaned close and said with a combination smile-frown. "It's all moved to his back."

Aunt Louise continued to tell Uncle Andrew he looked ridiculous, but she let him take her to the only drive-in around, up in Eden. They drove the whole thirty miles with the top down, wind whipping as Uncle Andrew negotiated the country curves. After ten minutes, Aunt Louise quit complaining about her hair and how fast they were going, and turned the music up louder. She was laughing and singing to the oldies station by the time they arrived and told Helen they even made out during the movie.

"And when we got back home that night," she continued with a smirk, "We did some other things we hadn't done since we were seventeen."

Helen laughed. "If he's going to have a mid-life crisis, at least he's happy having it with you."

Aunt Louise nodded. "He wants to go to the Outer Banks before the summer's out. Take a four-day weekend and drive the whole coast. Even mentioned doing the Blue Ridge Parkway when the leaves start to turn. Just drive all day and find somewhere to stay when the sun goes down."

Helen rolled her eyes. "Gene's idea of a midlife crisis is when the price of milk goes up a quarter."

All Tommy knew was that he had a dependable car at a fraction of the cost. It had a CD player instead of a tape deck, air conditioning that worked, and a set of practically new tires his uncle had bought to pass inspection four months earlier.

But by the end of summer, something happened that changed Tommy's good fortune. As a wise sage once wrote, the best laid schemes of mice and men ...

Tommy and Gene were in the middle of unloading the dry goods shipment from their distributor, SD Products. Melvin, the usual driver, was checking items off his clipboard as Tommy's dad loaded up the hand truck and rolled it down the truck ramp into the back of the store.

Tommy was waiting for his dad to come down the ramp when his dad's hand truck listed to the right. Gene looked up, his face distorted, and said, "Bacon is blue tarp tomorrow."

Tommy was about to laugh when Gene's hand truck rolled off the ramp, its boxes filled with cleaners, oil, and various hardware. The boxes crashed to the hot pavement, and Tommy's dad tumbled after, his body collapsing in a heap.

Tommy threw his own hand truck aside and rushed to his dad's side.

He rolled Gene over and cradled his head. There was a large gash over his left eye that leaked thick red blood. Melvin dropped down from the truck and covered the gash with his handkerchief.

"Dad? Dad? You alright?" Tommy almost yelled. Gene's eyes weren't focusing. "Dad?" Tommy yelled. "Dad?"

Gene's face was contorted as if in pain. The left side was slack, but the right was grimacing. Tommy would remember later how he immediately thought of the comic book character, Two-Face.

Gene mumbled.

"What? Dad, what are you saying?"

Melvin grabbed Tommy's arm. "I'm calling 9-1-1. Stay here."

Tommy looked up, wild-eyed, tears forming. Melvin ran inside while Tommy held his dad. Gene's eyes danced around like stick-on rolly eyes found at hobby stores. "Dad? Say something!"

Another car had pulled up to get gas, and the driver jumped out. He ran over to them and knelt down. It was Mr. Sprague; he had a son Brant's age. "What happened?" he asked.

"Somebody's already called the ambulance," Tommy said, still cradling his dad in his lap. "I ... I don't know what's wrong. He just fell."

"Looks like a stroke," Mr. Sprague said. "See the way his right side is limp?" Mr. Sprague grabbed Gene's right hand. "Gene? Gene? Can you hear me? Can you grip my hand? Let me know you're still in there; squeeze my hand."

Two more cars had pulled up, and a crowd began to form. It was late Thursday afternoon, and people were starting to return from work. Melvin usually came by around two or three, but he was running late today. If he'd come on time today, Tommy thought, this wouldn't be happening. They would have unloaded the truck, had a laugh or two, and gone home for dinner.

"Heart attack!" All of a sudden Tommy remembered the heart attack his dad had a few years back. "His nitro pills. I've got to get them." He left Gene with Mr. Sprague and the surrounding crowd, and ran inside to the office.

Tommy found the bottle in the top drawer and slipped a pill into his dad's mouth. Then he thought of his mom. She needed to be called, but he didn't want to leave his dad again. A fear had overtaken him that if he left again, when he got back, his dad wouldn't be there.

He looked up into the crowd and found Mrs. Finley. She was part of the Ladies Club at church with his mom. He asked her to make the call.

It didn't seem real, this scene in the side parking lot of the store. It was something you see on TV, on some drama show, or a snippet on the news. An interview with a witness. "I saw him fall. Like a sack of wet oatmeal. I remember seeing oil all over the place, running on the pavement, and wondering if it was his blood, then looking around to see if anyone was smoking."

A siren wailed in the distance, syncopating in repetition as it grew closer.

"Dad, hang on. The ambulance is coming." Gene made no response that he'd heard or understood.

But his eyes had locked onto Tommy's, no longer floating around in their sockets. It was a good sign, Tommy thought, it had to be. The ambulance showed before his mom did, but she pulled up a moment later. Helen held her husband's hand as they raised him onto a gurney, and loaded him inside the truck.

His eyes, the entire time, until the moment the double doors closed on the back of the vehicle, remained on Tommy. Tommy tried to read them, but the right side of his dad's face was slack, unmoving, frozen in an expressionless void.

The left side, however, was contorted in a mixture of emotions. His dad was the strongest person he knew. He laughed at inconvenience, grunted his way through pain, scoffed at his first heart attack, and fought the nurses during his entire stay.

The pain was evident now, its effects written in the deep lines creased in Gene's forehead, his taut cheeks, his distorted mouth. But most expressive were the eyes. In them, Tommy saw something he'd never seen in his dad, and never thought he would.

Fear.

Chapter 32

Two weeks passed. Gene had come home but still didn't have full use of his right side. His face remained slack and so did his right arm. He could move his legs, but his right one was lethargic, almost as if it was on a time delay.

Helen fed him, clothed him, bathed him. She was his wet nurse and personal assistant while he played the ungrateful patient to a tee. No matter what she did, it wasn't good enough.

"I said iced tea. Two cubes of ice does not make tea 'iced.' All that's gonna do is piss the tea off, like you're pissing me off giving me two cubes of ice in my iced tea."

"You trying to freeze me out in here? What's the thermostat set on? You got any idea what the power bill's gonna be this month? You trying to bring winter on early?"

"Do you always got to put so many onions in your meatloaf? You should start calling it onion loaf; leave the meat out altogether. Just make me a hamburger next time, and you can keep the onion loaf for yourself."

Helen took it with a smile. Gene had always been ornery. When they were young, she called it high-strung and bull-headed, but she knew when they grew older, it would turn into orneriness. She'd accepted that. Gene's mom had been the same way, right up until the day she passed.

Even though she expected his attitude, Helen didn't mind making Gene wait a few extra minutes when he started yelling for her. The way she figured, if he was yelling, he was okay. It was when he got quiet she had to worry.

So she took his gruff manner and never-satisfied complaints with solace. With a certain kind of peace. With the knowledge that if Gene was ever beckoned to the pearly gates, he would give St. Peter absolute hell about his timing. He'd mention how disappointing the gates looked and how they weren't really pearly, were they? *And since they looked more like ivory, why were they called pearly gates instead of ivory gates? That was misleading, and if you're lying about the freakin' gates, what else you been hiding?*

St. Peter would send him back.

"What are you smiling at?" Gene asked. The right side of his face twitched like it wanted to join the left side in its scowl, but had forgotten how.

"Nothing, honey," Helen replied.

"I tell you my soup's lukewarm, and you smile at me? You do something to my soup?" He craned his neck to peer into the soup bowl.

"No, Gene."

"'Cause you know if you're gonna call this stuff chicken noodle soup, there ought to be more chicken in it than two pathetic cubes the size of dimes." Some broth dribbled out the right side of his mouth, and Helen wiped it with a napkin. Gene continued, "I mean, what's the point if you're just gonna ..."

Helen tuned him out and thought of her older son. Tommy had done so much for himself despite constant opposition from Gene.

She asked Gene once a few years ago why he was so hard on Tommy, why the man never told his son he was proud of him when it was so obvious to her. He was hard on the boy, he said, "To make him strong, Helen. If we make growing up too easy, he'll get out there in the real world, and it'll rip him apart like a pack of hungry wolves. The world won't care, and you won't be able to protect him. You want to send him out there coddled like a baby or hardened with some teeth of his own?"

There's got to be some middle ground, she argued.

He never answered back.

And now, at that very moment, Tommy was doing the hardest thing he'd ever done in his life. It was a decision he'd made on his own, and their discussion had been less of an actual discussion, and more of him telling her his decision.

A decision that broke her heart because it was Tommy's one dream, and he'd achieved it. Few people in this world ever get to live their dream. Tommy Chandler was one of the lucky ones.

Until now.

Chapter 33

"I have to quit school," Tommy said. He was in Coach D.'s office, the door shut. "It's my dad. He had a stroke a few weeks ago. He's at home now, but he can't do anything by himself."

"And you're gonna take over the store." It wasn't a question. Coach D. knew most everything about his players' lives. Their families, their majors, their girlfriends. He wanted to know every fact that affected his boys because when they became a part of his team, they were part of *his* family too.

Despite not being around very much due to the demands of a college basketball coach, Coach D. also made it a point to know everything about the boys his daughter had dated.

Tommy's gut was wrenched into a knot before he entered the office, but he relaxed a little now that he'd gotten the first words out.

"I talked it over with my mom," he said. "We both think it's the best thing right now. The store's my family's only source of income. My mom hasn't worked since I was born and taking care of my dad is a full-time job anyway. If she ran the store, she'd have to hire a nurse, and the nurse would cost more than the store would make. Plus, she doesn't know how to do the books or when to order the—'"

"It's okay, Tommy. You don't have to explain. I understand. Family comes first. Believe me, I know." Coach D. sniffed and looked off in the distance. He leaned forward and propped his elbows on his desk. "I lost my dad about ten years ago. Colon cancer."

An acid expression slid across his face. "Nasty stuff. Near the end, he was wearing diapers because he couldn't control ... well, you know. The point is, there was my dad, the most capable man I knew … used to get up every morning before the roosters, milk the cows, slop the hogs, feed the horses and mules, and then come in for breakfast. This man would work in the fields all day, never complaining about blisters or being tired or the weather. He took what God gave him and he made it work. He was a man's man, chewed tobacco and drank whiskey. Never backed down from a fight, not if it was a neighbor encroaching on our land, a drunk trouble-maker raising hell at the local watering hole, or the IRS man threatening us over back taxes that couldn't be paid before the family was fed."

Coach D. clenched his jaw. "Here was this man, the strongest man I knew, wearing diapers the last few months of his life, depending on his wife to wipe him and clean him five, six times a day. I asked my mom why she didn't put him in some care facility where they could handle all that. Told her I'd pay for it. I was making enough money it wouldn't have been a problem. And do you know what she said?"

Tommy shook his head no.

"She told me he was her husband, for better or worse. They'd had the better times and now were the worse. She wasn't going to abandon him because his body was failing. He was still her husband, the love of her life, and every night, after she'd put him to bed, they talked and laughed like they were still kids. She wanted every one of those moments she could get because she never knew when the last one would come."

The words hung in the air between them like a silent cloud of anticipation, the emotions palpable and real as the cement floor beneath them. And just as hard.

"Tell you what we're gonna do," Coach D. said. "We're gonna redshirt you this year. You take the year off. Get your life in order, get things straight at home." He shrugged. "Maybe take a part-time load. Surely you can get somebody to look after the store a few hours a week. You don't have to grow up just yet."

Tommy grinned.

Coach D. continued, "I'll have a scholarship for you next year. I want you on this team, but more than that, I want you to graduate with your degree. I mean that." He paused. "Think you can make it to one or two practices a week?"

Tommy frowned. "I don't know."

"I'll make you a deal. You get to a few practices a week, take a couple of classes, and I'll get the school to pay for it. You'll still be on the team, but you gotta make me one promise."

Tommy hesitated. "What?"

"Promise me that in the end, you'll do what's right for you. Not what's right for me or the team or your family, but what's right for you. Because ultimately, Tommy, you have to lead your own life." He paused. "That's one of the lessons my dad taught me. He never wanted me to go into farming unless it made me happy, and believe you me, he knew early on the only thing that made me want to get up each day was a bouncy orange ball."

Coach D. laughed, and Tommy joined him.

"You got a good head on your shoulders, Tommy. You're quick, and you make good decisions. Hell, you have to be when you're a point guard, right?" He didn't wait for an answer. "Just promise me you'll do what's right for you, okay? Can you do that?"

"Sure, Coach." Tommy stood and smiled weakly. "I can do that."

Chapter 34

Tommy ran the store by himself for a month before he began to make changes. At first, they were just small changes, like removing some old signs and cleaning up the bulletin board. He replaced the ratty commercial doormat that had been there forever. He cleaned up the area around the register and one night, put down a new clear coat on the wooden countertop.

The first major change was to dust off the computer and purchase the inventory software the store's distributor used. Then, on a tip from the distributor, Tommy found a small store in Lexington that was closing its doors and liquidating inventory. Not only did Tommy purchase half their store at fifty percent off the normal wholesale price, he also bought the register.

The store's current register was one of the old kind that used receipt tape that was an inch wide and only printed dollars and cents. The new register had a small computer inside that could be synced up with the inventory program on the computer in the office. It also had a barcode reader.

Brant drove up from ECU and helped network the computer and register together. They pulled an all-nighter until finally, at four in the morning, an item purchased at the register deleted from the database inventory on the computer.

Tommy high-fived his brother and they grabbed a celebratory beer from the cooler.

For a whole week, Tommy brought Steve in for more hours, and together they entered the store's entire inventory by UPC code, incorporating the new product from the out-of-business store. He barely saw Leigh Ann that week except between classes.

Then the next Tuesday, Tommy closed the store for the day. He changed the sign outside to say they were "Closed for Inventory, Re-Open Wed. Gas pumps ON." It was an inconvenience, but at least people could buy gas with their credit card.

That day, he and Steve took a complete inventory at the store, down to the last bag of hex screws, and input all the numbers into the new computer system. They tested a few sales on the new register, and Tommy double-checked that the computer's inventory updated.

Tommy's mom knew what he was doing, and sent him to the store that morning with white chocolate-chunk muffins. He and Steve snacked on them all day long, working well into the night. Shortly past ten, Tommy declared the experiment a success.

He was glad they'd finished in a day; he'd missed an ECON class to do the switch-over, but he thought it was a fair trade. His dad was right about one thing: college didn't teach practical experience like this.

When Gene Chandler first heard about the store changes from Mrs. Patterson—she visited the house with a chicken pie the following weekend—at first, he didn't say a word. He listened intently as his visitor blathered on about how Tommy scanned all her groceries with a gun, just like at a big grocery store. "It was quite exciting," she said.

After she left, Gene turned to his wife, and before he could begin, she told him she'd known all about it, and what's more, she gave Tommy her blessing. Gene ranted and cussed and spit out the side of his mouth, his face turning red, until for the second time in their married lives, Helen out-shouted him and told him to hush his foul mouth.

Gene resorted to pouting as Helen wiped the right side of his face and chin. Saliva had dribbled out the sagging side. He was still unable to feel it.

When his self-pity-filled muttering stopped, Helen reprimanded him like he was a misbehaving child. "He's *your* son. What did you expect?"

"What's that supposed to mean?" Gene snapped, averting his eyes when she raised her eyebrows at his tone.

"He's just like you in so many ways you can't see it," she responded. Gene glowered.

Helen wiped a place on Gene's chin she'd missed before. "He's his own man, just like you were at that age."

"Well ... I never directly disobeyed my father. I specifically told that boy—"

Helen laughed. "You never what?"

"I said I didn't want all that fancy stuff in the store. No telling what it all cost me."

"You never disobeyed your father?" Helen repeated.

Gene jutted his chin out and met her eyes. "Never."

"Do you remember what we did on your eighteenth birthday?"

"That doesn't count." Gene looked away. "That was different."

"Was it that different?"

"The world was different; Commies were everywhere—"

"Gene." Helen smirked. "Commies had nothing to do with you stealing your dad's Chevy and driving us three counties over to get married by your cousin, a cousin who just happened to overlook the fact I was two years underage."

"Well, your dad wouldn't sign the consent paper. What else was I supposed to do?"

Helen shook her head. "This isn't about my father. It's about yours and the fact he forbade you from ever driving that Bel Air of his."

Gene frowned and tried to look away, but Helen cupped his face in her hands, smiling warmly. "I'm just making a point, honey. You said to hell with everyone else and did what you wanted to because you thought it was right. Your son's the same way. You told Tommy you weren't paying for him to go to college, so he spent his own money and got school loans."

"And a little help from you."

Helen shrugged. "I didn't see you stopping me."

Gene tried to look away again.

"Then you tell him *no computer* and the first chance he gets, he installs one with software he found himself. He's single-handedly dragged that store, and you, kicking and screaming into the modern age. Remind you of anyone you know?"

"I didn't make changes like that when I took over the store."

"No, not at all," Helen scoffed. "You closed the barbershop within a month."

"I needed that room for storage, and you know it."

"Your father got along just fine without that extra storage."

"Plus, how many haircuts was Uncle Robert giving a month at that point? Two? Three? The old man had to get so close to somebody to see what he was doing, it looked like he was trying to smell them instead of cut their hair."

Helen laughed. "Remember the last haircut he gave your dad?"

Even Gene laughed at this, the right side of his face twitching, straining to join in the mirth. Gene continued the thought, "He had to go to Wayne Greeson's to get it fixed. His hair was so short, for a while people thought he'd enlisted again."

Helen ran her fingers through her husband's thinning hair and laid her head on his chest. "He's just like you, Gene. You raised him to think for himself, to make his own decisions. You can't get upset at him for doing what you taught him."

Gene closed his eyes and sucked in a deep breath. He allowed the rest of his anger to seep away.

Helen knew what was on his mind, and also knew he wasn't the type of man to talk about it. So she said instead, "You've always implied the store would be Tommy's one day, right?"

"Yeah, but ..."

"But what?" Helen sat up and met his eyes. "But not yet? Is that it?"

Gene tried to turn his head, but Helen reached her hand out and pulled his face back. "Gene, honey." She took a breath and waited until his eyes met hers. "We both know you're not going back."

The statement struck him hard as if the words had actual weight now that they'd been said aloud. It was a thought he'd tried not to think about. After a hesitation, he said, "But the doctors—"

"I don't care what the doctors said. They're not married to you. That store almost took you away from me twice now. It's not going to get a third try."

"But—"

"No buts. From now on, you're officially retired. Maybe Tommy'll let you run the register on Saturdays." She smiled. "If you can learn how."

Now Gene smiled. "That's mean."

"No, that's not mean. *Mean* is when I make you finally take me all the places I've wanted to go. Like Paris and London. You thought you'd get out of traveling because of the store."

She laughed at his expression. "Don't worry. We have a few more years before I make you do any of that. Right now, you just rest up and work on getting the right side of your body jump-started back into motion."

Chapter 35

Tommy, Brant, and Steve decorated the store for the holidays that year. It was a true first and had Gene been in the grave, he would have rolled over. As it was, he was at home lying on the sofa watching basketball when he learned of the decorations, and he rolled over anyway.

Lights were strung around the windows, doors, and the "Chandler's" sign. They draped silver garland around a fake tree Tommy had dragged to the roof. Icicle lights hung from the roof's edge, and a waving light-up Santa was installed beside the ice machine. And of course, the same lights and decorations they used were also for sale in the new holiday section of the store.

Tommy placed speakers throughout the building and tuned the radio station to one that played holiday music 24/7. The stereo was a late 1970s table-top console with a built-in record player and 8-track cassette deck. He constructed a new shelf beside the register just for the system.

Sometimes, when Tommy was at the store alone, he played old Christmas records he'd found at Remember When Records in town: Bing Crosby, Andy Williams, Paul Anka. To him, *White Christmas* wasn't the same without a few hisses and pops.

The day after Leigh Ann's final exam that semester, she surprised Tommy at the store with lunch. She brought a Hawaiian pizza from New

York Pizza, the same place they'd gone on their first date, the very day they met on the tennis court.

That was more than a year earlier. After Tommy's unofficial practice, he dropped by Leigh Ann's dorm as she'd asked, and they went walking around campus. They wandered for more than an hour, talking and laughing, before they found themselves emerging onto Tate Street.

Leigh Ann suggested they grab a bite to eat and nodded towards the pizza joint. Tommy blanched. He didn't have any money, he told her, he'd just come out to play ball with the guys. Didn't even have his ID on him. Leigh Ann smiled and said she'd pay, he could get the next time.

Tommy studied her for a moment, and she said, "Come on, I won't even expect you to put out afterward."

Tommy shook his head, a smirk forming, and graciously accepted.

"Besides," she continued, "if we ever get married, how cool will it be to say I paid for our first date?"

They had Hawaiian pizza that first night, too.

Tommy was cleaning The Andy Williams Christmas Album when Leigh Ann popped into the store, pizza box in hand. His scowl immediately transferred into a huge smile. It was amazing how she brightened every room she entered.

"Whatcha doing?" she asked as she set the pizza on the counter and kissed him.

Tommy held the record up. "It's skipping. Andy keeps dreaming of White Christmas nuts roasting on an open fire."

Leigh Ann grinned and asked him to get some napkins. He returned the record to the player and reset the needle as Leigh Ann grabbed two Mountain Dews from the cooler. Tommy tore off some paper towels from a roll under the counter and they dove into the pizza.

Conversation moved from sports to school to how the price of gas was fluctuating. They wondered how long New York Pizza had been on Tate Street and whether or not the restaurant was the original tenant of the space since it looked like it'd always been there.

A few customers came in, each buying a few small items. Mrs. Tattinger asked if that was Andy Williams crooning away, and Tommy beamed, pointing to the album cover he'd put on display above the register. Oh how she loved her Andy Williams, she exclaimed. She offered to buy the album, but Tommy told her it was his personal record. It wasn't for sale.

She told him he had an old soul and left with a huge smile across her lined face, refusing Tommy's offer to carry her bag, saying, "I'm not that helpless yet."

Then, thirty seconds later, while Leigh Ann was laughing at Tommy as he took an extra-large bite and sliced through a pineapple—its juice ran down his chin and dripped onto his shirt—Laura Novak strolled through the door.

Laura paused for the remotest of moments as she locked eyes with Leigh Ann, then smiled at Tommy. Tommy, his mouth full of pizza, brought his hand up in a weak wave as Laura turned left toward the coolers.

As soon as Laura was safely down the aisle, Leigh Ann leaned over the counter and said in a low voice, "Who's that?"

Tommy, still chewing, held up a finger as he chewed, finally covering his mouth as he said, "Cawa."

"Cawa?"

Tommy shook his head, chewing, and swallowed some more. He tongued the rest into his right cheek and said again, "Laura."

"Uh-huh." Leigh Ann nodded, glancing over her shoulder, then back at Tommy. "And who is this Laura?" Her eyebrows were raised slightly.

Tommy swallowed some more. "Just a friend from school. High school."

"A friend?" Leigh Ann raised her eyebrows.

"Yeah, just a friend."

Leigh Ann glanced over her shoulder again, then said, "She's pretty."

Tommy took another bite of pizza.

"Isn't she?" Leigh Ann urged.

"Yeah, I guess so," Tommy answered, taking another bite of pizza.

"You guess so?" Leigh Ann glanced toward the back again. "You were never more than just friends?"

Tommy swallowed. "You mean like did we date?"

Leigh Ann crossed her arms and leaned sideways on the counter, eyeing Tommy.

Tommy tried his best to look indignant, as if the very idea was absurd, then thought that would make him look guilty of something instead. He relaxed a bit. "Laura and me? We've been friends since like the second grade."

"And you've never dated?"

Tommy realized he'd still not answered the question when Leigh Ann asked it again. He said, "No, we never dated." He paused, then added with a shrug, "We went to the Homecoming Dance together one year."

"What year?" Leigh Ann asked, her face registering triumph.

"Oh, I don't know. Senior year maybe?"

"You're not sure?"

Tommy began to feel warm as the memories of that night flooded back to him. He hadn't thought of it for so long. Meeting Laura's mom, the laxative cookie story about his dad, dinner at TK Tripps, dancing with his arms around Laura, her heady scent making his knees weak, the Hall and Oates song "Kiss On My List," and finally, the fateful kiss that drove a wedge through their friendship.

"Yeah, it was Senior year."

Leigh Ann narrowed her eyes as Tommy sipped his Mountain Dew. Laura came from behind her and set some groceries down on the counter: a half-gallon of skim milk, a loaf of Merita wheat bread, a package of cheddar cheese, and a frozen Totino's supreme pizza.

"Sorry about your dad, Tommy." Laura had stolen a look at Leigh Ann again but addressed Tommy. "Has he gotten better?"

Tommy shrugged. "He still has trouble with his arm and his face isn't quite back to normal yet. But Mom says at least his attitude's gotten worse."

Laura laughed, and Tommy smiled. Leigh Ann didn't.

"I'm Leigh Ann." She stuck her hand out.

Laura turned her laugh into a wide smile as she shook hands. "Laura."

"So you've known my Tommy a long time?"

Laura grinned and glanced at Tommy. "Yeah. You could say that. He sat in front of me in Ms. Mim's second grade class. He was my first friend at school."

"Uh-huh. And where do you go to school now?"

"Hollins," Laura answered. Then added, "In Roanoke. Virginia."

Leigh Ann was nodding. "I play tennis for UNCG. That's where Tommy and I met." Leigh Ann reached out and grabbed Tommy's hand from the counter. She squeezed his hand and shot him a smile. "On the tennis court."

"Tommy was always an athlete."

Tommy straightened at this remark; he wasn't aware Laura had ever paid too much attention to him on the court. It was then he realized how much taller than Laura he'd become.

It was one of the revelations that hit him once he thought about it, like seeing his little brother hop behind a steering wheel and drive off. People tended to get caught up in the moment, concerned with the circumstances and time immediately surrounding them. But every once in a while, something happened to remind them how far they'd come, how much the world—their world—had changed in just a short time.

Something like running into an old friend, or going to a family reunion, or years later, seeing the first girl you ever had a crush on. Tommy hadn't run into Laura in almost two and a half years, not since the summer before he began college when she'd stopped by the store and they'd sipped drinks on the roof. It seemed like so long ago; he was such a kid back then, unsure of himself, green, so gullible and ignorant. He felt like it was a lifetime ago.

Yet at the same time, looking at Laura now, the last time he saw her felt like just days ago. Her hair was different, lighter now with subtle curls, but her eyes were the same, always bright, emanating kindness with every glance. Her hands still looked delicate, her skin unblemished, her demeanor forever Laura in every way. There was a lilt to her words Tommy thought would never disappear, a definite cadence to her speech that added to her gentle personality.

Sixty more years could pass, Tommy thought, Laura could be wrinkled and stooped, her perfect complexion mottled with age spots, her outside beauty faded with time, and she could say hello behind him in the line at the K and W. Before he turned to face her, himself balding and sporting a cane, he'd know it was her. Laura Novak. Just by the way she said his name.

Just by the way it rolled off her lips and tickled his ears.

He'd know.

"Tommy's the starting point guard on the basketball team," Leigh

Ann said.

"I thought you were taking the year off," Laura said, turning toward him.

Tommy did a double-take. "Oh, yeah. For the store. I'm still going to school part-time. Coach red-shirted me. I hope to be back in uniform next year. Full-time."

Laura nodded. "And what's your dad think of that?"

Tommy grinned. "I haven't asked him."

Laura snorted, then said, "Is he planning on coming back to the store?"

"I don't know. That depends."

Laura laughed. "Brant said the same thing."

"Brant?"

"I was in here, oh, about a month ago. Brant was running the register. He said you were out. He didn't know what your dad was going to do either. I guess it's still too soon to tell." She looked around. "It's just weird thinking of this store without your dad in it."

"Tommy's made a bunch of changes," Leigh Ann chirped.

"I can tell," Laura said. "Mr. Chandler never decorated for the holidays." She looked around again, then at Tommy. "It's nice. I like it."

Tommy said thanks, and there was a moment of silence. Leigh Ann squeezed Tommy's hand, and he said, "Oh. I guess you want to check out." Tommy scanned the items and bagged them as Laura pulled a twenty out of her pocket. He rang the sale, tore off the receipt and gave her change.

"Thanks for coming in," he said as Laura headed for the door with the bag of groceries cradled in her left arm.

"See you later," she said. Then to Leigh Ann: "It was nice to meet you."

THE WALK-ON

Leigh Ann smiled thinly. "Likewise."

Tommy waved, and when the door closed, Leigh Ann pulled her hand away from his. "What was that all about?" she asked.

"Huh?" Tommy swiveled toward her. "What?"

"That ..."—Leigh Ann waving her hands around, face tightening—"all of it. That's what."

Tommy's eyes widened. "All of what?"

"You two should've just gotten a room."

"Huh?"

"Don't tell me you didn't see the way she looked at you."

The record began to go *sssss-tum, sssss-tum*, and Tommy knelt down to turn it over, saying, "You're imagining things."

"Tommy." Leigh Ann waited until he'd flipped the record and straightened back up. "I know that look."

"What look?" Tommy was becoming frustrated. "I didn't see any look. Laura always looks like that."

"Ha. Right. And I'll bet she always dresses like that when she drops by the store for cookies and milk." Leigh Ann had her hands on her hips now, her expression sarcastic, incredulous.

"Dressed like ... she had on a sweater and jeans."

"A *tight* sweater and jeans. And I see you noticed."

At that moment, Tommy realized this was one of those arguments a girl and a guy had where the guy always lost. No matter what he said, it would be construed to whatever meaning Leigh Ann expected, the interpretation from point A to point B not following any logical path in his mind.

Tommy felt he'd done nothing wrong, but still, Leigh Ann had perceived something imaginary. It was an impossible task to dissuade her of whatever phantom occurrence she'd observed.

Tommy threw his hands up. "Okay. You caught me. I'm too transparent; I can't hide anything from you."

Leigh Ann frowned.

"The sweater. It was the sweater. If she wore red, we were to meet outside her house tonight. If it was blue, like the one she wore, we were gonna meet here after I closed up. The cookies and milk were for us."

Leigh Ann pursed her lips and glared at him.

"I was supposed to think of an excuse to get rid of you. Something like having to wash my hair or do laundry—oof."

Leigh Ann punched Tommy in the gut. He laughed and guarded his midsection, continuing, "And once you were gone, I was supposed to strip down to nothing but a Santa Hat—"

Leigh Ann lunged at him, but he was ready, fending off her hands, gripping her wrists. "I'll jingle your bells," she said, struggling to free her hands.

"Ooh ... promises, promises. That's why we devised such a complicated code." He was having a hard time containing her. "You know what the cheese meant?"

"Keep it up," Leigh Ann said, still wrangling for freedom.

"If she got regular cheese, that meant nothing. But cheddar?" Tommy shook his head. "It was gonna be a kinky night. Cheddar meant she was gonna show up in an elf's costume, and I was supposed to show her how we made the naughty toys."

Leigh Ann twisted free as she hopped on the counter and rolled. Tommy braced himself, but when she landed in front of him, she wrapped her arms around him and pulled tight. Tommy returned the gesture, and they stood there, swaying to "The First Noel."

Tommy gazed down into Leigh Ann's eyes, and he smiled, saying, "You know I love you."

"Even my neuroses?"

"Especially your neuroses. In fact, mainly your neuroses."

They kissed until the bell and swoosh of cold air signaled a shopper entering the store. They separated and Tommy waved to Mrs. Caruthers, wishing her a Merry Christmas.

She regarded them with a raised eyebrow.

Tommy smiled. "Just testing out the best places for the mistletoe."

Mrs. Caruthers rolled her eyes and walked to the coolers.

"Ooh, I almost forgot," Tommy said. He reached under the counter and pulled out a Christmas tin, popped the top. "Mom made cookies."

"Ooh ... what kind?" Leigh Ann reached for one.

"Chocolate chip with three kinds of chips. Dark chocolate, milk chocolate, and white chocolate."

"Mmmm." Leigh Ann bit into one, and her eyes closed as she savored the sensation. "Your mom is a God-send."

"Yeah," Tommy said, devouring a cookie in one bite. "She knows what she's doing in the kitchen."

Tommy offered a cookie to Mrs. Caruthers when he checked her out. "Just the milk and flour," she said, begging off while staring at the open cookie tin. She left with her willpower and waist size intact.

Leigh Ann kissed Tommy again. "I have to get out of here."

"So soon?"

"I just wanted to surprise you before I headed to Ohio."

Tommy pulled back. "I didn't think you were heading back until after the weekend."

"Me too. My uncle's deploying out before Christmas gets here so we switched things around; my mom's family is getting together this weekend now."

"I'm going to miss you," Tommy said, pulling her close. "Stay for a little while longer. I'll wear my Santa's hat."

Leigh Ann laughed. "That would be a sight." She took in a deep breath and nuzzled Tommy's chest. "But I have to go. I haven't even packed yet."

"You're not leaving tonight are you?"

"No, but I'm going to bed early and getting up early." She rubbed Tommy's chest through his shirt. "And if I stayed here much longer, I might not be able to leave at all."

Leigh Ann finally left, and Tommy watched her go, waving and blowing her a kiss when she looked back before getting in her car. His heart ached each time they parted, but it was a good ache, the pain a lover experiences from temporary separation. The kind of pain that fades quickly, secure in knowing the void will soon be filled with an overflow of love.

Chapter 36

The spring semester went smoothly for Tommy. He finished his fourth semester of Spanish and an Information Systems course on databases. The ISM course gave him a better idea of how the software system at the store worked, how the underpinnings treated the data he entered. Now he wouldn't have to depend on Brant every time the system hiccupped.

Tommy also made it to several practices a week and every home game. It was difficult watching DeJuan Flores run the point with the new Division I recruit, Derrick Thompkins, backing him up. They both did alright, but there were so many small mistakes made. Errant passes. Missed opportunities. Bungled plays.

Thompkins had raw talent but played like a freshman. Give him another year or two, Tommy thought, and he'll be ready. The two other Division I recruits were a different story, however.

They immediately made an impact. Scott McManness was a 6-10 center with a smidgen of athletic ability. He could block shots and intimidate anyone who drove the basket, and then step outside for a ten-foot jumper. Alvy Hanes, a 6-8 power forward from Garner, NC, was said to be one of those steals who could have gone to a bigger program and started. The critics were right. Hanes quickly gained a loyal following of fans who went wild every time he dunked on an opponent, which was an average of 3.7 times a game.

It was UNCG's first year in the Big South conference so they weren't eligible for the conference tourney, which also meant no shot at going to the Big Dance unless they secured an at-large bid. Which meant no chance. UNCG's last regular-season game was their last game that year. With a 10-12 record, there was no NIT invitation either.

Neither was there an expectation.

Life outside school also ran as smoothly as it could have. Gene Chandler continued improving each day until he slowly regained full use of the right side of his body. Every once in a while, though, a tic would erupt on the right half of his face, jiggling his cheek uncontrollably for a second or two, as if the muscles were showing off their regained mobility.

But even in his self-declared 'cured' state, Gene was not allowed back into the store except to retrieve an item needed for home. The doctors said he was fine to return to work, but there was a power greater than doctors that said no ... his wife.

Helen forbade any activity which created too much stress. Or *could* create stress. Which meant the store. So Gene took up building things.

First, he cleaned out his work shed that had filled with junk throughout the years. But when too much of that junk was declared "not junk" by Helen, Gene decided to build another workshop. His ideal workshop, one that would never be used for storage. Never ever.

In his initial designs, the shop started out fifteen feet square, but when he visualized the machines in there he wanted—compound miter saw, jigsaw, tablet router, drill press, etc.—he decided the place would be too cramped. After all, he needed a staging area to put his projects together after he'd readied the various pieces.

The design expanded to twenty feet square, but then he decided to add a bathroom and a small office with a couch for relaxing. Suddenly, the building was thirty by thirty, because he decided he himself would need storage.

In one weekend, the men of the family readied the foundation and had it poured. The next Saturday, they erected the walls and the A-frame roof. Sunday, they finished the roof, adding plywood, tar paper, and shingles.

Within a month, they'd built the outside walls, had the plumber finish the bathroom, paid a cousin with Helen's cake to wire the place, tiled the bath floor, finished the office with sheetrock and paint, and painted the outside walls a deep maroon. The double doors were outlined and adorned with a bright white X like barn doors.

Gene bought a window unit out of the classifieds and stuck it in the office, then installed a huge industrial fan in the wall opposite the double doors so that in the dead heat of summer, he could prop the doors and create a cross breeze.

After the building—or "shop" as Gene called it—was finished, there was no doubt where Gene could be found at all times of the day.

Projects began small. Birdhouses were the only finished items that emerged for the first few weeks.

Then Gene bought a used lathe and began making chairs. He experimented with different designs and styles and building techniques.

In the end, Gene decided he was a purist, opting to use only dowels, biscuits, wood glue, and special cuts to join wood. He bought design books at Lowe's and switched from chairs to basic furniture: small tables, bookshelves, bed frames.

Slowly, furniture in the Chandler house began to be replaced by Chandler exclusives. All pieces were finished and varnished by hand, and after much study, Gene found that he was drawn to the Arts and

Crafts movement made popular by Gustav Stickley shortly after the turn of the century.

Not only were the Craftsman pieces simpler to make, they were more pleasing to the eye, focusing on quality and aesthetics instead of "frilly crap," as Gene called it.

Craftsman pieces had a certain appeal to a man who believed in keeping things as simple as possible at all times. The smooth plainness and clean lines of his furniture pleased him.

Helen no longer worried about her husband's stress levels. At first, when he began spending the majority of his time in the shop—Gene eventually built a sign with raised letters that read THE SHOP in black and screwed it over the double doors—Helen had been concerned.

But then she noticed how her husband had an undercurrent of happiness she'd never seen. A burden had been lifted from his back that he hadn't realized was a burden at all. There was a hop in his step, and he couldn't wait to begin work each morning. And more than once, she could have sworn she saw him smiling as he stepped out the back door, coffee mug in hand.

For Tommy, the store wasn't the burden it was before he took it over. Now that he made the decisions, it was almost like a game he got paid to play.

Even so, he was serious about finishing his degree, and during the summer, he made preparations in that respect. Homer Persons was Joey Persons' grandfather, and this past spring, the old man had been forced to retire from the United States Post Office. As such, he'd begun to hang out at the store more and more, bored to death with the prospect of retirement.

"Who wants to sit home and talk to Glenda all day?" was a mantra Homer had repeated more than once to customers who came and left while he hung around the store chatting with Tommy.

Homer became such a fixture at the store that summer that the few times he didn't show, he was inquired about. And thus, Tommy offered Homer a chance he couldn't say no to.

Would he like a job?

Homer Persons was thrilled beyond speech and nodded profusely while shaking Tommy's hand. "I'll do a good job fer ya," he said when he'd recovered enough sense. "You won't be sorry."

Homer was a huge fan of Big Band and beginning that fall, the likes of Tommy Dorsey, Glenn Miller, and Cab Calloway could be heard in Chandler's, filtering from the speakers at a pleasant volume. Homer had dug up his old record collection, albums he hadn't heard in decades because the old console stereo at the house hadn't worked since 1976 when a lightning surge rendered it merely another piece of wooden furniture to pile knick-knacks on.

Tommy returned to school with a full slate of classes: an economics class, an accounting course, Western Civ, and two business classes—one on management, the other on supply chain management.

He checked in at the store once a day around lunch and usually stopped by at night or early the next morning to run reports, check receipts, and get the deposit money. He still ran the business—ordered new supplies, clearanced slow-moving items, made decisions regarding inventory and accounting—while Homer ran the daily operations of the store. Steve filled in here and there, like when Homer's wife forced him to get check-ups at the doctor to make sure his pancreatic cancer stayed in remission.

"Like there's anything the doc can do about it," Homer would say to Tommy. "Because between you and me, I ain't doing no more chemo. That stuff about killed me the first time, and I'd rather let the cancer get me instead. At least I'd be able to keep down my supper."

Six years ago, Homer's doctors discovered the cancer and put Homer "through goddamn hell" to cure him of it. He had enough vacation built up at the post office that it didn't set back his retirement so at least there was that.

At times that semester, Tommy felt like a kid, the times he was in class or concentrating on homework or dribbling down the court. He was just another college student.

But there were other times he felt old, having responsibilities that the kids he saw every day knew nothing about. He didn't have time for partying or lounging around the Quad.

And still, other times when he was with Leigh Ann—sequestered in the library, stuffing down lunch between classes, or simply holding hands and watching the fountain in front of The Caf bubble over—he felt neither young nor old.

In those moments, time had no meaning because he was living in the now. And the moment lasted as long as he could possibly make it. In the back of his mind, he knew this period of his life was "the good ole days" he'd remember forever, like he and Nick had talked about once, and he wanted to experience every second to its fullest.

There were some memories that already stuck out.

The day his Accord ran out of gas, and one of his classmates happened to be driving by as Tommy was walking to find a phone. Avery Simpson became a new friend that day as they talked about everything from basketball to President Bush's foreign policy and how it affected the U.S. Economy in the long-run.

The night he and Leigh Ann dressed up to see a play in Aycock Auditorium put on by the UNCG drama department. A jazz quartet from the music department provided the music, and afterward, Tommy took

Leigh Ann out to Bianca's where they were served a four-course Italian feast amidst soft lighting and background music. "Is that Verde or Puccini?" Tommy asked.

"No, it's Dan Fogelberg. Drink your wine."

The day Tommy borrowed a pair of rollerblades, and he and Leigh Ann bladed around the entire campus, finally bailing out in the soft grass after she took them down the crazy hill to The Caf just as a crowd of students popped out the front door. "Why'd you do that?" Leigh Ann asked after she'd made her way back to him. He was lying prone on the ground breathing hard, his chest heaving partly from exhaustion, partly from fear of how the hill could have turned out. "I started getting a blister," Tommy lied, rubbing his rollerblade. Leigh Ann shook her head and collapsed beside him in the grass. They talked about the most amazing things that day; lying in the grass staring at the puffy clouds spilling over the roof of The Caf: how big the universe is, what souls actually are, how come corduroy makes that sound when you walk.

He learned life was made up of those small memories, and you had to do everything you could to hang on to them.

Chapter 37

UNCG's first official game in Tommy's junior year was at the University of Maryland. Even in Maryland's down seasons, they were always tough. Gary Williams never had a bad team; his squads rarely dropped games to opponents they had no business losing to.

This game was no exception. Maryland won by twenty-two.

And what's more, Tommy had a miserable game.

In his first game back in uniform, Tommy started but put up dismal numbers. Six points, three assists, one steal, three rebounds, five turnovers.

Tommy didn't mind having an off game with his shooting or defense or rebounds. But five turnovers and only three assists? As a starting point guard, that reeked.

The first thing he did after the game was apologize to the coaches. "Don't worry about it," Coach Fulton said. "First game."

"But I played awful. You'd have been better off with DeJuan or Derrick in there.

"You realize the kid you were playing against was a two-time All American? He was MVP of the ACC tournament last year, and Maryland didn't even win."

Tommy shrugged.

"He normally scores twenty a game. You kept him to twelve points and what"—he glanced at Coach D.—"five assists? No, where this team beat us was in the paint. They out-rebounded us by twenty-three. They were just too big. We needed a miracle to win this one, and we didn't get it."

The coach was right, Tommy finally conceded to himself as he showered and changed. The loss wasn't Tommy's fault. But still, if he could've done more, turned the tide with a few more plays, anything could've happened.

On the long bus ride back to Greensboro, Tommy sulked alone in his seat. He tried to skim through his ECON textbook, but his mind wasn't in it. After an hour, he wandered up front and asked Coach D. if he had a minute.

"Sure," the coach said. He picked up the folders and clipboard from the seat next to him and motioned for Tommy to sit down.

Tommy did, and Coach D. said, "You sucked pretty bad tonight, huh?"

Tommy looked up, surprised. Coach D. smiled and said, "That's what you wanted to hear, right? How bad you played, how you could have done better?"

"I ... uh ... I guess."

"Tommy, you're quite a piece, you know that?"

"I don't understand, Coach."

Coach shook his head. "No, you don't. You wouldn't. I'm gonna explain something to you now nobody's probably ever told you. It's not a judgment, mind you, just an observation."

Tommy nodded.

"Your bar is set too high, Tommy. No matter how good you are, or how good you become, you never let yourself reach the bar. Understand?"

Tommy shook his head no.

Coach D. exhaled and turned in his seat a little more. He was an animated teacher and being cramped in a seat on a bus where he couldn't wave his arms wasn't helping him get his point across. "It's not a bad thing. Okay? I want to say that. Too many kids get to a certain point in their abilities and think they've made it, but not you. You're never satisfied, always hungry. If more of my kids had your work ethic ... well, now that I think about it, if they had your work ethic, they'd have been grabbed up by programs like Maryland. But Tommy, do you want to know what your greatest weakness is?"

"Yeah." Tommy rubbed his leg and sniffed.

"Your biggest weakness is also your biggest strength. You're never satisfied."

Tommy cinched his brow.

Coach D. continued, "It's good to have high standards, high expectations for yourself, Tommy. But you have to learn to accept that every once in a while, you won't reach them. You might have a stellar game against an All American now and then, but not every time. It's okay to come in second sometimes. It's how you learn."

"Yeah," Tommy scoffed. "I learned I can't go left as good as I thought."

"No, you learned you've got to protect the ball better against a kid with a quick first step. Get your right arm out there like a guard if you go left. Use your left arm if you go right. Make your defender work. That's what you learned."

Tommy nodded. "Okay."

"And you should've learned that you can't win them all. Let me ask you something." Coach D. leaned back in his seat. "Why do you think I scheduled so many money games against big programs so early in the year?"

"To punish us?"

Coach D. grinned. "No. To get you ready. To play you against the best talent out there so you'll learn from each game. So that when conference play begins, you'll hopefully be a leg up over other Big South players. So by the time we play the conference tournament, our team will play at another level. Maybe not the top level, but a level above our other conference teams. We win that tournament, and we go to the NC-Double-As. And that's the goal, isn't it? The final goal? To play the big game on TV against a bigger opponent, and then, in that game, play the best you've ever played. That's why we play Georgia Tech and NC State this year. Why we play Richmond and Syracuse. Why we played Maryland and got our butts handed to us."

The coach, animated now, turned in his seat toward Tommy, facing him full-on with his hands active. "Tommy, you've got a leg up on every kid on this bus. Do you know what that is?"

Tommy shook his head. "Good looks?"

Coach D. grinned. "Besides that. Tommy, you've already grown up. Because of what's happened in your life, you've already taken on more responsibility than these kids will see in the next ten years. You've got a business, and you're already supporting a family. These guys behind us?" Coach tilted his head. "Their parents are sending *them* money. You're doing the opposite."

Tommy hadn't thought of his situation like that. It was just the way things turned out.

"I know you're playing because I gave you a scholarship, but why are you really playing? Why'd you play as a walk-on?"

Tommy thought for a second. He wanted to come up with a good answer, one that impressed the coach. But he couldn't. He shrugged and said, "It's fun."

Coach D. smiled and relaxed in his seat. "See, you've already got it figured out and don't know it yet. You're so hard on yourself sometimes you forget it's just a game. You play for the fun of it, for the love of the game. You know I interviewed for the coaching position at Florida?"

"Really?"

"Yeah. I could've been the head coach for the Florida Gators. They offered it to me, you know." He leaned closer. "The money was amazing. The salary alone was triple what I make here. Add in the licensing bumps and coaching camps and promotional perks, and it was more money than God himself makes." He shook his head. "But it's different at a school like that. Kids are there to get to the next level. You're not fighting to keep them in school to get their degree, you're fighting to keep them from going to the pros too early. They're not there for the education—oh, some of them are, but those are the exceptions. It's a stepping stone for them."

Coach D. fiddled with a folder he'd kept in his lap. "You know, when I was the head coach at Iowa, one of our kids woke me up. He was losing his father to ALS. You know what that is? Lou Gehrig's disease?" He closed his eyes and took a deep breath. "It's awful. You slowly waste away, losing control of all your bodily functions until at last, even your lungs won't suck in air by themselves.

"This kid had mediocre talent, but it was his attitude that drew me to him. No matter what happened—win, lose, good game, bad game—he was always in the most amazing mood. So one day I pulled him aside after practice. I'd just made them run wind sprints after an excruciating loss on last-second free throws, and I was wearing them out and making them shoot free throws, you know, to get them used to it.

"And here was Andre Brunson, smiling as if he'd just hit the lottery, joking around with his teammates, none of whom were in a joking mood. So I pulled him aside, and I asked him, why? Why was he always in a good mood? Why was he, no matter what had happened, always smiling, always peppy?"

Coach D. was grinning now. "You know what this eighteen-year-old kid said to me? Here he was about 5-10, no more than a buck-fifty fully clothed, biggest white teeth you ever seen because that's what you usually saw on him, his teeth. You know what he said?

"He said, 'You don't know, Coach? 'Cause it's just a game. My dad loves to see me play. It makes his day.' I told him I'd never seen his dad make it to a single game. That's when he said his dad had ALS. It wasn't evident when we were recruiting Andre, but it had gotten worse, so bad he couldn't go in public because he couldn't control his bowels anymore. At forty-seven, the man wore diapers."

Coach D. bit his lip. "This kid's telling me about his dad wearing diapers. Then he tells me how his uncle comes to every game, every single game, and tapes them with his camcorder. Tapes every game so his dad can watch them."

Coach D. cleared his throat. "So you see? Here's this kid telling me his dad watched all his games, wearing diapers, pausing the games when the diapers needed changing. He's telling me it's just a game, it's just a game ... but it made his dad happy. You see?"

Tommy nodded slowly. "I think so, Coach."

"No, you don't. Hell, I don't know if I do anymore. But what I'm saying is, Andre played because it made him happy to make his dad happy. It was just a game to Andre, but to his dad, it was so much more. It was a reason to live. Andre's dad had never been good enough to play, but Andre was, and that was enough for his dad. Look, I'm not telling this right. Let me just say, I didn't take the job at Florida because the kind of kids I wanted to coach ... I wanted to coach more Andres, you know. Kids that played because it was a game. And not a job. Kids that played for the right reasons. Basketball purists."

The look on Tommy's face must have said it all because Coach D. shook his head and sighed. "Just do me a favor, Tommy. Don't be so hard on yourself. You're here for your degree, and all things considered, basketball is just a stupid little game. Have fun with it. Take as much joy away from the losses as you do the wins because in the grand scheme of things, instead of running up and down a hardwood court throwing a bouncy ball through a hoop, you could be at home hooked up to a respirator shitting yourself every thirty minutes." Coach paused. "Now go back to your seat and listen to your Walkman or whatever. I'm losing my voice."

Tommy said thanks and left. Coach Fulton leaned forward and peeked around the seat. He said, "That's the craziest story I ever heard."

"Yeah, well. I never told it before."

"I didn't know you got offered the job at Florida."

Coach D. shook his head. "Never even interviewed for it. You kidding me? I only had two winning seasons out of five at Iowa. Why would they want me?"

Coach Fulton grinned and shook his head. "The part about Andre and the diapers. That was good. How'd you come up with that?"

Coach Denton turned completely around in his seat and faced his assistant. "It was *my* dad in diapers."

Chapter 38

The school year flew by. UNCG lost its money games to the big programs but gave a scare to Syracuse when UNCG led by four at halftime. Syracuse surged out to a six-point lead early in the second half and never relinquished, winning the game by ten points after the final minute became a free throw shooting contest.

But the conference games were more even-suited. UNCG finished second in the Big South just behind Charleston Southern University—formerly known as Baptist—who UNCG had played numerous times in both of their pre-Division I years.

In the fall, Tommy made the dean's list for the first time since he'd begun college. His courses in the spring semester were going just as well.

Homer Parsons took care of the store as if it were his own. As Tommy's basketball season had kicked in, Homer took on more responsibility. He made deposits and stayed late some days to lock up. He worked with the distributor and reorganized the stockroom for better flow.

One Saturday during the season, Laura's mom stopped by while Tommy was manning the register. Tommy put away the paper he was working on and asked about Laura. Ms. Novak told him Laura was graduating this year with honors.

"She was always smart," Tommy replied.

"How about you?" Ms. Novak asked.

"Well, I took last year off. You know. Went part-time. So I won't graduate until next year."

"How is your dad, by the way? I hear he's better."

"He thinks he's Bob Villa now." Tommy laughed. "He practically lives out in his shop."

"I've seen some of his work. It's really beautiful."

"Oh yeah?"

Ms. Novak nodded. "You know my cousin, Phyllis Hancock? He built her a beautiful set of side tables for her living room. Best furniture in her whole house."

Tommy smiled and waved at Mr. Peterson when he entered.

Ms. Novak continued, "I came in a few weeks ago and Homer was here. He's such a nice man."

"Yeah. Homer's been great. Without him, I don't know what I'd do."

"You wouldn't be able to put up twelve points a game."

"Huh?" Tommy looked up.

"Isn't that your average? Twelve points, eight assists?"

Tommy stared. "Yeah, how'd you—"

"You didn't know there was a write-up in the paper today?" Ms. Novak smiled. "That's what made me remember I needed some eggs and bacon, seeing your name in there, so I thought I'd come see if the star was working today."

Tommy blushed and nudged a pen on the counter. "I'm not a star ..." He hesitated. "What else did it say?"

Ms. Novak grinned. "Oh, it gave your game averages. Assists, rebounds. All that. Told how you took last year off, red-shirted I think they said? And how you helped out the family business. How you're back, and your impact is felt. That kind of stuff."

"Really?"

She nodded. "It was very flattering."

Tommy continued to redden and—eager to divert attention from himself—offered Ms. Novak a muffin. She began to say *no thanks* until he opened the tin and the aroma wafted out.

She balked, craning her neck, saying, "What kind are they?"

"Oatmeal bran with cinnamon. Mom made a batch for my dad, but she had some left over." Tommy pushed the tin across the counter. "There's no way I can eat them all. You'd be doing me a favor."

Ms. Novak snatched one up. "If you insist."

"And they're laxative-free."

Ms. Novak chuckled. "Well then, how can I resist?"

Chapter 39

The end of the school year approached, and the unspoken tension grew between Tommy and Leigh Ann. This was Leigh Ann's senior year, and her plans to go to law school hadn't changed.

"We need to talk," Leigh Ann said. It was a Friday, a week before classes ended and exams began.

"There's nothing to talk about," Tommy replied.

"Yes, there is." Leigh Ann paused. "I'll come by your dorm room after my two o'clock class."

Tommy shrugged. "Whatever."

For his final year, Tommy had moved to campus. He roomed with another point guard, Derrick Thompkins, in the basketball dorm right across the street from the gym. It was Hinshaw, the dorm beside Leigh Ann's in the Quad.

Leigh Ann arrived at five minutes after three. Tommy was looking out the window, watching two guys throw football on the grassy expanse of the Quad. He offered her something to drink. She refused and sat on his bed.

Tommy sat beside her and stared out the window. The room was on the second floor so all Tommy could see from his seat was a huge oak and the dorm across the way.

"Tommy," Leigh Ann said. "Look at me."

"What is there to say?"

"It doesn't have to be like this."

Tommy stared out the window. Two girls were laughing somewhere below.

"We knew this was coming, Tommy. I'm going to law school."

"But in Chicago?" He turned toward her, eyes rimmed in red.

"It's where I got in."

"You got in at Duke, too."

"But Chicago was my dream school. Duke was my backup. Chicago's where I've always wanted to go."

Tommy huffed. "That's the first time I've ever heard of Duke as a backup school."

"Chicago's law school is highly respected. You graduate from there, and you're practically guaranteed a job."

Tommy turned to the window again.

"Don't do this." Leigh Ann put her head on his back, and he shook it off. She bit her lip. "Don't do this Tommy."

"Do what?" he mumbled.

"Don't shut me out."

Tommy laughed and twisted around. "*Me?* Shut *you* out? You're moving to Chicago. You call that including me in your life?"

"That's not fair."

"You're damn right it's not fair." He shook off her hand again and stood. "You keep saying we knew this day was coming, but you want to know what I thought would happen?"

Leigh Ann shrank at Tommy's sudden outburst.

"I thought you'd get into Duke—which you did—and then you'd go there, and we could continue to see each other. Duke's only about forty-five minutes away. It's not that far. But Chicago? Chicago? Chicago might as well be on the other side of the country."

"Tommy." Leigh Ann was in tears now. "I love you."

"Well, you sure have a funny way of showing it. Most people I know who love each other actually try to stay together. They do it different in Ohio?"

"Tommy. Please." Leigh Ann was reaching for him, tears streaming down her face. "You think this is easy for me?"

Tommy still pulled away. "Dropping out of school to run my family's store wasn't easy either, but I found a way to do both." Tommy stood and walked to the window. He'd been preparing himself for this moment all day. He was hurt and angry but determined not to cry. There was no point.

Suddenly, he wheeled around. "I love you so much, Leigh Ann. I thought we'd get married one day. I was already picturing our house, our children. You're practically part of the family."

The last outburst did it. Tommy felt the warm tears trickling down his cheeks.

"Damn it, Leigh Ann." Tommy sunk to the floor, his back to the wall, and hung his head as the tears flowed.

Leigh Ann leapt to him and enclosed him in her arms. She held him tight as if she could squeeze the tears into happiness.

Tommy blubbered on. "I had it all planned out. Where we'd live, where our kids would go to school, how we'd make it the next few years with you in Durham."

"Oh, Tommy." She held him for a moment, her tears dripping into his hair. "I'm ... I'm not ready for any of that. Not yet. I still want to travel the world before I settle down."

Tommy lifted his head. "Travel? I can't travel, I have too much responsibility to just take off."

"I've told you my dream is to travel while I practice law."

"But I thought ..."

"You thought I'd grow out of it?" She shook her head. "That's why I want to specialize in international business law. To travel. Tommy, I'm not even sure I want to live in the U.S. ever again." She was smiling now. "There's so much world out there to see, so much to do ... that's why I wanted to go to college away from Ohio."

"Huh?"

"I got offered a scholarship to play tennis for Ohio State also, but I've lived in Ohio. I don't want to live there again. That's why I came to North Carolina. Now I want to live in Chicago, in a big city."

"Why didn't you tell me any of this?"

"I did, Tommy, I did. I told you lots of times, but you heard what you wanted to hear. I told you how I wanted to see the world. I told you all the places I wanted to visit. All the wonders out there; the Parthenon, Moscow, the Great Wall, Machu Picchu, the Pyramids."

"I said I wanted to see the Pyramids. I said I wanted to travel, too."

"But Tommy, you want to go when you retire. I want to go when I can still hike Machu Picchu without having to take a nap halfway up."

Tommy snorted and wiped his face. He looked into her eyes. "You really want to travel like that?"

"Yes, I do. More than anything else in the world. And I figure international business law will give me the opportunity to travel to all kinds of places while still making the kind of money I need to do it first class. Plus"—she smiled—"I'll get to write off all the expenses. It'll be like traveling for free."

Leigh Ann kissed Tommy on the lips, then caressed his face. "We're totally different, Tommy. You're a planner. You can see exactly what your life ten years down the road looks like; you set your goals, plan how to get there, and then, you do whatever it takes to accomplish those goals. You're amazing like that, but me? Looking more than four years ahead suffocates me."

She shuddered. "The very thought that I know where I'll be ten years from now is ... unthinkable. It's unnatural. I want to be able to pick up and go at a moment's notice. Be living in Italy one day, then in Brazil the next, then in China a month later."

Leigh Ann sighed and laid her head against the wall.

"I do love you, Tommy," she said. "I love you more than I've ever loved anyone before. And maybe more than I'll ever love anyone in my life, but we have different paths, and that saddens me." She kissed his cheek. "I tried not to fall for you so hard but sometimes ..."

She nuzzled his neck as he said, "I'm gonna miss you."

"I'm gonna miss you, too." Her breath was warm on his skin. "But I know something, Tommy Chandler. You're gonna make some girl very happy one day. And she'll be the luckiest girl in the world."

Tommy exhaled with effort. "Sure. Maybe."

"I know it, Tommy. I know it."

Chapter 40

That summer, Tommy and Leigh Ann called each other at least once a week. Tommy even drove up to visit her in Chicago one weekend, and she showed him around. "It's a nice place to visit," he told his mom once he'd returned. "But I wouldn't want to live there. Too many people."

She understood. She'd been to D.C. once and felt the same way. Crime was rampant, people living on top of each other, roads congested. "It's no way to live," Helen told him.

On July Fourth, Gene Chandler finally sold the store to Tommy, the proceeds to be paid monthly from future profits. Interest-free.

Helen had put the pressure on him. She knew that as long as the store was in Gene's name, he would always be tethered to it in some way. So one night, as Gene was feeling particularly rambunctious, she asked him to sell the store to their son. Be rid of it. For good.

"Can't we talk about this later?" he pleaded, grabbing for her.

"No, not later. Now."

Gene had stripped down to his boxers, and Helen wore a piece of lingerie he'd been trying to get her to wear since he gave it to her the previous Christmas. It was just a simple silk teddy, but it was way more revealing than her normal nightgowns.

"But, right now?" He placed his hands on her waist and pulled her toward him.

"Yes, right now. It's practically his already. What with all the changes he's made."

"Well, there you go." Gene kissed her neck and began pulling the teddy up her waist.

Helen grabbed his hand and halted him. "No, I want you to promise."

Frustrated, Gene said, "I thought we'd save it for a graduation thing."

Helen smiled. "That's nice, but that's a whole year away."

Gene squeezed Helen's behind; she yelped and laughed, but pushed him away.

"Fine. Whatever," he said. "This summer. That make you happy?"

"Yes. It does."

They kissed, and three weeks later, after constant badgering, on July Fourth, the store changed hands.

Tommy was stunned when he signed the paperwork. It wasn't until later that night, after he'd caught the fireworks downtown with some of the guys from the team, that it hit him. He was a business owner.

He owned his own business before he even owned a home. It was a high he'd never felt.

The first thing Tommy did was incorporate as a Subchapter S, something his father had fought him on the last few years, even when Tommy made the case about personal liability and tax savings. "I want it kept simple," Gene had argued. "But this *is* simple," Tommy responded back.

Now Tommy made all the decisions himself. It was exhilarating and at the same time, frightening. There was no safety net, no do-overs. His decisions would make or break the store.

Tommy analyzed his inventory reports and decided to do away with some products, cutting down the number of brands available on some foods. After some wrangling, he was able to move half the storage out to the floor, and after another month, he emptied the storage room altogether.

That was when he approached his dad.

"I want to sell your furniture."

"What?"

Gene was adding the finishing touches to a bureau dresser and raised his head.

"I said I want to sell your furniture."

Gene straightened. "You want to what?"

"You heard me."

And Gene had. Gene set the stain brush down on his workbench and picked up his coffee mug. His mind was reeling. The store was one thing. But his furniture was an extension of himself. He frowned.

Tommy sighed. "I figure I can set you up a show area in the storage room—"

"The storage room?"

"Yeah, I've cleaned it out, and I'm not using it for storage anymore. I cut out some of the items that weren't selling and instead of replacing them on the floor with new stuff, I'm just using that shelf space to hold the extra stock. So I don't need the storage room for storage anymore."

"And you want to put my furniture in there? The pieces I make? These?" Gene swept his arm in an arc.

"Yes, Dad. Your furniture. Chandler Exclusives."

Gene leaned back against the workbench and sipped his coffee. "You don't have to do that because I sold you the store."

"That's not why I want to do it." Tommy paused. "I think we can both make some money."

Gene set the coffee mug down. "We?"

"Yeah. I figure a twenty percent consignment fee is fair."

"Twenty?" Gene's voice raised. "Twenty percent of my furniture? That's robbery!"

"Twenty percent is fair, dad. Most everything in the store is upwards of a forty percent mark-up. I figure an eighty-twenty split is a pretty good deal for you, and it works for me because it makes use of space in the store that's not currently making any money."

Gene shook his head, snorting. Disbelieving.

"And there's one other stipulation I'd make," Tommy said. "I'd want an exclusive on Chandler Exclusives. You can't sell it anywhere else, or sell it yourself."

"What?" Gene was picking up his mug for another sip and slammed it to the table, spilling coffee onto the dresser. He made no move to clean it up.

Tommy continued, "I can't have anyone cutting me on my price. Somebody could see a dresser at the store, then come straight to you to buy it. And that's not very fair since it was my valuable space that actually sold it."

"So what you're really saying is you want twenty percent of my business? That's what you're asking for."

Tommy scratched his leg. "I hadn't looked at it that way." He glanced around the shop. "Let me ask you something. That buffet you just finished right there." He pointed. "The one with the bubbly glass in the doors. How much do you want for that?"

"You interested?"

"Dad. How much?"

"Oh, I don't know. The materials cost me ..."

"If I came in the shop right now with my wallet open and told you I wanted that piece, and I was going to take it out right now. How much?"

"Four hundred."

"Wrong."

"Wrong?" Gene finally wiped the coffee off his hand. "What do you mean, wrong?"

"You're undervaluing it. I could sell it for six hundred. Easy. And if I sold it for six, my commission would be one twenty ... giving you four-eighty. Eighty more dollars than if you'd sold it yourself. Plus, during the time you'd have been dealing with a person, you could have been building, making more pieces, which means more money. Besides, dealing with people is stressful. Wouldn't it be easier to just do what you love? Build?"

Gene knocked back the rest of his coffee. He stepped into the office and poured another cup, then stared out into the shop through the Plexiglas window. He took a sip and came back out to Tommy. "Ten percent."

"Twenty."

"Ten."

"Dad—"

"You know how many loaves of bread you'd have to sell to make a hundred bucks?"

Tommy smiled. His dad, still a businessman.

"Fifteen," Tommy countered. "And I'll get Brant to design you a cutout logo to spray paint on the back of each piece with the store's phone number."

When they shook on it, their eyes never left one another.

The following week, Tommy yanked the coarse brown paper off the old barbershop's large front window for the first time in more than twenty years. He paid an artist to design a logo and paint it on the outside of the same window. His dad used his jigsaw to cut out the image from a thin piece of veneer and sprayed it in black on the backs or bottoms of all his pieces.

Chandler Exclusives was officially born when Tommy and Gene lugged in a set of nightstands, two different-sized dressers, three styles of sitting chairs, a rocking chair, two buffets, and a sideboard. During that week, Tommy had bought five vintage lamps at a secondhand store and set them on various pieces of furniture. He added a few green plants from The Oasis and two large paintings of the North Carolina mountains to fill out the room. At night, he would leave the lamps on and the furniture would sell itself through the big plate glass window.

The first week, Tommy sold the rocking chair, one of the buffets, and the pair of nightstands, and took a special order for a dining room table based on an old black and white picture Mr. Hayden brought in, saying it was his Great Grandpa's, and he wanted one just like it.

Chandler Exclusives was doing better than he'd ever expected.

Chapter 41

Two months later, during Fall Break, Nick Muller stopped by the store and surprised Tommy. It was shortly after lunch, and Nick popped in wearing a shirt and tie, a big grin on his face.

"Excuse me, can I get some help over here?" he said.

Tommy looked up from the furniture catalog he was scanning and laughed. He hopped off his stool and grabbed Nick's outstretched hand. "What's up, man?"

"Oh, nothing much."

"Nothing much? Look at you dressed like a million bucks."

Nick waved a hand. "This old thing? It's Casual Day."

Tommy laughed. "I heard you got a cushy job."

"Yep. Arthur Anderson. Can you believe it? I'm a consultant who's never done a damn thing to consult on."

"So they basically pay you to look good."

"They pay me *insanely* to look good." He twirled. "And do I look good or what?"

Tommy rolled his eyes. "What are you doing in here?"

"Are you kidding? I came by to see my old friend. They've got me in Greensboro for the next month or so, then I'm on to a state contract in Raleigh with the Department of Corrections. Anyway, I decided to take a two-hour lunch break today, see if you wanted to head up the road and grab something."

Tommy sucked in air through his teeth. "I can't. I'm the only one here right now. I can't go anywhere."

"Sure you can," Tommy's mom said; she'd come in through the back. "Go take a break. I'll cover the store."

Tommy turned to her, smiling, shaking his head. "I smell a conspiracy in the air."

Nick sniffed. "I smell something else." He pointed with a mischievous grin. "What is that?"

"Oh, you mean this?" Tommy indicated his mom's carrot cake. It was going to be his lunch while he thumbed the catalog. "This is for paying customers and employees."

Helen had slid behind the counter and slapped Tommy's hand as he hovered over the cake like a *Price is Right* showgirl. She said, "That's my carrot cake with raisins and mangoes. You can have some when you get back."

"Is that a cream cheese layer?" Nick asked, leaning forward.

Helen waved him away. "Go on now, it'll be here when you return." She set a silver dome over the cake.

"Alright bud," Nick said, straightening. "No excuse now. Wings and beer on me."

"Wings and cake," Tommy's mom corrected.

Tommy grinned and shrugged. "You heard the woman. Wings and cake."

When Nick ordered a beer for himself, he said, "What? She's not *my* mom."

They were at Ham's, sitting in a booth near a window. The clientele was a mix of college students and young professionals. The TVs were set to ESPN and ESPN2.

THE WALK-ON 263

"This place has barely changed," Nick said, straining to look around. "Except for all the UNCG stuff on the walls now. That's new." He looked at Tommy. "How's that feel?"

"How's what feel?"

"Being a basketball star?"

Tommy laughed hard. "It's UNCG. Half the people on campus don't even know we have a basketball team. And the half that do are surprised we play teams like Wake and State. They don't even know we're Division I."

"Still, man. You're at the beginning. In twenty years, when UNCG wins something big, they'll do a reunion and bring back all the old guys. Probably have some alumni game for charity, and you'll be leading the team. One of the original stars."

Tommy was shaking his head. "Yeah, right. You have an active imagination. They pay you for that, too?"

"It's a package deal."

They ordered buffalo wings and chips with ranch dressing and talked about old times.

"Remember when Angel had that birthday party, and we played spin the bottle?" Nick said, sipping his beer. "I kissed Kim Fleming that night. Full-on lips and all."

Tommy nodded.

"I wonder what she's doing right now? You ever think about stuff like that?"

"She's going to nursing school at ECU."

Nick set his beer down.

"What?" Tommy shrugged. "Mrs. Fleming comes in the store. I know what everyone's doing."

Nick laughed. "So Chandler's is the hub of social knowledge in your little corner of the world? You got all the dirt, don't you?"

"Good dirt and bad dirt. I don't have a choice."

Nick leaned close. "So what's Laura up to right now?"

Tommy started to answer, but their waitress brought the wings and chips. Tommy thanked her, and Nick watched her walk away. Nick turned back to Tommy, saying, "Well?"

"She's moved back home."

"And?"

"She's getting her Masters."

"At UNCG?"

Tommy nodded and dug into his wings.

"Hold on," Nick said. "You're a single man now, and Laura's back in town ... she single?"

Tommy tried not to grin. "Her mom made that very clear."

Nick kicked him under the table. "Oh man, her mom's in your corner? You can't go wrong. You gotta go for it."

Tommy scrunched his face and said, "I don't know, man. I got a lot going on right now. Plus, I already tried that once. Didn't work out so well."

"Man, you're crazy. You're both different people now. In high school, girls go for the flashy guys, the guys that treat them like crap, the Patrick Harts in this world. But once they grow up, they give up looking at the bad guys. They look for the providers, the stable guys, the good guys. You ever notice how nerds always end up with the hot chicks?"

"You calling me a nerd now?"

Nick laughed. "You gotta have good grades to be a nerd."

"Hey. I didn't have bad grades."

"You didn't have good ones either. What I'm saying is, things are different now. You're both older with different experiences. You've both had your hearts broken a few times and that changes people, wakes them up. Matures them."

Tommy thought about Leigh Ann and the way her laugh always put him in a good mood.

They ate for a while before Nick said, "Speaking of Patrick Hart, you hear the news about him?"

Tommy nodded.

"They say he's as good as new. That torn tendon early last year healed up better than they expected."

"Yeah, that's great."

Nick laughed. "I hear Coach K had to beg for him to be redshirted so he could play this year."

"Nah. His parents probably bought him an exception. It'll be known as the Hart Rule from now on."

Nick shook his head. "Guys like him have it so easy. And it never changes, does it? I hear he wants to go into politics."

"Figures. He'll buy his way into office like everybody else."

"Hey," Nick said. "You guys don't play Duke this year do you?"

Tommy shook his head and bit into a wing.

"It's a shame. I'd like to see you go up against him now."

Tommy's blood had warmed just thinking of Patrick Hart. He'd like to go up against him, too. The memory of that day behind the school was still fresh. Tommy had a feeling it would always be. Memories like that had a way of never fading into the background.

Chapter 42

UNCG blew through the year under Tommy's leadership. They dropped a two-point game at NC State that was UNCG's up until the final minute when a flagrant foul was called on hot-shooting freshman, Skeet Harzell. Coach D. came off the bench so fast, the nearest ref had to walk him back so he didn't get a technical.

But the UNCG Spartans proved themselves a week later, routing Georgia Tech in Atlanta by fifteen points. Although the Yellow Jackets possessed a bigger team, UNCG outrebounded and outplayed them. A ten-point halftime lead was stretched out further by Harzell's five second-half three-pointers. Despite Tommy's twelve points and eight assists, his dad chastised him for his sloppy play.

Maryland escaped with a hard-fought six-point win but not before Tommy recorded his first twenty-point game of the season. According to Gene, the Terps won because Tommy was a ball-hog.

UNCG dispatched their next three non-conference foes with little effort: Austin Peay, Akron, and Old Dominion. Then they stole a last-second win at SMU, fueled by Tommy's defense. He deflected an inbounds pass that ended up in Alvy Hanes's capable hands. Alvy immediately threw the ball down court to a speeding Tommy Chandler who caught the pass and laid it in without a single dribble.

After securing victories against Davidson and College of Charleston,

UNCG traveled to West Virginia for their last non-conference game and came back home with a solid ten-point win over a tough Big East program.

Big South Conference play began with UNCG rated forty-eighth nationally in the RPI rankings. They were 8-2.

Against Radford, Tommy set a team record of twelve steals in a single game. At Liberty University, he set another team record, this time with fourteen assists. Conference foes had no answer for a 6-4 point guard with his quickness and ball smarts. Captain of the team, Tommy led them through a comfortable schedule of contests, emerging at the end of the season with a perfect conference schedule.

With a 22-2 record at the end of the regular season and several wins over quality teams, UNCG saw its RPI ranking rise to thirty-nine, virtually unheard of for a young team from one of the weakest conferences in the nation.

The starting five—Tommy Chandler, Skeet Harzell, Manny Cuthrell, Alvy Hanes, and Scott McManness—combined to set nine different team records over the course of the season, including Harzell's fifteen treys over Towson State and Alvy Hanes's eight blocks at UNC Asheville.

The team entered the conference tourney ranked first, playing a battered Winthrop team who'd began the season strong but faltered after two of its strongest players were lost to injuries. The thirty-point win set the mood for the Spartans' march through the rest of the tournament. Tommy's dad said they should have won by forty, easily; they played like lazy kids.

Coastal Carolina, the conference champs in 1991 and 1993, was having another great year, despite accusations of academic fraud. Rumors were that the NCAA had opened a full investigation into the program. But after dispatching UNC Asheville in the first round with relative ease, the Chanticleers went no further.

UNCG plowed over them with a twenty-three-point win; Tommy recorded twelve points, five assists, four rebounds, and three steals. Gene made sure to point out Tommy's two turnovers and missed free throw.

Liberty University, a private college founded by religious icon Jerry Falwell, is nestled snugly in the little mountain town of Lynchburg, Virginia. Housing an impressive basketball facility, it was a natural choice for the Big South tournament.

As such, the final game between top-ranked UNCG and second-ranked Liberty felt more like a home game for the Flames and an away game for the Spartans.

Liberty began the game hot, hitting six of its first seven shots, and before Tommy could calm his team down, the Flames commanded a 12-4 lead. But under his command, UNCG launched a 10-2 run, capped by an alley-oop dunk from Tommy to Alvy Hanes. UNCG tied the game at 14.

Two straight treys, courtesy of Skeet Harzell, and a driving lay-up by Tommy after a steal put them up 22-16. The Flames coach called a timeout, but it didn't matter; the rest of the first half was all Spartans.

By the time the break came, UNCG was up comfortably, 42-32.

But the Flames began the second half in the same fashion they began the game, and under the crowd's frenzied urging, they closed the gap to tie the game at 44-44.

Liberty wasn't impressed by UNCG's RPI ranking or their win-loss record or their upsets over ACC foe Georgia Tech and Big East's West Virginia. They were only concerned with winning this one game; the champ would represent the Big South Conference in the NCAA

Tournament.

Liberty opened the lead back up to four, but Skeet Harzell answered with a three from the far corner. A dunk from the Flames' Nigerian center prompted a trey from Tommy and the score was tied again.

The teams continued like this, back and forth, until the final minute. Tommy brought the ball down after a Liberty miss, and UNCG held the ball in a four-corners-like offense until there were only seven seconds on the shot clock.

The team spread out so Tommy could take his man one-on-one to the basket. Tommy was shooting well that night—6 for 8 including two three-pointers—so it was natural to have the ball in his hands. Liberty expected it too, but each man had to stay with his defensive assignment because Tommy had also dished out seven assists during the game.

Tommy drove right, dribbled through his legs and faked left, then went down awkward on the hardwood. His left foot slid in a puddle just below the free throw line, and he splayed out in an unnatural split. He grabbed his leg as the ball bounced right into the hands of Liberty's point guard, who, with six seconds left, drove down the court lightning fast to lay it in with a second on the clock.

Tommy struggled to his feet as the ball dropped through the hoop.

Liberty won 72-71.

Coach D. raised hell about the puddle, which had been wiped up several times during the course of the game—there was a steady leak in the domed ceiling fed by a constant rainstorm. The contest was televised on ESPN2, and the slow-motion footage of Tommy's fall was replayed all the next day, complete with graphic pointers highlighting the puddle and a footage montage of the different times the ball boys had wiped it up during the game.

Tommy's injury was superficial. Within ten minutes, he was walking normally; the only thing permanently injured was his ego. He couldn't believe his luck. They had this game. It was theirs to lose. And they had.

He had.

Everyone on the team patted him on the back, asking if he was okay, and told him it was just a thing, man, just a thing. There was nothing he did wrong, nothing he could have done differently. It was just a thing.

Tommy knew that, knew it wasn't his fault, but it didn't matter. He'd let his team down. Their dream season had ended at 24-3 although odds were, they'd probably get an NIT invitation and end up playing some team like Georgetown or St. Johns in the first round.

But there was to be no NCAA tourney for UNCG. No invitation to the Big Dance. No Cinderella run for the little college in Greensboro.

All his dad said that night was, "You shouldn't have tried to get so damn fancy."

Chapter 43

The team's mood picked up the next day when, right after the replayed puddle-and-fall footage, ESPN announced UNCG would be one of those bubble teams that might get into the NCAA tournament through an at-large bid. They had played well against quality opponents throughout the year, their only losses coming to two other Top 50 teams—and of course, the tourney final loss to Liberty. Add to that, the announcer said, the wins over Georgia Tech and West Virginia, and you had yourself a true mid-major bubble team.

UNCG's strength-of-schedule was respectable and their RPI held at thirty-nine, even after the final loss, because Liberty had a strong season also.

The team's fate would lie in other tournament outcomes. College of Charleston had won the TAAC Conference tourney as expected, but Old Dominion had edged out the first-place contender in the CAA, George Mason. George Mason was another mid-major with a 20-win season and quality victories under its belt.

Hampton took the MEAC and Davidson, the Southern Conference. In all, the mid-major conference tourneys wouldn't matter as much as how well the mediocre teams did in the power conferences.

The following week was saturated with bubble-team speculation. Every sports show under the sun focused on them: UNCG, NC State,

Butler, Maryland, Iowa, Oklahoma State, Syracuse, Indiana. Some shows included West Virginia, others Drexel or UNLV.

But all of them included UNCG, the little team in the heart of ACC country, who, in their third year of Division I athletics, had put together a legitimate Top 50 team under the leadership of a former Division II walk-on point guard, a kid who had once been a high school teammate of Duke's star point guard, Patrick Hart. The story was picked up everywhere, even on non-sports shows.

Tommy Chandler, a walk-on who had taken a year off for "family reasons," and then returned to a full-blown athletic scholarship, ranked fourth in the nation in assists-per-game. His dean's list achievement was usually mentioned, and one news outlet had even announced he'd once dated the coach's daughter in high school.

The Greensboro News and Record wrote a feature story that Thursday; it included a huge picture of Tommy behind the counter at Chandler's, a basketball in one hand and a loaf of bread in the other. The story and picture covered the front third of the sports section.

It seemed like Tommy's entire family called him that week. Other students gave him high-fives as he went to class, then stared and smiled at him once class began. There was a full-page write-up in The Carolinian, the student newspaper, that featured a small profile on all the players, along with some generic information on that year's bubble teams.

The guys on the team ribbed Tommy about having dated the coach's daughter; he'd told no one.

As the week progressed and the power conferences held their tournaments, bubble speculation grew more focused. NC State goofed early in the ACC tournament with an embarrassing twenty-two point loss to Florida State. According to most sports announcers, this dropped them out of consideration. Maryland, however, made it to the finals before UNC edged them out in a hard-fought contest. This more or less pushed them to the top of the bubble list, and ahead of UNCG, a team they'd beaten during the year.

Just like every other basketball season, Tommy was glued to the TV coverage during tournament weekend. But this year he had a vested interest in the outcomes. He wondered if he might get ulcers. On UNCG's tourney hopes, Gene Chandler told his son not to hold his breath.

By the following Sunday night, several teams had been eliminated from bubble contention, while others had been added, the teams having not done as well in their tourneys as expected. The Spartans gathered at Coach D.'s house that night for the tourney selection party, prepared to be exhilarated or disappointed as one entity. CBS had a camera crew there to capture the moment for the whole nation.

Helen Chandler made the team orange-vanilla cookies she iced with black lines so they looked like basketballs. The coach was chomping on one when the cameras went live and Dick Vitale asked him how he felt his chances were.

"We've got a talented team," Coach said, lowering the cookie to his knee. "It would be a shame for the boys to have such a great season not be rewarded with a trip to the NC-double-As."

Dick Vitale replied, "Coach, I've gotta say, you guys are Awesome Baby!" Vitale fluttered his hands around as he talked. "I've nominated all you guys to my All-Rip Van Winkle Team. I mean, you're the Darlings of the tournament and you've not even gotten in yet." He was getting more animated the more he talked. "You are totally Prime Time and I think it would be a shame, a damn shame, if the Spartans weren't invited to the Big Ticket. In fact, the only people who wouldn't be upset if you were left out are the other bubble teams."

Coach D. smiled and said thanks, and the camera turned off.

Dickie V continued to talk to the other announcers about UNCG's year, the Prime Time wins over Georgia Tech and West Virginia, the wins over the other conference tourney winners—Davidson and College of Charleston—the Knee-Knocker misses at tough ACC opponents, Maryland and NC State.

"They even routed one of my favorite sleepers, the Austin Peay Governors," he added. "And I tell you what, I'll stand on my head if the Spartans don't get in." The TV once again showed the puddle-slip footage as Vitale explained about the leak in Liberty University's dome, then said how it would be a shame if such a talented team was left out of the Big Dance because of the weather.

"They've got a Diaper Dandy in the form of sharp-shooter Skeet Harzell," he said, as footage of Skeet shooting treys appeared. "This kid shoots the area-code J!"

Everybody in Coach D.'s house oohed; the players closest to Skeet shoved him in jest.

"Then they've got a kid at the power forward position"—a slow-motion shot of Alvy Hanes dunking over Maryland's center popped up—"This kid is only a junior, and he's a beast. You see that Slam, Bam, Jam right there? You could pick him up and drop him into any program in the nation; he'd be a starter."

Alvy stood and bowed, flexing his muscles to laughs and a barrage of crumpled napkins.

"And then they have a 6-10 center." They cut to a shot of Scott McManness shooting a jump-hook. "Another junior in their first class of Division I recruits. He's a Space Eater *and* he's athletic ... a tough combination."

McManness smiled and shook his head.

"They've got senior leadership from a steady player, Manny Cuthrell, who puts up Q. T. every game. He's kind of the cool guy on the team who plays the same no matter what the score is."

Everyone in the house nodded thinking the same thing. Cuthrell didn't even smile when he heard his name mentioned on national TV.

"But I think the kid that's captured America's hearts the most," Dickie V. continued, growing calmer, "is the team's senior point guard, little Tommy Chandler."

Footage played of Tommy's dribbling, shooting, passing, running a timeout meeting.

"Here's a kid who wasn't recruited in high school because he was too small. He went to UNCG and made it as a walk-on. In the program's first year as a D-1 contender, Chandler's father had a stroke, and the kid dropped off the team to run the family store.

"He returned to full-time status the following year, and now, in his final year at school, he'll graduate with a double-major in Business and Economics. He's the Engine of the team; he's led them to a 24-3 season, and he's ranked nationally in assists and steals. He's a 3-D man ... he drives, he draws, he dishes ... but he can shoot the Trifecta too."

Vitale squared his body to the camera. "What Coach D.'s got there is a special kid. A real special kid."

Tommy was embarrassed at his life being laid out in such a fashion. The team didn't care; they ribbed him with baby-talk remarks and marriage proposals. They ran fingers through his hair and asked for autographs and bowed, repeating over and over, "We're not worthy."

Tommy took it in stride, and then the East bracket was announced. Everyone hushed.

It was no surprise; the Carolina Tar Heels were the number one team, and they played the Big South representative, Liberty. As the announcers unveiled the other teams in the bracket, everyone in the coach's house held their breath, even the camera crew. UNCG was not among the teams announced.

Maryland and Syracuse were listed as number ten and eleven seeds. Players spat out analysis of whether this was good or bad for the team. The general consensus was that since Maryland made it, UNCG had a good chance. If Maryland hadn't been invited, how could the committee justify inviting UNCG, a team Maryland had beaten.

The top of the South bracket popped on the screen next. The number one seed was Florida, playing Hampton. Georgia was listed as a nine seed which surprised the announcers—they were a bubble team that was barely under consideration. Dickie V. pointed out how well they'd done in the last half of the season and that sometimes the committee weights that more than the overall record. "After all," Vitale explained, his hands fluttering. "It's how you're playing at tourney time that makes you tourney bound, baby!"

The bottom half of the bracket flashed on the screen and the room erupted! UNC Greensboro was listed as a tenth seed, set to play seventh-seeded Vanderbilt. The winner would play the victor of number two Duke and number fifteen Middle Tennessee State.

When the announcers finally got to the match between Vanderbilt and UNCG, Dick Vitale was fixed in a goofy smile. He said, "Now here's a selection the committee can be proud of. This team, headed up by coach Robbie Denton, is the Real Deal. I'm naming them to my Bracket Busters list. All you people out there making up your brackets in the office tomorrow, be careful who you have down to win this one."

The TV switched to the video of the UNCG players exploding into cheers and high-fives with the announcers voicing over, "And there's that Spartan team in Greensboro just a few seconds ago."

They switched to an analysis of Duke versus Middle Tennessee State, and Dickie V. added, "And here's a piece of trivia. Guess who UNCG's star point guard, Tommy Chandler, played backup to as a junior in high school? That's right. Duke's senior point guard, Patrick Hart. How fun would it be if these two met each other on the court as opponents?"

The Midwest bracket graphic popped onto the TV, but no one in Coach D.'s house was paying attention anymore. Players chatted excitedly amongst themselves while the coaches huddled in a corner, planning strategy.

Tommy glanced over at Britney. She had a huge smile spread across her face. She shot him a thumbs-up, and he returned it.

He was still too numb to do anything else. Their season wasn't over.

Chapter 44

The following week, ESPN and every other news outlet was awash with NCAA news: stories of the perennial powers that always garnered the first and second seeds of the tournament; stories of the teams who'd won their conference tourneys for a second straight appearance in The Big Dance; stories of Cinderella teams; Bracket Busters who had come out of nowhere, burst onto the scene with virtually no basketball history, no famous NBA alums, no famous coaches ... schools that when their name was mentioned, people said, "Where are they?"

At the top of that list was the little team that could, UNC Greensboro. A team in their third year of Division I competition, with their seniors originally part of the Division II squad, led by a former walk-on. The school itself was over a hundred years old but didn't go coed until the sixties. And so on ...

It was the same information, rewritten and rehashed, over and over, all week long.

The team flew down to Orlando and practiced a few days before their Friday game. Coach D. said they had to focus on Vandy's point guard and big man. Don't let the point penetrate, and double-team the big man every time he touches the ball. No open shots for anyone, make good passes, use your picks, play smart.

It was no different than prep for any other game all year long.

Vandy's point guard, Avery Smith, was a sophomore student who had wrestled the starting position away six games into the season. His prowess on the court was apparent from the opening tip-off, when he snatched the ball from mid-air and blew by two Spartan players, then faked Scott McManness out of his shoes for a left-handed lay-up.

It was 10-2, Vandy, before UNCG mounted any kind of an offense. Skeet Harzell connected for a trey, then after Alvy Hanes swatted a shot, Manny Cuthrell launched the ball down court to a sprinting Tommy Chandler. Tommy elevated for a swift dunk and all of a sudden, UNCG was in the game.

The butterflies were officially squashed, and the guys had asserted themselves. This little team was there to play, and the crowd was on their side.

It was a phenomenon that occurred each and every year. As a game wore on, if the underdog was hanging in, showing its teeth, the undecided fans began pulling for them. The blocked shot and subsequent dunk had begun the changing of the tide.

Ten minutes into the first half, Alvy Hanes slammed home his own dunk, a thundering rim-shaker that began when he caught a pass at the free throw line, then used a Scott McManness pick to break free of his man. Before McManness' man could switch, Hanes was by him and in the air. The crowd went wild.

And the dunk gave UNCG its first lead, 20-18.

The half ended on a textbook play to isolate Skeet Harzell on the wing for a three-pointer. It worked beautifully, and his shot dropped through the hoop just before the buzzer sounded.

UNCG led at the half, 35-30.

Vandy surged out of the gate in the second half. For the first two minutes, they dominated the court. But then Tommy Chandler took control; on three straight possessions, he drove to the basket for lay-ups. After that, Avery Smith had to pull back and try to deny the lane, and it left Tommy enough breathing room to do what he did best, create scoring opportunities.

Tommy finished with an individual and school record of fifteen assists as UNCG topped Vandy, 83-75. Tommy's dad was as impassive during the game as every other game, and the only thing he said afterward was that he should've taken care of the ball better, there was no excuse for three turnovers.

The press embraced the Spartan Cinderella team, and in the same breath lamented on their chances against the probable winner of the next match-up, Duke. After Duke dispatched Middle Tennessee State with ease, the Tommy Chandler-Patrick Hart connection was highlighted every time the future contest was mentioned.

Chapter 45

On Saturday, it seemed that everywhere Tommy turned, the UNCG vs. Duke game—David versus Goliath—was at the center of conversation. Could this nobody team put up a decent game against a program that had churned out NBA players year after year? Could they compete against a true basketball powerhouse?

On paper, the team's numbers were comparable: points per game, points allowed, rebound margin, three-point percentage. Duke was a bigger team, topping the Spartan players by an inch or two at every position except point guard, where Tommy enjoyed a two-inch advantage over Patrick Hart.

It was an advantage Coach D. planned to use. He brought Tommy aside as the teams were warming up and told him to shoot.

"Okay, Coach," Tommy replied.

"Every chance you get, Tommy. You understand? I want you scoring no less than twenty points tonight. Got it?"

"Yeah."

"And when they pull out to cover you better, drive by them. Get the ball to Alvy or kick it out to Skeet. Duke's inside guys are big, and we're gonna need every advantage you can make out there. I want them having to double-team you wherever you go so there'll always be someone open. Got it?"

Tommy nodded and went back to warming up.

UNCG won the jump, and Tommy brought the ball down. Patrick Hart was on him, having picked him up at half court, and didn't look much more different than he did the last time he saw him in person five years earlier.

Patrick was still a talker.

"You know you guys haven't got a chance, don't you?" Patrick said. "You're lucky to have gotten this far, but you don't belong here. This place is for big boys only." He sneered as he mirrored Tommy's movements.

Tommy called the play, then pulled up for a jumper almost immediately. He was just beyond the three-point line and Patrick had no chance to guard him; Tommy shot the ball uncontested and when it hit nothing but net, Patrick glanced at him.

Tommy said nothing; he just winked and smiled, then jogged down the court.

Dickie V., who'd drawn the announcing duty for this game out of luck or persuasion, said to the viewing audience after a prolonged *oooh,* "Did you just see that? I don't know if you could see that, but Hart was talking to Chandler all the way down the court, and Chandler just pulled up for a three. He threw down the gauntlet; Chandler just told Hart to bring his best game because he's a P.T.P. Oh, baby, baby, it's game on in Orlando tonight! This is gonna be a barn burner!"

Duke answered with a play that picked Alvy Hanes off his man who slammed home an alley-oop dunk pass from Patrick Hart.

The game went back and forth for the next ten minutes, the lead changing hands seven times. Duke's shooting guard hit two treys, and Skeet Harzell answered both times. Then Tommy stole the ball on an inbounds pass and put up a quick two.

But UNCG ran into a dry patch where nothing fell. Alvy Hanes missed a dunk, Manny Cuthrell had his shot from the baseline bothered, Skeet Harzell missed a trey, Scott McManness had the ball stripped as he went up for a shot in the paint.

And just like that, Duke was up by nine.

Coach D. called a timeout when one of Duke's big men slammed home a dunk to a thundering response. Scott McManness tried to block it, but instead of getting the ball, he got all shoulder and upper arm, and was charged with a foul for the privilege. Duke's fans let him know it.

"Alright guys," Coach D. said. "They're up by eleven, but there's a lot of game left. You're playing good defense, but you're giving up the back door. You can't do that against Duke; they'll take advantage every time. Scott"—he grabbed McManness' jersey—"stand your ground under there. Your man likes to lower his shoulder before he goes up. When he does that, take a flop. See if you can get a charge. I wanna see you get nominated for a goddamn Oscar, you got me?"

This garnered a few smiles.

"Skeet. Smart shots, buddy"—Coach D. tapped his temple—"Smart shots. Use those picks. Slide by them so close you couldn't squeeze orange juice between you, and make sure to square up before you shoot."

The coach surveyed the faces crowding the huddle. "And everybody just calm down. You're letting them get you riled. You're letting them take you out of your game. You're letting them play *their* game. Don't. They like to run, and they're good at it. Slow them down. We can beat them in the half-court."

The buzzer sounded, and Coach D. pulled Tommy close. "This is up to you. You have to control the momentum, calm them down. Your confidence has to guide them; they'll feed off you." He paused. "Catch us up by halftime."

Just before heading out on the court, Tommy glanced into the crowd. His mom beamed at him, Brant whistled, Britney cheered. Gene blinked at him a few times with a blank expression.

Duke's guy missed his free throw, and Alvy Hanes yanked down the board. He bulleted a pass to Tommy at the hash line, and Tommy took off down the court at top speed. The only defenders between him and the basket were Duke's center and Patrick Hart.

Hart was tracking Tommy from mid-court while the center hung out at the free throw line. Tommy started to hold up and wait for help, but something urged him on. Patrick came up on him quick and mirrored his movements. Tommy faked left and went between his legs as Patrick committed for the steal. With Patrick's weight shifted, Tommy burst past him toward the last waiting defender.

Tommy drove at him, went right, and then stopped and spun left to pin the center against his back as he committed the wrong way. The move was quick enough to isolate him but also allowed Patrick Hart to catch up. Tommy caught a glance of Patrick in his peripheral as he prepared to jump toward the basket. Tommy's plan was to dunk the ball to get the crowd back into the game, but he didn't make it.

He left his feet just in time to get clothes-lined by Patrick Hart. Patrick later told the interviewers he was just going for the ball, and Tommy jumped a little sooner than Patrick thought he would.

Tommy was propelled into a cartwheel as the ball flew from his hands; he landed on his back, his head snapping against the hardwood like a crash test dummy.

Coach D. leapt from the bench, but the trainer beat him to Tommy's side. Manny Cuthrell, the quickest player on the court, dove for Patrick Hart and threw a right-hand roundhouse that caught the Duke star on the side of the head.

Refs blew whistles, benches cleared, and it was a full five minutes later before the melee was quashed. After reviewing the tapes, Manny Cuthrell was ejected—he walked off the court, his face as passive as always—and a Duke forward was also forced to leave the game after it was determined he left the bench to throw a punch, even though the shot only connected with the empty part of Erik Brunson's blue and gold jersey.

When Tommy finally stood—with the help of the trainer and Coach Fulton—the crowd went wild. Tommy shook his head a few times in an effort to clear the cobwebs as they directed him straight back to the locker room.

Everyone in Tommy's family section was all frowns, his mom with her hands covering her mouth. Everyone except Gene, who's expression was more of a scowl.

Junior Derrick Thompkins filled in at point guard during Tommy's absence and at halftime, Duke was up fifteen.

Chapter 46

Patrick Hart's hard foul on Tommy Chandler was replayed and analyzed at halftime by the announcers, and after all was said and done, Dick Vitale had the final word. "Regardless of what happened, without the leadership of Tommy Chandler, I don't see UNCG having a chance to keep this game respectable."

There was a certain amount of anticipation when UNCG marched onto the court for halftime warm-up drills. Tommy Chandler was not among the team. He wasn't there when Duke threw the ball in to begin the second half and ran a set play designed to give Olden Minor an open three, which he made. Tommy wasn't there when Skeet Harzell's shot was blocked, and Patrick Hart broke away for a long pass from Ian MacKay, then laid the ball in for two.

Duke's fifteen-point lead stretched to twenty in less than a minute.

This was the moment Tommy Chandler chose to trot into the arena from the locker room. The crowd erupted into a roar so loud that all the players on the court looked up to see what happened.

Alvy Hanes inbounded the ball to Derrick Thompkins while the crowd was still going wild, but Thompkins got immediately trapped in the corner by Patrick Hart and Olden Minor. After struggling to pass the ball, he opted to bounce the ball off Hart's leg and out of bounds.

Tommy had been chatting with Coach D. and now ran to the scorer's table. The scoring ref pressed the buzzer and Tommy subbed for Thompkins, Derrick giving him a high-five on the way to the bench.

This was the final straw for the crowd. Any undecided fans were now swept up in the following frenzy. Tommy received the inbounds pass from Alvy after a referee's whistle no one could hear.

He dribbled out of an incoming trap, crossed the half-court line, and pulled back to set up the offense. But then he saw something that only the great point guards can innately see, a sliver of open air in the defense's armored layers.

It's an ability that can't be taught, akin to the second sight quarterbacks have when they thread a pass through an impossible wall of defenders and into the hands of their receiver at the perfect speed and trajectory so that the catch looks almost like an afterthought.

Tommy broke to the basket, faked left when King Simms popped out to pick him up, then went wide right so Noah MacKay had to pull off his man to pick him up. Tommy glanced at Scott McManness and offered a slight nod just before he tossed the ball over the basket. McManness got the hint and rose into the air, grabbed the pass, and slammed it home in one fluid motion.

"OOOOOH BABY!" Dick Vitale yelled into his microphone. "This kid is the real thing, baby! A real Surf and Turfer!"

Tommy stole a look into the crowd. His dad still had no expression, while everyone around him was jumping and screaming.

In the next three minutes, UNCG cut the lead from eighteen to eleven on two Skeet Harzell three-pointers, an Alvy Hanes jumper, and two driving lay-ups by Tommy, only allowing Duke a trey by Olden Minor and a jumper by Ian MacKay.

Halfway through the second half, the deficit was corralled to seven, and after Tommy drilled a three from the top of the key, UNCG was only down by four.

Duke held UNCG back for another five minutes, the teams trading baskets so that UNCG never got closer than four or farther away than eight.

And then Tommy stole an inlet pass King Simms was tossing to Noah MacKay. He stepped in the lane, grabbed it with his left hand, dribbled twice, and launched it down court to a streaking Skeet Harzell.

Harzell surprised everyone when he put on the brakes and let Olden Minor fly by him, then shot a three right in front of the Duke bench. Minor recovered and leapt for Harzell but only succeeded in clipping him. The whistle blew as the ball swished through the hoop.

The noise was overbearing, a physical force that stunned the players for a split-second. With Harzell's following free throw, UNCG tied the score at 74.

Duke's next possession was a bust as Scott McManness fouled Noah MacKay. The shot was missed along with the subsequent free throws. Duke's Coach K. was visibly upset.

Tommy brought the ball down, held up the sign for a play that ideally would end in a six-foot Alvy Hanes jumper if all the screens ran according to plan. But like most plays, the defense adjusted and forced the offense to improvise.

It was precisely those times that a team's cohesiveness and ability to predict each others' movements came into play. A true team could always beat a squad of superstars that played as individuals. Communication was the key.

Tommy shot around a Scott McManness pick on the block and received a pass from Erik Brunson at the same time Alvy Hanes flew around a Skeet Harzell pick. This is when Tommy was supposed to bounce-pass to Alvy, but Tommy's radar picked up Olden Minor cheating off Brunson, anticipating the pass.

Tommy faked the pass and sent Minor stepping into the lane, which left Brunson an open path to the basket. Tommy yelled Erik's name and led him with a pass toward the center of the paint.

Brunson sped down the lane, grabbed the pass, and elevated for a finger-roll lay-up.

With just under four minutes to go in the game, UNCG plucked the lead back from Duke, a lead they hadn't enjoyed since the midway mark of the first half.

Coach K. called an immediate timeout.

"Okay, guys," Coach D. said when they'd gathered in a huddle. "They're gonna come out of this timeout with a set play to try and score a three. It's what they do. Fight around your picks and don't let them shoot without smelling the French fry grease on your hands." Everybody chuckled.

"Now listen closely; after our first made basket, press. Press hard. We've done this a million times in practice, and this is why. I want a steal and some quick points, but be ready for them to run it hard. If they break the press, get your asses down the floor."

The buzzer sounded, and the teams took the court.

Duke did just what Coach D. said they would. They ran a play designed to get Olden Minor open for a three. Skeet Harzell hopped around his pick before it caught him, and by the time Minor received the pass, Harzell was close enough to ask him for a dowry.

Minor sloughed off a pass down to Noah MacKay, and Alvy Hanes pulled off his brother Ian for a double-team. Noah sensed it and tipped a pass to Ian who rattled the backboard with a slam dunk that brought the Duke fans out of their seats.

Tied at 76 with three minutes to go.

Tommy brought the ball down, and the Spartans tried to find an open man unsuccessfully for thirty of their allotted thirty-five seconds. But Duke being Duke, their defense was oppressive and unrelenting. Skeet Harzell had to fire a leaning jumper that clanged off the rim into King Simm's hands.

He threw an outlet pass to Patrick Hart at the hash, and the race was on. Tommy slid into the backcourt, keeping himself between Patrick and the basket, and when Patrick made his move—a twisting loop-de-loop—Tommy fouled him.

Patrick pumped his fist as the ball ricocheted off the backboard and into the basket to the sound of the whistle. He strutted to the free throw line and dropped the ball through the net with barely a ripple.

Duke up by three, 2:18 left in the game.

Tommy received the inbounds pass, and just before he was trapped in the corner, passed to Alvy at half court. Alvy dribbled five feet and got rid of the ball to Skeet, who bounced it back to Tommy as he held up the sign to set the offense.

They ran the call, but Duke continued to overplay which made getting a man open difficult. Erik Brunson almost lost the ball when he bounce-passed it back to Tommy; King Simms got a hand on it. Tommy had to break left to grab the loose ball; it was enough of a disruption to open a hole because, at the same instant, Patrick Hart lunged for the steal. Tommy spun, took two dribbles toward the basket, and dropped in an easy ten-footer.

Duke up by one, 1:51 to go.

This time UNCG didn't press. All too often, when teams were expecting a press, they could break it and turn it into a three-on-two fast break. And Duke was a master at breaking the press.

Instead, the Spartans picked them up at half court. Coach D. knew

Duke was going to run as much time out as possible before taking their shot, so he yelled to his guys not to foul. There was still a chance the game could be won without a foul fest.

Duke passed the ball around the perimeter between Patrick Hart and Olden Minor and King Simms while the MacKay brothers flashed through the paint to try and isolate their man. Noah got the ball once, but Scott McManness was instantly on him. There wasn't going to be an open shot.

Finally, with eight seconds on the shot clock, Olden Minor fired one over Skeet Harzell from the corner. It wasn't the prettiest looking bucket, but it garnered Duke three points to make the contest a two-possession game.

UNCG down by four, 1:23 in the game.

Tommy hustled the ball down the court at top speed, and when Olden Minor pulled off Skeet to double-team him, Tommy threw an over-the-shoulder left-handed pass behind him to Skeet. Skeet, expecting this possibility, had set up at the three-point line. He caught the pass and immediately launched a textbook shot with perfect rotation. Swish.

82-81 Duke, 1:16 left.

Duke and UNCG traded shots again. King Simms broke away from Erik Brunson for a backdoor lay-in, and Scott McManness put back an Alvy Hanes miss after a sweet one-handed rebound.

Duke up, 84-83. 48 seconds to go.

Coach D. called a timeout.

"You know what it is," he said when the team had huddled around him. "They can keep the ball almost the whole time. We gotta foul. No choice."

"Coach," Tommy said. "Let us play defense first."

"You think you can get the ball without fouling?"

Tommy surveyed the determination of his teammates' faces. "Yeah, Coach. I do. How about this ... if the big MacKay gets the ball, we foul. Other than that, we try for the steal and don't allow the three."

Coach D. smiled and held out the clipboard. "You wanna draw up a play, too?"

Tommy chuckled. "That's alright, Coach. You gotta earn your money somehow."

"Okay, guys. You heard the man. You think you can get the ball? Prove it to me. You got us here, now bring us home. Get the ball and do your thing."

The buzzer sounded, and Coach D. grabbed Tommy before he ran out.

"It's yours if you want it, Tommy. Question is, how bad do you want it?"

Tommy picked up Patrick as soon as Ian MacKay passed it to him. He played Patrick close but not so close a foul could be called. He hounded Patrick so hard, it took eight seconds for Patrick to get the ball over the timeline.

Patrick passed the ball to Olden Minor, who got it to King Simms, and then back to Patrick. Erik Brunson got a finger on the pass to Patrick but knocked it farther away from Tommy rather than closer. Patrick caught it without a problem.

Tommy stepped in closer now. Retrieving the deflected pass had sent Patrick into the lower corner, and when Skeet sensed what Tommy was doing, he dropped down to help double-team Patrick.

Patrick was in trouble and he knew it. He twisted away, hugging the ball, and called timeout.

26 seconds on the clock, 13 seconds on the shot clock.

"Good defense, guys," Coach D. said as they came to the bench. The players were pumping their fists and high-fiving. "But the game's not over. This is the hardest part. They're gonna come out of this timeout with one thing on their minds ... scoring. They got thirteen seconds, and they're gonna shoot for the dagger."—he was nodding—"The three."

He shoved his whiteboard out for all to see and began pointing to positions. "Watch out for Minor or Hart setting up for the three. Don't let them have it, but if they do get it, for God's sake, don't foul them. If they get a three off, we gotta make something quick, then foul. They make a two, we gotta get a three to tie"—he was looking at Tommy and Skeet—"You guys understand?"

Everybody nodded, and the coach said, "Anybody got anything to add?"

Tommy spoke up. "They're not gonna score."

Coach D. grinned. "I hope not, but we've been through this before. It's not much different than that game against SMU."

"Except this time we're the team that's behind." Skeet said.

"Well let's be better than SMU," Tommy said, getting a few snorts and grins.

Duke did indeed run a set play designed to get Olden Minor open beyond the arc, but knowing that, Skeet skipped around Noah MacKay's pick the opposite way and almost stole the ball. Minor clipped a quick pass to Patrick Hart who immediately launched an alley-oop pass to a breaking Ian MacKay. The Duke forward rose high into the air for the pass, a foot from the rim, but Alvy Hanes was ready. He rose in front of MacKay and snatched the pass down inches from MacKay's hands.

Before he landed, the crowd erupted into an explosion of whistles and shouts. Alvy got the ball to Tommy with eighteen seconds on the clock.

Tommy brought the ball down, pressured by Patrick Hart, Hart riddling him with words the whole way. "I'm gonna get the ball, Tommy. I'm gonna steal it right out of your hands because no matter what, you'll never be as good as me. As long as I'm in the building, you'll always be second best."

Tommy passed to Skeet who got it right back to him. Then he passed to Alvy, and back to Tommy. Duke was smothering them with defense.

Time slowed as Tommy frantically searched for the open chink in the Duke defensive armor. He couldn't find anything. No one could break free from their man. Tommy couldn't find a weakness.

Then, with nine seconds to go, Tommy lowered his eyes at Patrick and began dribbling. "Hey Patrick," he said, facing him at the top of the key. "You remember this move?" He started toward the basket, Patrick tracking him backward. "You ready? I'm gonna fake left, then go right. Got it? Ready?"

Patrick matched him step for step, his eyes recognizing the words.

Then Tommy did it. He lunged left, committing his whole body so fast that Patrick committed also. But he dribbled to the right between his legs and pushed hard off his left. Patrick tried to recover, but Tommy was too quick—he was beside Patrick before Patrick could adjust his footing. He dribbled once more to separate himself.

Tommy elevated over the outstretched hand of Noah MacKay, but the defender was too late to bother the shot. It was a standard ten-footer at the edge of the free throw line, a shot Tommy had popped thousands of times since he first picked up a basketball.

Two seconds on the clock ticked down to less than one as Tommy's high-arcing jumper nicked the back of the rim, ricocheted in the cylinder a few times, and dropped through the hoop.

The buzzer sounded just as it did.

Game over.

85-84.

UNCG over Duke.

It was the upset of the tournament.

Dickie V yelled into his headset. The crowd screamed and shouted and jumped in triumph. Coach D. and the other UNCG coaches leapt from the bench, arms in the air, fists clenched. The team descended upon Tommy, bouncing him around, high-fiving, shouting glee with renewed energy. They toppled onto him, then lifted him up, and toted him on their shoulders.

That was when Tommy saw his dad. Gene Chandler was hopping up and down, arms raised. He was screaming to Tommy's mom whose expression was a mixture of surprise and disbelief. Tommy couldn't hear him, but he could read lips.

"That's my son!" Gene was shouting. "That's my son!"

Chapter 47

UNCG's March Madness was to end the next Thursday, however, as they ran into a UCLA Bruins team that would later go on to the finals. It was a bittersweet moment. UNCG had made program history and enjoyed a weeklong national exposure that no amount of money could buy.

The unknown university from Greensboro had beaten an ACC powerhouse in a story that spun off more subplots than a Latin soap opera. Coach D. and several of the players had turned away more interviews in that short week than they'd given in their whole lives.

Tommy and his *walk-on-turned-starter* bio was every reporter's perfect storm. Gene did an amiable job fending off calls and requests, telling them his son had to concentrate on the game at hand. Call back after they'd won it all. When the reporters started badgering *him* for an interview, he said it wasn't his story to tell and promptly hung up on them.

With all the hype that was thrown around in the sports and news shows, Coach D. did his best to keep the team grounded. They were prepared for UCLA, but they weren't the better team. It just wasn't to be.

A month passed after the loss, and Tommy's life returned to normalcy. He focused on graduating from college and running the store. Every time someone bought something, there was a fifty-fifty chance there'd be a conversation about the NCAA Tourney. They'd congratulate him or tell him how much they hated Duke or ask him what he was going to do next. The sting of losing to UCLA had dissipated to a dull memory, and only the high points remained.

That part of his life was over.

The bell on the store's front door rang, and Tommy yelled from the back, "Be there in a sec." He emerged to find Laura Novak at the register. She wore a pair of jeans and a plain blue T-shirt, and she was smiling at him in a way that made him pause.

"Hi," she said.

"Hey, Laura," he replied, continuing to the register where he set a bottle of Greased Lightning under the counter. "What can I do for you?"

"I was just coming in to see if your mom had made any more orange macaroons." Laura glanced toward the shelf beside the register where Tommy kept the second product line of Chandler Exclusives—baked goods. Since this past Christmas, at the request of the store's customers—who constantly nibbled on Helen's goodies at checkout—Tommy had convinced his mom to turn her baking talents into more than just a hobby.

At any given time, Tommy carried more than two dozen different confectionary creations on his shelves—everything from cookies to brownies to cakes. He kept tally of which ones customers asked for when they weren't on the shelves so his mom could step up production on those. It was early April and still, they were experimenting with the base product line.

"So you like the orange macaroons?" Tommy asked, grinning.

"My mom. She can't get enough. She ate the last batch in one night." Laura's eyes widened. "Don't you dare tell her I said that."

Tommy chuckled and zipped his lips with his right hand. "Your secret is safe with me."

Laura grinned and took a breath. "Looks like they're selling pretty good." She nodded toward the half-bare shelves where Chandler Exclusives usually sat.

"Yeah. Hard to keep some of them in stock. Still trying to figure all that out. I'll make a note about the orange macaroons." He paused. "Your mom's birthday is coming up soon, right?"

Laura raised her eyebrows.

"Well, I was just thinking. Mom has started taking special orders. How do you think your mom would like an orange macaroon cake?"

"She could do that?"

"Mom can pretty much do anything with a mixing bowl and oven. I'll ask her about it."

Laura beamed. "Thanks."

A moment of silence passed.

"I saw you on TV," Laura said.

"TV? Oh. The tournament."

"You sound disappointed. You guys did great."

Tommy shifted his feet. "UCLA waxed us."

"Waxed you?" Laura shook her head. "They beat you by eight points. And then only because they made their free throws at the end when you had to foul."

Tommy tilted his head.

"You forget I used to play a little?" she said with a sly grin. "I particularly enjoyed the win over Duke."

This brought a smile to Tommy's face. "Yeah, that was pretty fun."

"I loved the part when they showed the replay of that last move you made, and Vitale said you broke Patrick's ankles like they were made of Silly Putty."

"Yeah, I saw that on Sportscenter the next day. That was pretty funny."

"And hey, you guys made it to the Sweet Sixteen. Everybody was pulling for you. You couldn't turn on a TV that week without seeing a clip about UNCG and Tommy Boy."

"Oh God. Don't remind me."

Tommy Boy was the nickname Dick Vitale had given Tommy after the Duke win. Every time Vitale referred to the Spartans, he mentioned the senior leadership of Tommy Boy.

Tommy continued, "Someone had a Tommy Boy poster up in my dorm room by the time we returned from Orlando."

"That first shot you put up? The three right over Patrick?"—she was shaking her head—-"Classic. You should've seen the expression on Patrick's face when you winked at him and jogged down the court."

"I did." Tommy's mouth curled up in an embarrassed smile. "Mom taped the game."

Laura smirked.

Tommy pushed a paperclip around the counter, then said, "So. Have you tried the macadamia nut brownies?" He nodded toward the shelf.

"No, not yet." Laura scooted toward the shelf.

"I'll give you a twenty percent discount if you want to try them."

"You don't have to do that."

"I know."

Laura picked up the package and slid it over the counter. "I guess I shouldn't come home empty."

"Make sure you tell your mom they're laxative-free."

Laura laughed. "The story that just won't die."

Tommy rang the brownies up. "So, home? You living with your parents now?"

"No, but I did move back to Greensboro this past winter."

"Oh?" Tommy looked up.

"Yeah. Just a little apartment near UNCG. I'm planning on starting there in the fall. I'm gonna get my Masters."

Laura paid for the brownies, and Tommy bagged them. "So," she said, "I guess I'll see you around."

She turned to walk out the door, and Tommy cleared his throat.

"Laura?"

Laura stopped and swiveled toward him. "Yes?"

It was now or never. "Are you doing anything tonight? I mean, you know, would you like to go out for dinner or something?"

She sucked in air through her teeth. "I'm having dinner with my parents tonight."

"Oh, okay. Well, maybe some other time?" Tommy fidgeted with the register keys.

"How about tomorrow night?"

"Really?"

"I'll call you tomorrow." Laura smiled. "I look forward to it."

She waved and left.

The rest of the day was a blur.

Chapter 48

The next afternoon, Tommy's luck changed. Homer was supposed to relieve him at three, but he called in sick. Between the hacking coughs and throat clearing, Homer apologized profusely. Tommy told him it was no big deal.

Tommy never mentioned the date with Laura that night because he knew Homer would come in anyway, even though he sounded like he was steps away from his deathbed. Homer Persons was that type of guy.

Tommy would have tried his brother, but Brant had his own spring break at East Carolina that week. He called Steve, but Steve had promised his wife they'd visit her parents in Pinehurst that day. They were almost there when Tommy rang his cell phone.

Tommy didn't want to ask his mother to cover for him because Saturday was one of the few days she took off from baking. Saturday was errand day, and Sunday was hang-around-the-house day.

So when Laura called him at the store at a quarter past one, Tommy had to tell her he was canceling.

"Nobody can cover you?"

"I tried everyone. Sorry."

Laura was silent a second, then said, "How do you feel about a late dinner?"

"I don't close up until nine. By the time I get home and ready, and then to Greensboro, it'd be near ten. That's kind of late, don't you think?"

"I was thinking more along the lines of picking dinner up and coming to you. It's supposed to be a beautiful night. You still have your oasis set up like you used to?"

Tommy laughed. "You mean on the roof? Sure."

"How about we eat up there and pretend we're at a fancy restaurant?"

"Sounds fine with me. If you don't mind—"

"Mind? It sounds perfect, Tommy. I'll bring Chinese, you provide the wine."

"Uh ... sure."

"See you at nine." And Laura hung up.

Tommy floated through the afternoon. He whistled and sang and grinned until his cheeks hurt. Mrs. Jacobs told him he looked like the cat that got the canary, and all he could think was, *not yet.*

Tommy had a hard time believing Laura wanted to go out with him. Sure she'd said yes, but she'd do that to be nice. After all, they'd known each other since second grade. But then, when he had to cancel, Laura was the one who found a way to make the date happen. And now, in a way, she was the one taking him on the date.

To say he was giddy with anticipation was a vast understatement.

Around six, Tommy called his mom to relieve him for about an hour while he went up to the roof to clean and fix it up nicer.

And then nine o'clock arrived and passed. Tommy closed the store down and turned off most of the lights inside. Fifteen minutes went by. He'd picked out a light Merlot from the small wine selection he carried in the store, a bottle from a local winery that promised to be smooth and fruity. Laura was supposed to be bringing Chinese, but that could be anything from beef to chicken to shrimp. Surely Merlot would match, right?

Headlights lit up the store's parking lot, and Tommy watched as a car pulled around to the side and parked next to his car. He unlocked the double doors and met Laura as she was getting out.

"I was beginning to get worried," Tommy said.

Laura rolled her eyes. "Tonight was busy at the Szechwan Kitchen. The normal ten-fifteen minutes turned into twenty-thirty minutes." She reached back into the car and pulled out a brown grocery bag.

"Are we expecting company?" Tommy said, lifting the weighty bag into his arms.

"I didn't know what you'd like"—she drew her eyes together—"so I kind of got a little bit of everything."

Tommy hefted the bag up and frowned. "Just as long as you don't expect us to finish it all."

Laura glanced at the sky as Tommy led the way to the metal stairs in the back. "It looks cloudy," she said.

Tommy looked up. "It'll hold off." But secretly he wasn't sure.

When Laura made it to the top, the roof was pitch black. "Where are the lights?"

Tommy handed the bag of food to her and reached down to plug an extension cord in. Laura gasped as the roof lit up.

It had been years since Laura last saw the Oasis. Tommy had added more plants, a resin storage bin, and more lights. For this night, he'd set up a bistro table with two chairs.

"Wow," Laura said. "You've done some things." She set the bag of food down on the storage bin and began setting the table. She paused and beamed, nodding to her right. "Nice sign by the way."

When Laura had named the roof, Tommy got his dad to make a wooden sign with "The Oasis" etched into it. He shellacked it and built a small stand for it. It stood off on the side.

On the table were two wine glasses, the bottle of Merlot, silverware, linens, and a large three-wick candle surrounded by glass. Tommy pulled a wand lighter out of one side of the storage bin and lit the candle, then pulled out a radio and turned it on.

Laura watched all this with amusement. "You expecting to get lucky tonight?"

Tommy's eyes widened and he stuttered, "Uh ... uh ... no, I ... just ... I was thinking ..." His face warmed.

Laura giggled and sat in the chair closest to her. "Relax," she said. Tommy sat across from her, and she continued, "It's very nice." She took a breath and looked around again. "It's been a while since someone went to this much trouble for me. I'm very flattered."

Tommy closed his eyes and shook his head. No matter how old and mature he grew, Laura Novak still had this effect on him. Her very presence gave him butterflies and turned his usual confidence into mush. He took a deep breath and tried to regain some of himself.

"What is it?" Laura asked.

Tommy pulled a wine tool from his pocket and began uncorking the wine. "Truthfully?"

Laura nodded.

Tommy hesitated, then continued, "I've had a crush on you ever since I first met you. You do something to me." He waved his hands. "Even now, we haven't really spent any time together in years, but just being around you makes me feel like I've forgotten how to walk."

He popped the cork off and poured wine into Laura's glass.

"Ever since you first met me?" she said, skeptical.

Tommy nodded. "Mrs. Mims' class on the first day. I got moved to the desk in front of you. I remember turning around when she made us pair up for some stupid writing practice. And there you were." He poured wine into his glass.

"You really remember that?"

"It was like you had a spotlight on you. Like in a movie when the director wants the audience to look at a specific character in a crowd. And the character will wear red or something bright." He paused. "Only you were wearing a blue thing with a flap and white buttons. I remember thinking it was like a sailor's shirt."

Laura laughed and sunk her face into her hands. She lifted her head, saying, "That was my sailor's outfit! I loved that thing. I wore it all the time."

"You showed me how to write cursive that day."

Laura lifted an eyebrow. "I remember some of that day. I remember you and Nick chasing me and Angel. Michelle too."

Tommy shrugged. "Boys do that at that age."

"And you threw rocks."

"Boys only did that to girls they liked."

Laura narrowed her eyes. "Well, you threw rocks at Angel and Michelle, too."

"But I threw the biggest ones at you."

Laura shook her head rolled her eyes. "Boys are bizarre."

Laura picked up her wine glass, still shaking her head. Tommy said, "Wait, a toast." Laura held her glass up and Tommy continued, "To the friendships that life brings us."

They ate and talked about school. Their families. The store. Raleigh. Greensboro. The things that had changed. The things that hadn't. Old friends. Old girlfriends and boyfriends.

"I'm sorry about the Homecoming Dance," Laura said.

Tommy was grabbing a second bottle of Merlot, and they were reclining on the chaise loungers. "Don't worry about it," he said.

"I know I hurt you that night."

Tommy shrugged it off. "It was a long time ago."

"Just let me say this." Laura was sitting up now, facing Tommy. "I'd had a bad break-up with Patrick, and I was needing to be with someone I trusted. That's why I went to the dance with you. But I wasn't thinking about your feelings. I knew you liked me, and I have a confession." She paused. "I liked you too ... but right then, at that very moment, I just couldn't be more than friends with anyone."

Tommy wasn't sure he'd heard her right. Did she just say she'd liked him too?

She continued, "I've wanted to say this for a long time now. You apologized to me once, but it wasn't your fault. It was mine. I was giving you all the signals, and you couldn't be blamed for reading them. I was just so confused. I wanted to feel needed, but without any strings." She took a breath. "And that was unfair. It was unfair to you."

Laura leaned back in the chaise and looked into the sky. "And then you were with Angel and what could I do then?"

"Wait. Hold up a sec ... you *liked* me?"

She turned her head. "Of course I did. But by the time I came out of my funk, I realized how much I'd hurt you. And I couldn't do that again. You were the nicest boy I knew, and I'd already hurt you once."

Tommy was speechless. He sipped his wine and focused on a light twinkling in one of the ficus trees.

"Say something," Laura said.

"I don't know what to say."

"Well, I do. I really like you, Tommy."—Tommy turned to her—"And I want to take this slow because I don't want to screw it up this time."

Tommy wanted to say a million things to that. He wanted to bask in it, wallow around, and coat himself with her words. He wanted to soak in that very moment for the rest of his life, submerge himself so deep he could never return to reality.

And then the clouds opened up without a sound of warning. A few drops of rain turned into a mixture of rain and hail, and within seconds, hail the size of BBs pelted them from every direction. Laura shrieked with laughter as she jumped up to gather the leftover food. Tommy shoved the radio back into the safety of the storage bin and unplugged the lights, then grabbed the wine bottle and glasses.

"Go, go, go!" he urged Laura down the stairs.

He fished the keys from his pocket and unlocked the door to the office. They rushed in, laughing and soaked, Laura gripping the deteriorating bag of food from the bottom. Tommy set the glasses and bottle on his desk, and shook his arms, holding them out like that would help them dry. Like his clothes weren't completely drenched through.

He turned, saying, "I guess you were right about the—"

Laura's kiss was firm, and yet, gentle. Her arms embraced Tommy, and he quickly followed suit. They kissed for what felt like hours before breaking.

"That was long overdue," Laura said, holding Tommy, their foreheads touching, noses nuzzling, eyes closed.

They kissed again, this time initiated by Tommy. Slower, more sensual, tongues flirting, lips caressing.

They broke, and Tommy said, "I have always loved you, Laura."

Their eyes held each other, communicating more emotions in those few seconds than words could ever say.

The next kiss was forceful, heated, frantic. Bodies excited, skin tingling, hands exploring. Actions frenetic, fluid, then halting.

They pulled back, breaths ragged. Laura tugged at Tommy's soaked shirt.

Tommy, eyes questioning, said, "I thought you said you wanted to go slow?"

Laura ran her hands under his shirt to his chest, lightly tracing her fingernails over his skin. Goosebumps rose. She said, "I think we've waited for this long enough." She broke Tommy's embrace and—still holding his eyes with hers—peeled her saturated shirt off.

"Well," Tommy said, "I *have* always heard not to stay in wet clothes."

Laura giggled as she helped him remove his shirt. "And there's that, too."

Chapter 49

Six months later, Southeast Guilford held its five-year reunion for the class of 1989. There was a bigger turnout than expected; the party was held at the Koury Convention Center in one of its larger ballrooms.

Nick Muller arrived shortly after Tommy and Laura.

"Wow, you look amazing!" Nick said to Laura.

Tommy ran a hand over his gut. "Gee, thanks. I've been watching what I eat. I think bran is the answer."

Nick shot Tommy a half-lidded look while Laura chuckled.

"Aiyyy!!!" Angel screamed as she came up behind Laura. Laura turned, and they embraced with huge smiles. "I hoped you would come!"

"I wouldn't miss it," Laura answered.

"And look at you!" Angel lunged at Tommy and hugged him, kissing him on the cheek as he straightened. "Mr. Basketball Star himself."

"Just call him Tommy Boy," Nick quipped.

Tommy blushed.

Angel turned to Nick saying, "And just where have you been hiding yourself all these years, handsome?" She smiled and embraced him, pecking him on the cheek also.

"I've been around," Nick said, laughing. "You look even more beautiful than I remember. How have you been?"

Instead of answering, Angel pointed at Tommy's hand clasping

Laura's. She addressed them both. "Is this something you'd like to share with the group?"

Laura glanced at Tommy, then said, "We've been seeing each other since April."

"April? Omigod! That's amazing!" She took a step back and looked at both of them with appraising eyes. She grinned, saying, "You look perfect together." She punched Tommy in the arm. "And it's about time, huh?"

Tommy twisted to look into Laura's eyes. "I guess you could say it was worth it."

Angel shouted again. "Aiyyy!!" She lunged at them, squeezing them both in a tight hug. "I'm so happy for you guys!" She stepped back again. "You look so in love." She shook her head and grabbed Laura's hand, saying, "Come on. We have some girl talk to catch up on. You'll never believe what's happened to Melody Bruner ..."

They walked off, and Tommy turned to Nick. "I think I'm gonna need a drink. You?"

"You don't have to ask me twice."

The bar was off to the right just inside the ballroom. Tommy slapped his nametag on as they moseyed over to it.

"Geez. You see that guy over there?" Nick nodded to his left.

"The one in the big charcoal suit?"

"Yeah. You know who that is? Wait till he turns this way. There. You know who that is?"

"Is that Stanley?"

"Yep. He got fat, didn't he? I heard he married this chick from Europe. A model or something."

Stanley was laughing and moved to one side. A gorgeous young woman with flowing blonde hair appeared behind him. Tommy said, "I'd say you heard right."

Nick ordered a seven-and-seven from the bartender, and Tommy opted for a glass of red wine. They moved off to the side as Nick said, "So, you and Laura, huh?"

Tommy nodded and sipped his wine.

"Six months?"

"Yep."

"Aw, come on. Spill. You got the girl of your dreams, and all you can say is *yep*?"

Tommy grinned. "What do you want me to say? She's the most amazing girl in the world."

"I want details. That's what I want."

Tommy laughed. "All I can tell you is that part's amazing, too."

They discussed Nick's job at Arthur Anderson, the store, and how well UNCG and Carolina were supposed to do this year. The whole time, they watched people pour in, some exclaiming and hugging like long-lost lovers, others shaking hands like dignitaries representing foreign countries.

They were interrupted several times by guys coming over to say congratulations on making it to the Sweet Sixteen. Most of them particularly loved the game against Duke, and how Tommy had shown up Patrick. Several mentioned the last play and repeated Dickie V's rant on Tommy breaking Patrick's ankles.

Former basketball players stopped and high-fived them both. Jalen Carter. Miles Flaherty. Terrell Baker.

"Hey," said Jalen. "I heard you and Laura were a thing now."

Tommy smiled. "Yeah."

"It's about damn time, huh?"

Tommy, Laura, Nick, and Angel ate dinner at the same table with some others. Discussion was light, flowing from basketball to the hussy Bobby Black brought with him to the dress choice of Michelle Garrick—too much cleavage, said the girls: the guys saw no problem with it—and back to basketball.

Music and mingling followed dinner, and Tommy found himself chatting with Nick once again.

"Hey," Nick said. "I need to ask you something."

Tommy saw the seriousness in Nick's face. "Sure."

"I know you dated Angel back in high school. I wanted to ask, you know, would it be weird if I asked her out?"

"You mean like best friend incest?"

Nick shrugged. "Something like that."

Tommy laughed. "You have my blessing. Just have her home by midnight."

Nick chuckled. "Jeez. How'd you get to be such a big dork?"

Angel's voice sputtered over the speakers just then, and the music lowered to the background. She told everyone to grab a seat, she was going to hand out some recognition.

"First of all, I'm so glad all of you made it here tonight for our five-year reunion." She paused as applause broke out and one drunk guy in the back let loose a raucous yell. Everyone laughed and she continued.

"I think we should all give a hand to Laura Derry and Kim Fleming for organizing this little get-together." Applause. No redneck yell. "I think you would agree it's pretty difficult to keep up with hundreds of us all going our separate ways. They did an amazing job." More applause.

"Now I know many of you came a long way to be here. Can I have a show of hands for everyone who's moved out of the state? Out of the country?"

Angel presented the winner who'd moved to England with a travel bag containing a mini-toothpaste, mini-mouthwash, etc. More applause with laughter. The couple with the youngest child received a box of Pampers. The couple who were the most pregnant, due next month, received a bag of marshmallows, a jar of dill pickles, and a bottle of Texas Pete hot sauce.

When the laughter died down, Angel asked if anyone would like to say something, make a speech or anything.

Suzy Hinshaw strode out and took the microphone. She said she would like a moment of prayer for all those who had passed on, remarking it was a shame they'd been taken so early in life. She relinquished the microphone to Angel after a fifteen-second pause during which most people looked at their shoes or drinks.

"Thank you, Suzy," Angel said. "It's important to remember everyone." There were murmurs of agreement. Then in a perkier tone, Angel asked if there was anyone else who had anything to say.

Catherine Stimpson stood hesitantly, then made her way to the dance floor. She took the microphone and said, "I just wanted to say that I'm so happy I came tonight. I'm sure that some of you were undecided like me when the invitation came in the mail, but now, I'm really glad I decided to come." She smiled and turned to give the microphone back to Angel as moderate applause rippled through the room.

Angel smiled and said into the microphone, "Thank you, Cathy. I, for one, totally agree with you. I'm glad all of you came, too. It's fun catching up with so many people I've lost touch with through the years."

She looked around the room. "Anyone else?"

No one waved or spoke up, and she repeated herself.

Just as she was about to say something else, Tommy stood. All eyes turned to him, and he exhaled the breath he'd been holding.

Now or never.

Chapter 50

Tommy navigated through the tables, sidestepping people he hadn't seen in five years. He nodded to the DJ as he stepped onto the dance floor. Angel smiled and announced, "Tommy Chandler," before handing him the microphone.

Everybody clapped. There were whistles and woot-woots from some of the guys who'd been on the team. Somebody yelled, "Duke sucks!" A laugh rippled through the crowd.

Tommy shook his head and nodded with a smile. He brought the microphone up. "Yeah, that was fun," he said. He paused. "First, I'd like to repeat what Catherine just said. I'm glad I came tonight. Because I've been doing the school thing for the last five years, at first I couldn't believe it was time for a reunion. Then I was like, 'Five years? What's the point ... nobody's even bald yet.'"

This got a laugh.

"Sorry, Miles. Didn't mean to call you out."—hard laughter as heads turned to find Miles Flaherty; Tommy touched the top of his head while leaning forward—"I couldn't help but notice."

He shrugged while Miles yelled out, "I was pulling for Duke."

More laughter.

"Seriously," Tommy continued. "I didn't think enough time had passed, but showing up and seeing so many familiar faces really brought back a lot of great memories. Makes me wonder what the ten-year and twenty-year reunions will feel like."

He took a breath.

"I had forgotten some of the friendships I'd made. Lasting friendships. It's a good feeling to reconnect. And in fact, I made such a connection not very long ago." He glanced toward his table and found Laura beaming up at him.

"The other day, I took a trip by my elementary school. Of course, it was the same size it had always been, but for some reason, it seemed so much smaller than I remember it. The walkways, the steps, the monkey bars." Laughter.

"Remember when we could fit through those monkey bars? When the merry-go-round was the size of a bus? Or when our feet barely touched the ground from the big swings?"

Nods and murmurs of agreement.

"While I walked around the playground, I thought about those days when me and Nick used to strut around there like we owned the place. Dodge ball and tag and chasing girls, even though we had no idea what to do with them if we caught them." Hearty laughter followed; somebody yelled out, "Nick still doesn't know!" More chuckles as Nick raised his hand and pointed toward the voice.

Tommy continued, "Guys, remember when we used to chase girls and sometimes even throw rocks at them?" Nods and chortles. "Back then, it was how we tried to get their attention. We couldn't ask them to dinner or to a movie or to go park at The Rock."

This got guffaws and catcalls from everyone.

When they settled down, Tommy said, "But seriously, to all you girls, that was what us guys did to express our desire to want to be with you." Tommy leveled his gaze at Laura. "So when I was there the other day, on the playground, I thought about the first day I met this particular girl"—smiling faces turned to glance at Laura—"She sat behind me in class, and when I teamed up with her to practice cursive writing, I was mesmerized. She had the most beautiful eyes I'd ever seen, so gentle and so happy.

"And then when she spoke, I was dumbstruck. We were supposed to be practicing writing our own names that day but what she doesn't know, is that I spent the time writing her name instead ... and not just because it was shorter." A few chuckles erupted.

"It was because from that moment forward, I was pretty much ruined for all other women." Tommy paused as the women in the audience emitted a collective *awww*.

Tommy motioned at Laura. "Can you come up here, honey?"

Laura shook her head, face reddening, but the crowd urged her on. She finally stood and to light applause, she edged her way forward. "I believe most of you remember Laura Novak?" There was a *she's-hot* whistle from the back. Tommy smiled and brought the microphone close to his mouth. "You know it," he said in a deep voice.

More chuckles from the audience. Even some clapping.

Laura, clearly embarrassed now, joined Tommy on the raised parquet floor.

"So I guess you're wondering why I dragged you up here?" Tommy said into the microphone, looking at Laura. She nodded, looking around. He turned back to everyone. "Being on the school playground the other day got me to thinking about life. How short it is and how sometimes we have to get hit in the head to wake up and do the things we want to do, to quit wasting all our time wondering *what if?*"

Tommy took Laura's hand. "Six months ago, on our second first-date ... you asked me why boys threw rocks at girls. I gave you the same

THE WALK-ON

answer I shared here tonight ... to get your attention. Then you brought up how I threw rocks at other girls, too. And I told you what?"

Tommy held the microphone up to Laura and urged her to answer. She said, "The rocks you threw at me were bigger."

Laughter swelled through the crowd again.

Tommy said into the microphone, "And do you know why we throw the rocks at other girls?"—Laura shook her head—"It's because sometimes we're afraid to tell you just how we feel. We're scared to lay it all out on the line because then the fantasy of *what-could-be* disappears. And we're left with the reality of *what-is*." He paused. "And the fantasy with you is sometimes more desirable than the *chance* of a reality without you."

Tommy nodded at the DJ again, and a song crackled through the speakers. "Do you remember this song?" Tommy said to Laura, the microphone picking it up faintly. It was Hall and Oates, "Kiss On My List." She nodded.

"The first time we ever danced, this song was playing."—Tommy turned to the audience—"It was the fourth grade Valentine's dance, and on a dare, I asked Laura to dance." He pointed to Nick. "Thank you for that push, Nick."

Nick clasped his hands and raised them in triumph. During this, the DJ had come out on the floor behind Tommy and handed him a box slightly larger than the hand that held it. The DJ returned to his post.

Tommy turned back to Laura who now had both hands raised to her mouth. He smiled. "So, the other day, when I was on the playground, I started thinking about the symbolism of boys giving girls rocks and how that carried itself to later in their lives ..."

The air in the ballroom was suddenly thick. Everyone was leaning forward in their chairs, some with mouths opened a fraction, others with jaws slackened in huge Os.

Tommy flipped the lid off the box with his thumb. "I thought I'd give you a symbol of that first rock I threw at you." He held the box with his microphone hand and pulled out a gray rock the size of an oblong baseball and held it up. The silence in the room was blistering.

"I found this rock on the playground the other day," Tommy said into the microphone, holding it out as if it were on a pedestal. "I know it's not the same one I first threw at you, but I would like it to symbolize that first rock."

He looked at Laura. The confusion written across her face was visible from the corners of the room. She lowered her hands from her mouth and took the rock Tommy now held out to her.

Tommy frowned and shook his head at the DJ. The music disappeared with a slight scratch.

"You don't like it?" Tommy asked.

Laura forced a smile. "I love it," she said, her response barely heard to the group. "It's perfect."

"Are you sure?" Tommy said, his own face devoid of emotion.

Laura nodded and forced another smile.

Tommy cleared his throat as "Kiss On My List" began again. He said, "Because it looks like maybe you were expecting a different kind of rock. You know, judging by how big a production I made of all this."

Laura sucked in a breath as Tommy dropped to a single knee. She brought the huge rock close to her chest. Tommy reached into his pocket and produced a ring so brilliant there was no mistaking it for a clump of gravel. It wasn't huge, but it was shiny and sparkled as he held it up. Laura dropped the oblong rock and it hit the floor with a thud. Tommy didn't flinch.

"Laura Novak, I have loved you since that first day I lost myself in your eyes. You were the most beautiful girl I'd ever seen, and you still are. You make me laugh, you make me challenge myself, you bring a happiness to my life I never knew could exist, and more important, you make me the best man I can possibly be."

He paused and the DJ lowered the music a tad.

"Laura Novak, I know it's cliché, but you are the love of my life. I would be honored if you chose to grow old with me and share in life's struggles and accomplishments, no matter what gets thrown our way. Will you make me the luckiest man alive? Will you marry me?"

A tear trickled down Laura's cheek as she slipped on the ring and rasped out a weak "Yes." She took Tommy's face between her hands, leaned over and planted a deep kiss on his lips.

The place exploded. Shouts. Whistles. Hoots. Applause. The music grew louder and Tommy straightened, still keeping their kiss connected.

Slowly, the two danced once again as they had so many years ago. Other couples joined them on the floor and when the song was over, Tommy and Laura received a standing ovation.

For Tommy and Laura, the life of their love was just beginning.

Afterword

(Twenty-Five Years Later)

Jalen Carter and his wife live in Boone, NC, where Jalen is the men's head basketball coach of his alma mater, Appalachian State. They have six kids and no plans for more.

Miles Flaherty lives in High Point, NC, with his third wife. He owns a construction company and drinks a six-pack every night. He still talks about the good ole days.

Stanley Gattison resides in California with his second wife, actress Shauna Vaughn. They were married shortly after he appeared on a weight-loss game show. He won after shedding 157 pounds and three chins.

Alvy Hanes lives in Charleston, SC, with his wife and two children. After eight years in the NBA, playing for the Celtics, the Knicks, and finally, the Hawks, Alvy retired and invested in bounce houses. He now owns the largest bounce house company on the east coast, Bounce Happy, LLC.

Scott McManness still lives in Italy where he played pro ball for ten years after he graduated UNCG. He led the league in rebounding for three of those years and met his wife the night of one of his best games, at a pizza parlor in Venice. He didn't speak much Italian and she didn't

THE WALK-ON

speak much English, but none of that mattered. They have three little bambinos.

Erik Brunson lives in Dallas, Texas, where he began as a computer programmer at an engineering firm, but now manages the business. He is married with a seventeen-year-old son currently being recruited by SMU, UNCG, Drexel, and Eastern Michigan.

Skeet Harzell lives in Greensboro where he began life after UNCG as a textile salesman. He was invited to several pro camps but decided a life on the road wasn't for him. He married his college sweetheart, and they have two twin boys who now lead Page High School in three-point percentage and steals. They are being looked at by UNCG. Predicting the downturn in textiles, Skeet invested early in real estate and owns over two hundred rental units in the Piedmont Triad.

Manny Cuthrell graduated UNCG and went on to medical school at Duke University. He is now a respected surgeon—specializing in cardiothoracic surgery at Johns Hopkins in Baltimore, Maryland. He is married to the Resident Pediatrician and they have a thirteen-year-old girl and a nine-year-old boy.

Coach Barrows still coaches at Southeast Guilford, still loses some of his best players to Greensboro Day, and still treats every kid that plays for him as if they were his own.

Coach Denton, riding high on UNCG's meteoric season, accepted an offer to coach at Xavier for triple his salary. After eight humdrum seasons, his contract wasn't renewed, and he wished he'd never left UNCG.

Britney Denton stayed at UNCG after her dad left for Xavier and graduated with a degree in Communications. She is currently married to Len Duggers, forward for the Charlotte Bobcats/Hornets, and spends her time announcing college basketball games televised on ESPN and

ESPN2.

Nick Muller and Angel Keller were married within a year of their first date—the night after Southeast's Five-Year Reunion. Nick took a job as a programmer engineer for Norfolk Southern and they moved to Colorado. Angel began a conference planning business—Conference Services Inc.—and they are currently raising three blond-haired boys who drive them crazy.

Leigh Ann Pearson lives in Paris, France. Since graduating from the University of Chicago with her degree in International Law, she has lived in Italy, Spain, Vietnam, Russia, and England. She is still unmarried and breaking hearts all around the world.

Homer Persons continued working at Chandler's until the day he died when he was discovered slumped at the desk in the office. He had been auditing the books for inventory and had found no discrepancies. The funeral was said to be beautiful and everyone attended, even though it was January and the wind was bitter.

Patrick Hart graduated from Duke and went on to manage his father's business, an investment conglomerate. In the late nineties, he successfully ran for the U.S. Senate, backed by big money and a bloodline that called in favors. While being considered as a presidential hopeful for the 2008 race, Patrick was caught up in a scandal when he wrecked his Mercedes while intoxicated; the lone passenger was a scantily-clad seventeen-year-old girl. Investigators then uncovered a history of ten DUIs previously dismissed by a judge who happened to be Patrick's godfather, and in a flash, Senator Hart's political ambitions were squashed as flat as the front of his Mercedes. He is currently referred to as North Carolina Inmate #058261788.

Brant Chandler attended East Carolina and graduated with a double degree in Mathematics and Physics. He went on to receive his Masters at

NC State in Physics and now teaches Intermediate and Advanced Quantum Mechanics at UNCG. He is married to a transplant from West Palm Beach, Florida, and they have a five-year-old girl named Anna.

Gene and Helen Chandler are proud grandparents who still run the various branches of Chandler Exclusives, to much fanfare. Gene now walks with a cane, but his furniture is top-notch—he gets most of his sales from the internet on a site Brant built for the store. One of his pieces, a special-order sturdy sideboard of oak and mahogany, currently occupies a wall in The Blue Room at the White House. The presidential seal is intricately inlaid in its top, carved from California Redwood.

Helen expanded her company and now employees three other bakers. She does more than half of her business over the web and has provided sweets for everyone from Good Morning America's Christmas Special to Jenny Tamblin's sixth birthday party.

Tommy and Laura were married in spectacular fashion, by an Elvis impersonator in Vegas. They chose the 68 Comeback Elvis over the 50s Blue Hawaii Elvis. It was a short but fun ceremony attended by more than thirty of their closest friends and family.

Laura is currently an artist and works from home in a shop out back, and Tommy still runs Chandler's store. They have a girl and a boy, aged sixteen and eighteen respectively. Kiran has just gotten her driver's license, and Tommy worries every time she leaves the house. Tyler turned down basketball scholarships to Florida State, UNC Chapel Hill, South Carolina, and Virginia Tech.

He accepted the scholarship to UNC Greensboro.

The Actual Facts

(And other interesting tidbits)

First, thank you for reading *The Walk-On*. In my short writing career, I've written different types of books (fantasy, horror, crime, humor, suspense, and whatever this book is). Some of them will never be released because they're awful and nothing can fix them. But as every writer eventually does, I sat down one day and thought about writing "The Great American Novel."

Well, my version of it anyway.

I thought about themes and plot lines and characters and all the stuff you think about before ever starting a story. I eventually decided to write a combination of themes all mixed into one: a sports-underdog story, a love story, and a coming-of-age story. Because who doesn't love Rudy or Rocky? Who doesn't love long lost souls finally getting together? And who hasn't gone through the trials and tribulations of growing up?

I wanted to write a book that everyone could relate to, something fairly PG-rated. A book for *anyone* instead of a marketing niche for a certain type of reader. A book that wasn't geared toward any certain gender or age group.

So this is what I came up with.

My original title for the book was ***Throwing Rocks at Girls,*** and I thought that was the coolest title ever. Not many others thought it was, and I couldn't envision a cover concept. When my first readers said, "There's too much basketball," I replied, "But that's a central focus. I can't write less basketball." If anything, I wanted to write more, but there wasn't room if I wanted to get to all the relationship and growing up stuff. This was to be a story about Tommy's entire life, not just one aspect.

So eventually, after a few years and advice from a lot of writers, I got the magic answer: Change the focus of the book. Once I decided to focus on the sports underdog aspect, the new title became clear, even though John Feinstein already has a book out by the same name. But his is about football, and I'm a basketball guy.

The Walk-On is a happy book that mirrors my outlook on life, that anything is possible if you truly work hard enough. Of course, there's always the factor of luck, but I've always said that you have to put the work in first, then get yourself in front of luck.

The character of Tommy is very, very loosely based on me. I graduated from Southeast Guilford High School in 1989 and UNC Greensboro in 1994, just like Tommy, and that's pretty much where the similarities end. I didn't get a business degree, but I do have the distinction of receiving the very first BS in Computer Science from UNCG. I also started the first basketball pep club at UNCG, The Rowdy Crowd. We were a small but effective group of loud students that gave the opposing teams hell and cheered on our Spartans like there was no tomorrow.

Like Tommy, I was a late bloomer, still enjoying my growth spurt in my college freshman year: I'd grown 11 inches in 3 years.

I've got a nice twelve-foot jump shot, but I can't go to my left to save my life. I even dunked once in the UNCG gym, and promptly pulled a groin muscle. I never tried again.

I didn't play organized ball at any level above recreational teams and intramurals, although one of my best friends growing up did try out for UNCG as a walk-on.

He didn't make it.

He later transferred to UNC Chapel Hill and graduated with a Business degree, parlaying that into a job with Arthur Anderson. Later in life, he moved to Boulder, Colorado, where he made sure trains got places on time.

Laura, and every girlfriend Tommy had, is loosely based on an amalgamation of the girlfriends and wives in my life. Yes, I'm on my fourth *AND FINAL* marriage. What can I say? I'm a romantic optimist at heart; I always think things will work out.

All of the events in Tommy's childhood were based on actual events, with some artistic liberty, of course.

There is no real-world place called "The Rock" that I know of, but we all know a place like it, don't we? Wink, wink, nudge, nudge.

Patrick Hart's character is based on a real-life bully that to this day, I would love to poke in the eye. He was an ass as a kid, and as far as I can tell, that followed him into adulthood.

I do not have a brother four years younger than me, although my sister (four years my junior) was at times a tomboy. My relationship with my parents could best be described as "storybook." They are amazing people and even more amazing parents.

I was always competitive with my dad in everything, from video games to chess to sports. He never let me win. I had to earn every victory, and I'm forever grateful for that. It taught me the importance of continually bettering myself, and gave me a bar to measure against.

I drew on that father-son relationship for the dynamic between Tommy and Gene, and then blew it *way* out of proportion.

The first time I beat my dad at a game of one-on-one basketball was a momentous occasion that happened nothing like portrayed in the book. In actuality, we finished the game, and I may have even gloated a little like teenage boys are rote to do until they mature. My mom ran into him when he retreated to the kitchen to catch his breath and grab a glass of water. She took one look at his disheveled state and said, "What happened to you?" He finished his water and replied, "He beat me."

Growing up, my younger sister was as bratty as I tried to make Brant. We never got along, but in adulthood, we're as close as siblings can be. There, Cheryl, now you're in a book.

The "laxative in the cookies" story really happened, only it was perpetrated by my mom in grade school upon a particularly nasty teacher who allowed students to eat in class, and then regularly stole food off their desks. Mom was suspended for her efforts, but applauded by her fellow students.

When I was conceptualizing the book, I originally had Tommy playing baseball as a pitcher. By the time I got to the preliminary outline, he was still a pitcher. But when I decided to make the father-son dynamic a subplot, I changed the sport to basketball, because it's really hard to play your dad one-on-one in baseball. Basketball is much more exciting anyway.

Chandler's store in the book is based on a real store just up the road from where I grew up, Shoffner's. There was indeed a barbershop in the store that was later turned into an office. But there was no Oasis on the roof or storeroom turned into a furniture showroom. They also used the old-style registers and a ledger book (as far as I can remember).

UNCG athletics did indeed rise to the Division I level in 1991 and made it to the NCAA tournament in the 1995-96 year after winning the Big South Conference Tourney. The team relied heavily on its first Division I recruits: Scott Hartzell (UNCG's first retired jersey), Skeet Woolard, Jonathan Clifton, Eric Cuthrell, and Brian Brunson. They lost their game in Orlando as a 14-seed against 2nd-seeded Cincinnati, 61-66.

In 2001, UNCG won the Southern Conference Tournament and advanced to the NCAA Tourney where they were beaten in the first round by #1 Stanford, 88-60. I dubbed that team the "Comeback Kids" because they had a knack of coming back from behind to win games. In contests decided by 6 points or less, they went 10-4, including a heartbreaking loss to NC State in Raleigh by a single point. The team was led by point guard Courtney Eldridge (UNCG's second retired jersey) who averaged 5.8 assists, 2.6 steals, and 14.6 points per game. When the ball was in Courtney's hands at the end of the game, UNCG fans relaxed.

In 2007, UNCG opened the season at ACC foe, Georgia Tech. In front of a standing-room-only crowd, UNCG systematically dismantled the Yellow Jackets in the second half to win the game, 83-74. Kyle Hines (UNCG's third retired jersey) put on a clinic, shooting 10-12 from the field and 5-7 from the free throw line. It was the first time UNCG had beaten an ACC team, and the first time Georgia Tech had lost a home opener since 1980.

Since then, UNCG has taken down other ACC foes.

In 2013, UNCG traveled to Virginia Tech and left with a 55-52 victory after rallying in the final minutes. In 2017, UNCG finally beat NC State in Raleigh with the Spartans controlling the 2nd half to carry home the win, 81-76.

The 2018 UNCG team won the Southern Conference Tournament

and played #4 Gonzaga in the NCAA Tourney as a 13-seed. They narrowly lost 68-64 after finally taking the lead on a Jordy Kuiper tip-in with just under 2 minutes to go.

The 2019 team garnered its first NIT win in school history, led by Senior Francis Alonso. That year, he shattered the UNCG 3-Pointers-Made record previously held for 23 years by Scott Hartzell, completing 396 threes to top Hartzell's 309.

In 2011 (a year after I wrote this book), assistant coach Wes Miller took over the head coaching duties of the UNCG basketball program. Miller was a former sophomore walk-on at UNC Chapel Hill in 2005 when the Tar Heels squad won the NCAA Tournament. He earned a starting position in his junior year, and his final year saw him as a Team Captain. At the time of his promotion at UNCG, Miller was the youngest men's basketball coach in Division I.

The first I ever heard of a walk-on getting a scholarship at UNCG was Greg Williams. He began with UNCG in their Division II years, and by his senior year, he was awarded a scholarship by then coach, Mike Dement. He later went on to get his law degree and now practices in Durham, NC.

The saying goes that art imitates life, but sometimes, life imitates art ... let me explain.

This book was originally written around 2010 and not published until 2019. Some of the events that I fictionalized have almost come true. In 2010, it was laughable to write that UNCG would ever be considered as an at-large bid for the NCAA Tournament. That year, we finished with an RPI ranking of #296 out of 345 teams.

But the 2018-19 season saw an at-large bid become a distinct possibility. UNCG had just finished its third straight season of 25 wins or more, and the 28-5 team lost in the Southern Conference Tournament

Finals. We would have secured our first-ever at-large bid as the "last team in" if #1-seeded Washington hadn't gotten blown out by #6-seeded Oregon in the PAC Tournament finals, 68-48. Washington stole that final at-large bid.

So instead, UNCG became the overall #1 seed in the NIT Tournament where we won our first post-season tournament game in history against Campbell before eventually being knocked out by Lipscomb.

The UNCG Men's Basketball Team finished the season with a 29-7 record and a #32 RPI ranking, the highest in program history.

Also of note, I wrote in 2010 in the *Afterword* how character "Skeet Harzell" had twins that led Page High school in stats and were being recruited by UNCG. This upcoming year, in the 2019-20 season, UNCG welcomes its first legacy players, twins Keyshaun and Kobe Langley, whose father Keyford was a Division II player in the same years this book takes place. Interestingly enough, he was a point guard, and so are they. The twins also led their school, Southwest Guilford, in Assists (7.2 and 6.0), Steals (2.8 and 2.4), FT% (82% and 78%), and 3-Point% (Keyshaun with 40%) in their senior year. And if that wasn't enough, they also led the school to a 3A North Carolina State Championship.

So yeah, sometimes it's *life* that imitates *art*.

Hmm ... maybe I should write a book about UNCG's first fictional NBA star ... and maybe I'll name him Isaiah Muller ...

Written by
Ross Cavins

Cover Concept, Design, & Photography by
Ross Cavins

Published by
RCG Publishing

Please review this book on:

Amazon.com, Goodreads.com, and BN.com.

Your reviews help small publishers and independent authors thrive!

About The Author

Ross Cavins is a web developer and author of the award-winning book, **Follow The Money**, and Claymore Award Finalist, **Barry vs The Apocalypse**. A self-appointed disciple of Elmore Leonard, he writes from his home in North Carolina where he pretends people pay him to do what he loves. His sense of humor is sort of like Disco: you dance to it even if you don't admit it.

He has also edited and published the award-winning humor book, **Thing Go Wrong For Me**, by Rodney LaCroix, along with **Perhaps I've Said Too Much** and **Romantic As Hell**, also by Rodney LaCroix.

He is arguably the biggest fan of UNCG Basketball you'll ever meet.

You can find him toiling away on the web at **RossCavins.com, UNCGHoops.com,** and twitter (@rosscavins).

www.ingramcontent.com/pod-product-compliance
Lightning Source LLC
Chambersburg PA
CBHW050615300426
44112CB00012B/1513